San Francisco
As You Like It

San Francisco As You Like It

23 Tailor-Made Tours
for Culture Vultures, Shopaholics,
Neo-Bohemians, Famished Foodies,
Savvy Natives & Everyone Else

BONNIE WACH

Ulysses Press
Berkeley, California

Published by:
Ulysses Press
P.O. Box 3440
Berkeley, CA 94703
www.ulyssespress.com

ISBN 1-56975-387-3
ISSN 1545-5645

Printed in Canada by Transcontinental Printing

10 9 8 7 6 5 4 3 2 1

Editorial Director: Leslie Henriques
Managing Editor: Claire Chun
Editors: Ashley Chase, Lynette Ubois
Copy Editor: Richard Harris
Production: James Meetze, Lisa Kester
Cartography: Pease Press
Design: Sarah Levin
Front cover photography: Robert Holmes
Interior photography: *San Francisco Convention & Visitors Bureau*: pages 28, 38, 99, 112, 151, 287, 319; *Robert Holmes/Cal Tour*: pages 44, 61, 248, 252, 269, 276; *all other images* © Ulysses Press and its licensors

Distributed in the United States by Publishers Group West and in Canada by Raincoast Books

The author and publisher have made every effort to ensure the accuracy of information contained in *San Francisco As You Like It*, but can accept no liability for any loss, injury, or inconvenience sustained by anyone as a result of information or advice contained in this guide.

Table of Contents

ACKNOWLEDGMENTS

First and foremost, thanks to my dear beloved San Francisco, without whom none of this would have been possible. A heaping pile of gratitude and chocolate goes to my writing posse: Janis, Rosie, and Anita for all the fantastic editing and feedback (and tea and sympathy), and to my agent, Amy Rennert, for keeping this ball rolling. Thanks also to Kate Berland for her help with Nitty Gritty, and to my editors at Ulysses Press, Lynette Ubois and Ashley Chase, for their patience and understanding. Most especially, thanks to Pete and to Rowan, who make it all worthwhile.

Introduction

It's been a seatbeltless rollercoaster-ride-of-a-decade for San Francisco. Between the Internet implosion,  rolling blackouts, stratospheric gas prices, out-of-the-galaxy housing prices, the heartbreak 2002 World Series, and the fact that the city was bumped from its ivory tower in the Conde Nast Traveler Top Cities poll by Sydney, Australia—well, even the most L.A. Dodger-loving Frisco basher might have been moved to throw the city a "There, there."

But the truth is, for San Francisco, it's par for the course.

This, after all, is a city born of upheaval, a place that has reinvented itself time and again—sometimes because it had to (earthquakes) and sometimes because it could (Gold Rushes past and present). Down but never out, San Francisco always seems to exhibit a streak of irrepressible optimism just when things seem their bleakest.

And so we bided our time, safe in the knowledge that the things that truly make San Francisco, San Francisco—the red horns of the Golden Gate Bridge peeking out through a downy halo of white fog in July, the shaft of sunlight that streaks down California Street in September silhouetting the cable cars against the sky like a sentimental 1940s movie about lost love, the can-dancing garbagemen, the indefatigable barking sea lions, the pupusa lady—these things were never lost.

And of course, we quickly realized that nothing short of California breaking off and falling into the Pacific—not orange alerts, flight cancellations, epidemics, or economic Armageddon—would stop the folks in Minneapolis from hopping in the station wagon, landing on our doorstep, and demanding a tour of the town, Golden Gate Bridge, cable cars, crab stands and all.

The problem is that one man's Fog City is another man's Frisco: What's good for the grandma is not necessarily good for the grad student—and vice versa. Knowing that there are 150 Sichuan restaurants in the city won't help an artsy auntie find an emergency tarot card reading, or an erstwhile Ivy Leaguer locate the haunts of his ex-Princeton drinking buddies.

In this book you'll find tours tailored to suit every whim, idiosyncrasy, and taste (or lack thereof). From a parking place to pacify suburbanites' angst, to a celebrity graveyard tour to impress testy teenagers, to off-the-beaten-path options for people who prefer to be tourists incognito, there's an itinerary for every ethnically curious, environmentally aware, toddler-toting ex-flower child—and her gourmet grandparents, too.

The payoff, of course, regardless of whether you're host, houseguest, or hitchhiker from Hackensack, is when you have that only-in-San-Francisco epiphanic moment—a mixture of wonder, envy, and joy that reveals itself in a deep breath, a satisfied smile, a knowing nod, and the realization that San Francisco may not be perfect, but it sure as hell beats the alternative.

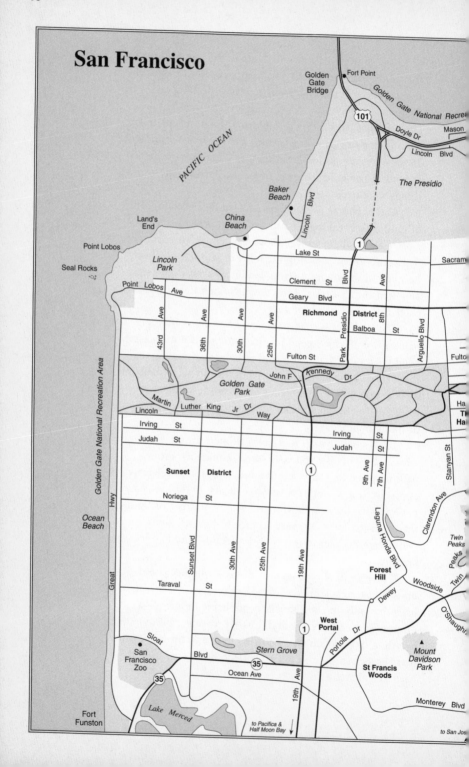

San Francisco

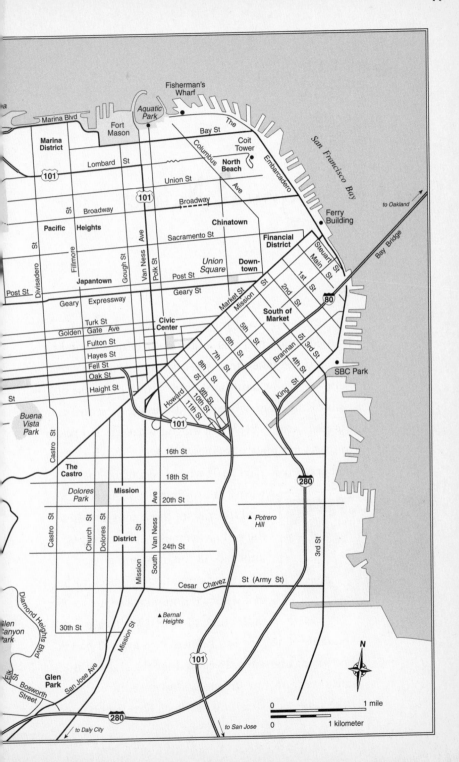

Cynical Natives

The few years that I was a Bay Area expatriate, I learned something that a lifetime here never taught me. You can take the city for granted. Hard to believe, I know. But there I was sitting in House of Chun King, somewhere in Milwaukee, Wisconsin, in the middle of February, staring at what was supposed to pass for a plate of cashew chicken (for which I had graciously paid $10) when it occurred to me: I

wasn't in San Francisco anymore. And like one of those movies where the girl has amnesia and then gets knocked on the head and all her memories come flooding back to her in a whirlwind montage sequence set to the tune of "I Left My Heart . . ." I suddenly ached for San Francisco in a way I hadn't known was possible. I yearned for the sight of the late afternoon sun streaming down California Street in October, for steaming bowls of Thai lemongrass coconut soup from Thep Phanom, for old Italian men playing bocce ball in Aquatic Park, and for movie watching as a participatory sport.

The following spring when I came back for vacation, the light, the fog, and the intoxicating goofiness of the city overwhelmed me. I got out my camera, went to the top of Russian Hill, and snapped away like a lovesick suitor. And I knew at that moment, as I sat on the steps near Macondray Lane—flower boxes overhead, Alcatraz dancing in the bay like an island paradise—that I had to come home.

Not everyone has such a volatile reaction. For some, this city is more like a chronic addiction, except without all the bad side effects (unless you count the shakes). Others may need a little reminding—something to stir the old embers, to rekindle the romance, to make 'em hug a total stranger and say, "Can you believe it? I live here!"

MORNING

As a populace, San Franciscans tend to be generally disdainful of anything that smacks of bandwagonism. We don't bound up to movie stars in restaurants for their autographs, we refuse to do the wave at sporting events, and we definitely don't do anything as obvious as ride a cable car (you might as well ask us to eat Rice-a-Roni). But if you haven't ridden the **Hyde Street Cable Car** (and I'd hazard seven out of ten residents haven't), you're cheating yourself out of the best E ticket in Friscoland. The problem is how to accomplish this without being mistaken for someone who's completely lost his or her sense of propriety. Best advice: set the alarm for 6 a.m., grab a trench coat and a pair of sunglasses, and head down to the Hyde Street turn-around at Ghirardelli Square. There, while the camera-toting, plaid-shorts people are still sleeping off those Buena Vista Irish coffees, you can indulge in this guilty pleasure without losing face. Buy the gripman a cup of Peet's best and he might even let you hang off the running boards Doris

Day–style (you know you've been dying to do it). As you swing in the sea breeze, soak up the city at dawn: the Pavlovian smell of roasting coffee and Chinese barbecued pork buns, the glint of dew on the tracks, the sultry harmonies of fog horns and seagulls punctuated by the thump, thump, thump of *Chronicles* being thrown at door-ways. Don't forget to turn around at the top of the hill for the cynicism-melting view of the wharf and the waterfront. All this for the low, low price of $3.

After you've worked up an appetite, take the streetcar up Market through the tunnel to Cole Valley and recharge your spirits as well as your batteries at **Zazie**. The soul-warming French-by-way-of-the-Mediterranean café is busy on weekends, but early mornings and weekdays there are just a few barely working folks drinking lattes from ceramic bowls, reading the paper, and watching the world roll by over gingerbread buttermilk pancakes, a bowl of oatmeal, or perfectly poached eggs Monaco (a variation on Benedict with prosciutto and tomatoes).

Alternative #1: On weekends, lots of people opt for a glamorama brunch at Sam's or Guaymas in Tiburon. Which is great if you're with your parents or first-timers. But there's something sublime about sitting in the morning sun, watching the ships roll in, and watching 'em roll away again at **The Ramp**. (Okay, so Otis Redding wrote "Dock of the Bay" in Sausalito; it should have been written here.) This industrial-waterfront fixture was actually my second-favorite spot for whiling away a Sunday morning in the company of rusted-out tankers and decrepit docks. My first favorite, Mission Rock, got bought up and made over into an upscale frat-boy bar and grill. Happily, the grotto charms of the Ramp seem (so far) to be lost on the current crop of Big Buck waterfront investors, and city dwellers can still enjoy brunching on the sunny driftwood deck with Bloody Marys in hand, as they bob to the rhythm of the sailboats and a seagull grabs their French fries.

Alternative #2: At the opposite end of the waterfront is another one of San Francisco's fast-vanishing institutions, **Louis'** at Ocean Beach. Never mind that it's right next to the Cliff House. None of that cheese rubbed off on Louis, a classic diner that has been overlooking the ruins of Sutro Baths since 1937. As you would expect with every good diner, the coffee's weak, but the cup is bottomless—leaving you lots of time to contemplate the mysterious cargos of those enormous barges as they head in and out of the Golden Gate. Try to get a table in the back corner, so you can truly appreciate your precarious position on the edge of the planet.

NOON

San Francisco long ago banished its dead to Colma, leaving only two cemeteries within the city limits—Mission Dolores and the National Military Cemetery in the Presidio. Graveyards are peculiar little time capsules—microcosms of a city's history distilled into a poignant shorthand of names, dates, and one-sentence epitaphs. But they tell volumes about a place: of battles fought and won, of love affairs gone awry, of family scandals and tragedies. Mission Dolores is more noteworthy for those who are not commemorated there (namely hundreds of Native Americans—see the Politically Correct tour). The Presidio's contribution is more subtle. Secluded on an enchanted sylvan stretch that gazes out over the Golden Gate Bridge, the **National Military Cemetery**, built in 1884, makes you look at the city's love-hate relationship with the military in a new light. Follow the stone fences along the rows of gravestones and monuments and you'll be swept up in tales of Civil War spy Pauline Cushman Fry, of Generals Funston and Kearny, of union busters and Indian guides, of Spanish-American war heroes, American war mothers, and the 15,000 young men (including thirty-five Medal of Honor recipients) who died in World War I. Most importantly, if you let the hush and soli-

Zazie
941 Cole St.
415-564-5332

The Ramp
855 China Basin Wy.
415-621-2378

Louis'
902 Point Lobos Ave.
415-387-6330

National Military Cemetery
in the Presidio, near the Lombard St. entrance

tude of this place seep into your overstimulated urban brain, you'll become one again with the gentle and noble underbelly of San Francisco.

It seems only fitting in San Francisco that just below this somber tribute to human war heroes lies a burial ground devoted to our fine four-legged friends. If you didn't need a hanky before, you'll need one now. Only the stone-hearted wouldn't melt at the sight of fresh flowers resting against the gravestone of Skipper, the "best damn dog we ever had." The **Presidio Pet Cemetery** (originally reserved for animals of military personnel, but usurped over the years by the general public) contains the remains of loved ones ranging from Afton the boxer to beloved rats Chocolate and Candy. There is something so endearing and so very EssEff about all these crooked little handmade markers with their poems and pictures that even the most blasé among us will be moved to wag a tail.

From here, head down toward the waterfront and the **Golden Gate Promenade**, a name which always makes me envision big-busted ladies in feathered hats and lace-up

boots carrying parasols and pushing prams. As you know if you've walked it, this 3.5-mile path is actually a lovely little slice of open space smack dab in the middle of the metropolitan maze. To truly appreciate the promenade, you must walk the entire trail, not just a piece of it, because various stations along the way are essential to revitalizing your sagging civic spirits. Start out at **Aquatic Park**, where you can watch members of the **Dolphin Club** don cheery orange swim caps and do the backstroke in the bay. Some of these folks, now in their seventies and eighties, have been treading these waters for forty-odd years. (If you're doing this walk in the fall, or on New Year's Day, try to catch the Alcatraz Island to Aquatic Park Swim.)

Follow the path around to Fort Mason, where you must stop at the bakery at **Greens** restaurant for an Acme baguette, a to-go bowl of black bean chili, or a buttermilk orange/currant/pecan scone, and at the public library's bargain **Book Bay** for a quick browse through the quality

paperbacks before you stroll down the path through the sailboat marina. Next comes **Marina Green**, a curious and
blissful cross-section of sunbathers in Speedos, gay volley-
ballers, East Coast private college grads on rollerblades and
mountain bikes, and Old Money spillover from the St.
Francis Yacht Club across the way. Five-star people
watching. Proceed down the road to **Crissy Field**, and plant
yourself on the beach to watch the windsurfers brave the
whitecaps as you take in the entire span of the Golden Gate
Bridge. (It's one of the few spots in all the city and Marin
where you can actually see the whole bridge.) Then
continue walking the trail past the offices for the State of
the World Forum and the Gulf of the Farallones Marine
Sanctuary, until you reach **Fort Point**. Here you'll likely be
joined by a number of tourists. Don't let that deter you.
Walk along the iron-link guard rail to the spot where the
waves crash on the rocks and spray the parking lot. Then
reenact the scene from Hitchcock's *Vertigo* when Jimmy
Stewart jumps into the bay to save Kim Novak (except
maybe without the jumping-in part). Next, walk across the
parking lot until you're directly under the bridge, look up,
and marvel at the awe-inspiring underbelly of one of the
Seven Engineering Wonders of the World. For an even
closer look, climb to the top of the wall inside the fort.
Before you leave, be sure to catch the film about the construction of the Golden Gate Bridge (complete with great
old newsreel footage) that's shown daily in the bookstore.

Zing, Zing, Zing Went My Heartstrings

Nostalgia and sentimentality are extremely underrated. When
I was in the Midwest, and San Francisco seemed but a distant
dream, just hearing Tony Bennett's voice was enough to send
me over the edge into slobbering sentimentalville. Living
here, you have to work a little harder to get that tear-jerk
reaction. But there are places that can help the process along.

Just a block from the dreaded Land-o'-White-Shoes
(a.k.a. Fisherman's Wharf) is the **San Francisco Art
Institute**, a place that will restore your faith in the notion
that not everything down here comes with a built-in ticket

**Presidio Pet
Cemetery**
just above Crissy
Field, corner of
McDowell and
Cowles

**Dolphin Club/
Aquatic Park**
at the foot of
Hyde St.
415-441-9329

Greens
Fort Mason,
Building A,
415-771-6222

Book Bay
Fort Mason,
Building C
415-771-1076

Marina Green
Marina Blvd.
at Lyon St.

Crissy Field
between Marina
Green and the
Golden Gate Bridge
415-561-4300

Fort Point
at the foot of the
Golden Gate Bridge
415-556-1693

**San Francisco
Art Institute**
800 Chestnut St.
415-771-7020

vendor. Walk up Chestnut Street from the big Tower Records store and you'll come to the entrance of this beautiful old Spanish colonial revival building, designed in 1926 by Brown and Bakewell, the same architectural team that gave us City Hall and the War Memorial Opera House. The doors open onto what was once a stately tiled courtyard and fountain. These days it has taken on the genteel, slightly melancholy air of an abandoned nineteenth-century Spanish villa, which somehow makes it all the more charming. On the west side of the courtyard, the skylit Diego Rivera Gallery houses a large mural Rivera painted in 1931 as a tribute to the American laborer. Sit on the bench in the center of the room, in the stillness of the fading afternoon light, and contemplate Rivera's backside—truly sublime. Then make your way to the roof deck and the café, where you'll find one of the best wharf views you've never had to pay a quarter for. (Residents with neobeatnik types in tow take note of the café sign that reads "Pseudo-Bohemians Welcome.") The café and surrounding sunny concrete pad

are walled-in castle-style, allowing you to gaze out through the trees and over the apartment houses, to smell the crab pots, to listen to the seals barking and the fog horns blowing, and maintain complete, blissful anonymity.

Now that the spirit is willing, walk down the street and seal the deal with a visit to the **National Shrine of St. Francis of Assisi** at Columbus and Vallejo. The church devoted to San Francisco's patron saint opened its doors in 1849 on the eve of the Gold Rush as California's first parish church.

Pause a moment to reflect on the men and women who came here seeking a new life, a spirit of tolerance and of adventure, and the promise of unimaginable fortune (some things never change). Be sure to check out the murals on the church interior. Several were painted by Luigi Brusatori, who was recently honored by the Vatican Museums. If it's Sunday, you'll also be treated to a free concert featuring the church's famed Schoenstein pipe organ.

Dago Mary's

**National Shrine
of St. Francis of
Assisi**
610 Vallejo St.
415-983-0405

Dago Mary's
Hunter's Point
Naval Shipyard
415-822-2633

On the opposite end of the waterfront spectrum, we have
Dago Mary's, which, considering its location amid the
splendid squalor of the Hunter's Point Naval Shipyard, is
not the likeliest place to rekindle the old San Francisco
flame. But this is one of the great ghosts of San Francisco's
reckless youth. Sally Stanford's bordello is gone, and you
can't visit Tessie Wall's parlor house anymore, but you can
still have lunch at Dago Mary's.

"Dago Mary" Chiorizio, an Italian madam, ran a posh
brothel out of these digs in the 1930s, just after the repeal of
Prohibition. The restaurant doesn't look like it has changed
much since its shady days. Highlights of the ornate
Victoriana decor include gold-flocked wallpaper, plush red
velvet drapery, and gilded chandeliers (apparently Mary's
tastes ran a bit to the gaudy side). In one of her more
acquisitive moods, Mary also picked up the marble fireplace
from the Flood Mansion in Menlo Park and deposited it in
the lobby. Don't let fear of Hunter's Point prevent you from
coming out here—at least during daylight hours. This is a
nice, white-tablecloth restaurant, serving large portions of
basic Italian food and catering to the business suit, shot-and-
a-beer crowd.

Shaken and Stirred

The 1906 earthquake hit San Francisco at an impressionable
age, when the city was still struggling to prove it wasn't
merely a flash in the Gold Rush pan. But disasters have a
funny way of bringing out the best in people, and San
Francisco proved to the world she was a real scrapper,
triumphing against the odds and rising phoenixlike from the
ashes bigger and better than before. Visit some of the
shrines of the 1906 quake and you'll feel a swell of pride
and a renewed sense of that can-do San Francisco spirit. Set
the tone by renting (or re-renting) *San Francisco,* the 1936
classic film starring Clark Gable, Spencer Tracy, and Jeanette
MacDonald. Between the earthquake scene (a chandelier-
swinging tour de force long before there were computer-
enhanced special effects), and the scene in which

MacDonald sings a soul-stirring version of "San Francisco," to win a contest and bail out her rogue gambler-boyfriend Blackie Norton, you'll find yourself cheering for the Little City That Did. Next, head over to Twentieth and Church streets and pay homage to the **fire hydrant** that saved the Mission district. Now painted gold and commemorated with a plaque from the city, the brave little hydrant was the only one that kept pumping during the great fire. It's the reason the Mission still has so many fine specimens of Victorian architecture.

From here, swing over to Golden Gate Park and the shores of Lloyd Lake, where perhaps the most poignant memorial to the old city lies moldering. Christened **Portals of the Past**, the stately marble portico is the only remnant of one of the grand Nob Hill mansions (and maybe the reason they always tell you to stand in a doorway in the event of an earthquake).

Lastly, make a pilgrimage to **Lotta's Fountain** down on Market Street, which began life in 1875 as a token of gratitude from a native daughter, and evolved into the unofficial

symbol of the city's indomitable spirit. In the wake of the quake and fires, the fountain became the meeting place for thousands of residents in search of missing loved ones. Four years later, on Christmas Eve 1910, a jubilant crowd of 250,000 gathered at the fountain once again to hear opera singer Luisa Tetrazzini pay singing tribute to San Francisco's recovery. Since then, every April 18 at 5:13 a.m., the few remaining survivors, along with politicians, history buffs, and legions of well-wishers, still congregate here to reminisce, celebrate, and polish their civic pride.

Swan Oyster Depot

There's nothing like fresh-from-the-ocean Dungeness crab or Tomales Bay oysters to remind you that in some places, Mrs. Paul's is top shelf in the seafood department. Swan's not only satisfies your seafood jones, it'll cure your hankering for talking with some unpretentious, honest-to-God San

1906 earthquake fire hydrant
20th and Church streets

Portals of the Past
on Lloyd Lake, JFK Drive, west of 19th Ave., Golden Gate Park

Lotta's Fountain
intersection of Market, Kearny, and Third streets

Swan Oyster Depot
1517 Polk St.
415-673-1101

Center for the Arts/Yerba Buena Gardens
701 Mission St.
415-978-2700

Franciscans. This fish market-cum-lunch counter was opened in 1912 by the Lausten Brothers and has been run since 1946 by an assortment of members of the Sancimino family. Swan serves up fresh, no frills seafood—filleted, cracked, and shucked before your eyes—along with healthy portions of friendly banter. Belly up to the marble counter and start with a bowl of clam chowder, served with a hunk of fresh sourdough and all the oyster crackers you can stomach. (Adventurous types will want to try one of the assortment of wacky hot sauces, which boast names like Ass in Space, Ultimate Burn, and Vampfire.) Then move on to a plate of fresh-cracked Dungeness crab, thinly sliced smoked salmon, a half-dozen Miyagi oysters, or mixed seafood cocktail/salad. Jimmy, Mike, or one of their brothers will pile on crab, prawns, bay shrimp—whatever's exceptional that day—and top it off with a dollop of cocktail sauce or homemade horseradish. Wash it down with a pint of San Francisco's own Anchor Steam beer.

Center for the Arts/Yerba Buena Gardens

San Francisco is one of those rare cities where "good" doesn't automatically translate as "old." Case in point: the TransAmerica Pyramid, which despite a rocky reception back in the '70s, is now San Francisco's second most-celebrated skyline icon (the Golden Gate Bridge, of course, being the first). The Center for the Arts and Yerba Buena Gardens are not nearly as controversial. In fact, they offer hope that urban renewal can really work. And there is no better spot for viewing San Francisco's eclectic downtown architecture.

On a sunny afternoon, begin your stroll through the galleries for an eye-opening introduction to the diversity and talent of local artists. Next, grab a sandwich at the top of the esplanade, sit at one of the outdoor tables, and look east, where you'll be treated to a vista that includes the Bay Bridge; Timothy Pflueger's magnificent Pacific Telephone Building (the city's first downtown skyscraper); the dramatically striped skylight of Mario Botta's Museum of Modern Art; the "jukebox" Marriott Hotel with its seashell windows; and a hodgepodge of other buildings—historic and modern—all thrown together in a happy architectural jumble. From here, head down to the Martin Luther King Jr. Memorial waterfall, and read the "I Have a Dream" speech, which never sounds like a cliché and never fails to remind me that we live in a town that tolerates all kinds with warmth and good grace. Finally, settle down in the grassy area for some peaceful R&R. If it's a summer weekend, chances are there'll be some kind of ethnic fair or a group offering a free performance on the outdoor stage. Free lunchtime concerts are also held across the street at the venerable **St. Patrick's Church** throughout the spring and summer.

NIGHT

Okay, so maybe it's a cliché, but there's something heart-warming and refreshing about seeing San Francisco through the wide eyes of a neophyte, someone who can sing "I Left My Heart . . ." sitting on the bench next to a piano man wearing a bad toupee and do it without a trace of irony. At **Lefty O'Doul's**, you may have such an experience, and you

may have it with or without the aid of whiskey. The Pacific Coast League base-ball legend's hofbrau and wonderfully schmaltzy sing-along piano bar is constantly fighting a high-rent battle that threatens to shut it down, but for now you can still cry in your beer and sing one for the gipper as you gaze at Marilyn Monroe's USO license and baseball memorabilia from the days when North Beach native son Joe DiMaggio played for the Seals and Francis "Lefty" O'Doul was his manager.

If you want to pay more sober tribute to Lefty O'Doul and the other working-class Irish folk who built this town, head to the Francis "Lefty" O'Doul Drawbridge on Third and Berry streets, next to SBC Park. It's one of two remaining drawbridges in San Francisco (the other's on Fourth Street), and the only one that you can still get a rise out of once in a while. Watching the enormous metal-grate roadway loom over Mission Creek, like a giant crocodile opening its jaws, never fails to put a lump in my throat. It somehow harkens to a grander, golden age of industry, when San Francisco worked hard, played hard, and was truly the "City That Knows How." Your best chance to see the drawbridge in action is during Fleet Week in October, when boats go in and out of the slips along Mission Bay.

Just up the street from Lefty's bar, the **Gold Dust Lounge**—a Gold Rush-style honky tonk in the heart of touristland—re-creates the era right down to the Dixieland jazz band and the can-can girls. (Okay, not the can-can girls, but you can picture them, can't you?) Where else in San Francisco are you going to find that old-time Bourbon Street sound now that Turk Murphy is gone? Grab a beer, surround yourself with vacationing couples from Ohio, and see if you don't find yourself wiping a tear from the corner of your eye during the clarinet solo.

Castro Theatre

If you haven't gone to a revival, a classic film re-release, or the sing-along *Sound of Music* at the Castro, you're missing out on one of the best "only in San Francisco" experiences. The theater itself is worth the trip, designed in 1920s art deco movie palace grandeur by Timothy Pflueger, the same genius who gave us the Paramount Theatre in Oakland, 450 Sutter, and the Pacific Telephone Building on New Montgomery. The elaborately painted and gilded ceiling and the Deco light fixture make pre-movie gazing almost as entertaining as previews.

For maximum enjoyment, go for a musical, anything filmed in San Francisco, or a classic Hitchcock flick where immortal sexist lines like "Change your hair color for me, Judy. It can't matter to you" bring down the house. Make sure you get there early enough to buy popcorn—with real butter—and so you don't miss the performance on the giant Wurlitzer organ. I invariably get goose pimples when I see that thing rise out of the theater pit just before showtime and the organist leads the audience in a clap-along of classic show tunes, followed by a rousing rendition of "San Francisco." I also love the fact that the biggest applause during the opening credits is not reserved for the stars, but for the costume designers.

Top of the Mark

In this sky room, World War II soldiers danced their last dance and vowed to be true to shapely gals they'd known for hours, before they shipped off to fight the good fight. It's also purportedly the view that inspired Tony Bennett to croon, "I Left My Heart in San Francisco." Though the room has been completely made over, some of that old SF nostalgia still lingers, especially on misty nights when the mournful fog horns blow like the unrequited sighs of a war bride. Order a Singapore Sling, stare out over the "cool, gray city of love," and get dreamy-eyed as the band plays "Isn't it Romantic?"

North Beach

Old stalwarts argue that North Beach now isn't what it was "back then." But frankly North Beach has never been what it once was. That's the beauty of it. When it became a predominantly Italian neighborhood in the late nineteenth century, the Irish lamented. When the beatniks moved in in the '50s,

everyone complained. And now that the neighborhood is becoming increasingly Chinese, the Italians are shaking their heads. Hopefully a little bit of every culture survives, and in some cases—as with the Irish and the gay communities (it did a brief stint as a gay district in the '40s)—revives.

For locals, the problem is distilling the neighborhood down to its essence. On the Italian side of things, there are a million-and-one restaurants between Broadway and Bay, all of which are run by authentic Italians, and all of which seem to capture the flavor of Old North Beach. For my money, Fior d'Italia, Sodini's, and L'Osteria del Forno do it best.

Fior d'Italia, purportedly the oldest Italian restaurant in the U.S., sits at the quintessential North Beach corner directly across from Washington Square. With its white tablecloths and two-spoon service, and its quasi-famous Tony Bennett Room (the singer made it a regular stop whenever he was in town), the restaurant is at once hokey and hopelessly romantic. No, the food won't win any James Beard awards, but it's traditional, hearty, and soul-warming—and none of this Italian-lite stuff.

Across the way, **Sodini's** feels like the Italian restaurants you see in old movies, albeit perhaps old movies about New York: drip-wax chianti-bottle candles burn in the window over white tablecloths, garlic wafts out the door, the proprietor offers you a glass of wine and motions for you to "come in, come in" out of the rain. It's a cliché, but in the best sort of way—and the food (which by all rules of cliches should be mezzo mezzo) is pretty decent, especially the pasta dishes.

Down the street, tiny **L'Osteria del Forno** does a brief, simple menu that hits the spot every time. Choose between the roast or pasta of the day or the thin-crust pizza made in the brick-lined oven.

Booster Shots

If Milwaukee taught me anything besides how to tear the blue ribbon off a Pabst Blue Ribbon for a free beer, it's how to find a good street festival. When you first move to a new place (or when you get old enough to appreciate drinking in the streets), you find yourself going to every single one of these things, and they all start to run together—the guy who makes those handmade rocking chairs, the Victorian house light-switch plates, lemonade slushies, et cetera, et cetera.

But all street fairs are not alike. And there's nothing quite like a good (emphasis on good) old-fashioned block party to soften the jaded soul. Maybe because of the location, the mix of cultures, or the colorful history, **North Beach Festival** in June–July, is one of the best—a glorious, uninhibited, yet splendidly Old World slice of San Francisco life (it's allegedly the oldest urban street fair in the country). Where else can you sit on a grassy knoll in front of the spires of the church where Joe DiMaggio went to school, with a glass of pinot grigio or a cup of espresso, and watch a

Top of the Mark
Mark Hopkins Hotel,
1 Nob Hill /
999 California St.
415-392-3434

Fior d'Italia
601 Union St.
415-986-1886

Sodini's
510 Green St.
415-291-0499

L'Osteria del Forno
519 Columbus Ave.
415-982-1124

North Beach Festival
Washington Square,
Union St. and
Columbus Ave.
415-989-2220

guy who looks like he just stepped off the set of *The Godfather* dancing to a band playing the "Hawaii Five-O" theme song? Other highlights include the world championship pizza toss, cheese sculpting, the official Blessing of the Animals, street vendors selling calamari with lime-garlic-dill aioli, a fantastic Arte di Gesso (chalk-art street-painting) contest, lots of men in tank-top undershirts and black socks, and a poets' tent featuring real, live, genuine Beat poets.

The other standout is the **Chinese New Year's Parade**. If you've never done this, you don't know what you're missing. A guaranteed flame rekindler. Giant dragons and lions dance through Chinatown; sleek Asian beauties wave from elaborately decorated floats; candidates campaign; firecrackers fly; and Grant Avenue is awash in the glow of a thousand tiny Chinese lanterns. After the parade, have a cocktail at **Li Po** or the **Bow Bow Lounge** for a *World of Suzie Wong* meets *Flower Drum Song* experience. It's Chinatown, Jake.

Enjoy Life, Sleep Out More Often

If you and the city are gonna stoke the old embers, why not set the proper mood? Leave the laundry, drop off the videos,

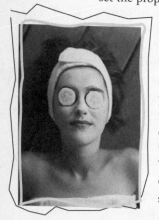

and head to a hotel. Best bets include the **Seal Rock Inn**, down by Ocean Beach. It's not fancy (in fact it could probably use an Extreme Makeover), but you get to wake up to the sound of waves crashing and fog horns blowing. Treat yourself to an early-morning walk on the beach, followed by breakfast at Louis'. Then walk on down to the **Beach Chalet** and reminisce among the WPA murals. Play the locals version of Where's Waldo and see if you can spot beloved Golden Gate Park superintendent John McClaren, sculptor Benny Bufano, and some of the lights of 1930s San Francisco society in these wonderful frescoes. Afterward, head upstairs for an amber ale at the microbrewery.

Those who feel they've gotten too comfortable and lost touch with the funky edge of hipster SF should make a beeline for the **Hotel Triton**. The court-jester-playroom-meets-Mount-Olympus décor is over-the-top eye candy: squiggly-back chairs topped with giant tassels, undulating pillars covered in gold leaf, spiraling floor lamps, walls painted in harlequin checkers, tables that jut out at odd angles, and royal blue carpeting emblazoned with stars. Splurge and stay in one of the suites designing by artistic celebrities, such as Graham Nash, Wyland, Carlos Santana, the cast of *Rent,* and the late Jerry Garcia. The rooms are small but nice, and—a bonus for natives who've forgotten how cosmopolitan a city we really are—the hotel lies adjacent to **Café de la Presse**, which serves a fabulous brunch at sidewalk tables and carries all the dishy international periodicals—*Paris Match* to *The Tatler.*

If you really want to feel like you've gotten away from it all, spend a weekend at the **Claremont Resort and Spa**, which is like a Palm Springs vacation, only better—you can sit on the terrace and gaze across the Bay at the San Francisco skyline. After your spa session and gourmet low-carb lunch, lie poolside and dream of the fairytale city that lies shimmering just beyond the horizon.

Chinese New Year Parade
Jan/Feb
415-982-3000

Li Po
916 Grant Ave.
415-421-0072

Bow Bow Lounge
1155 Grant Ave.
415-421-6730

Seal Rock Inn
545 Point Lobos Ave. at 48th Ave.
415-752-8000

Beach Chalet
1000 Great Highway
415-386-8439

Hotel Triton
342 Grant Ave.
415-394-0500

Café de la Presse
352 Grant Ave.
415-249-0900

Claremont Resort & Spa
41 Tunnel Road, Berkeley
510-843-3000

tour 2   San Francisco Virgins

Even though I grew up here and can never fully realize the wondrous revelation of seeing San Francisco for the very first time, I imagine that for many it's a life-changing experience.

I mean, if I can still get a lump in my throat at the sight of a cable car silhouetted against the evening sky atop Nob Hill, or the sound of an audience singing "San Francisco" at the top of its lungs before a movie at the Castro Theatre, just think what it could do for someone who's never been out of Kansas.

Playing tour guide to an SF virgin is a wonderful thing for a number of reasons:

1. It's easy—everything's new and exciting and amazing—even that lady with the space-alien lights in her hair who plays the accordion and sings "Feelin' Groovy."

2. You're required by the laws of hospitality to go to all those "tourist" places you'd never dream of visiting on your own (but were secretly dying to see), and you can blame it on your guests.

3. There's nothing quite like seeing your old, familiar haunts through the eyes of a newbie—a great way to renew your romance with the city.

MORNING–NOON

With first-timers, itineraries are a little more important than with other types of visitors, because there's a lot to squeeze into a day. Tours should be geared around areas where you can park and walk to a number of places, or where there's a logical progression in one direction. If your virgins are fairly fit and not afraid of a little traipsing, start out early Saturday morning in Chinatown, when the merchants are setting up shop. The streets fill with the smell of simmering soups and barbecued pork buns; in the windows hang roast ducks (heads still attached) and bizarre delicacies like armadillo, turtle, and pigs' noses; on the sidewalks are bins of embroidered slippers, wooden toys, and rice-paper candies. At about 10:30 or 11 a.m., scope out a dim sum parlor. The choices are endless, and it's actually hard to go wrong anywhere in Chinatown, but if your friends are not terribly adventurous, try the **Golden Dragon**, where you can get all the standards—pork and shrimp dumplings, roast duck, pot stickers, and sticky rice and sausage wrapped in a lotus leaf.

Location is the prime reason to try the **Hang Ah Tea Room**, which—in the tradition of the American "Breakfast Anytime" diner—serves dim sum until 9 p.m. Billed as the oldest dim sum place in Chinatown (established in 1920—the management claims some of the cooks have been here since then), it's located below street level on a tiny back

Golden Dragon
816 Washington St.
415-398-3920

Hang Ah Tea Room
1 Pagoda Pl., off Sacramento and Stockton streets
415-982-5686

alley called Pagoda Place, at the junction of even tinier Hang Ah Street. As you descend the steps, you half expect to see old Chinese men with long braids sitting cross-legged on pillows smoking opium pipes. But once you're inside, it's just your basic, no frills Chinese restaurant. For those who don't like weird food surprises, you can get traditional sweet-and-sour dishes here, as well as dim sum such as shrimp toast, foil-wrapped chicken, and steamed pork buns.

For more interesting variety and a Hong Kong atmosphere, try the enormous, three-story **Gold Mountain**, where steaming carts whiz by faster than traffic moves on Broadway, and where it's occasionally hard to hear yourself over the roar of the chattering—mostly Chinese—crowd. Dare your friends to close their eyes and point at a dish, regardless of what may be in it (the waitresses don't speak enough English to tell you anyway). Besides, half the fun is in the not knowing. (Hint to newcomers: if it looks like chicken feet, it probably is.) **Pearl City** is an inexpensive, good bet for the more adventurous palate. The mysterious-looking wrapped bundles are filled with everything from scallops and taro to sweet beans. (To my mind, three of the best dim sum parlors in the city are **Yank Sing**, **Harbor Village**, and **Mayflower Seafood Restaurant**—none of which is located in Chinatown. So if it's just excellent food and not atmosphere you're striving for, then skip the above and make one of these restaurants your morning destination.)

After brunch, wander through Ross Alley, making a requisite stop to watch the little old ladies carefully fold bits

You Will See An Increase In Profits

of wisdom into wing-shaped cookies at the **Golden Gate Fortune Cookie Factory** (more on this in the Nieces/Nephews tour), and up to Waverly Place. From the street, these apartment buildings don't look too inviting—a little run down, many with locked gates. But look up and it's a whole different world. Incense wafts from the ornate painted balconies, colorful Chinese paper lanterns swing in the breeze. Out-of-towners may feel apprehensive about going inside, but if they can handle four flights of stairs, they'll be rewarded with an amazing vision of pre-twentieth-century Chinese religious life. **Tin Hou Temple**, dedicated to the Queen of the Heavens and allegedly the oldest Chinese temple in San Francisco, is the one to visit with neophytes. Step inside the gate, and suddenly you're not in Kansas anymore. The ceiling is festooned with dozens of lanterns hung with red prayer papers and gilded miniature dioramas of villages. On one side, oranges, tangerines, flowers, and incense surround photos of loved ones who've passed away; on the other, there's an altar with ornate antique Buddhas and other intricately carved religious figures. On the balcony, an ancient Chinese woman burns incense and folds prayer papers. Encourage your friends to make a traditional offering by stuffing a dollar or two inside one of the small red envelopes at the front table.

From here, amble north along Grant Avenue until you hit the corner of Columbus. Prep your guests for the culture shock by stopping for a photo op at the intersection of Columbus and Broadway. Turn around and the Columbus Tower, in all its patina-green flatiron glory, is perfectly juxtaposed against the TransAmerica Pyramid, making it seem as if they're right next to each other. (If the architectural angle doesn't do it for them, be sure to tell them that Francis Ford Coppola's offices are located in the tower, and that the *Godfather* director can often be spotted sipping wine (his own) at a streetside table at **Café Niebaum-Coppola** in the base of the building.)

As you walk up Columbus into North Beach, start whistling "That's Amore" or the famous aria from *The Marriage of Figaro*. If your visitors are literary types, take a quick dip in **City Lights Bookstore** and **Vesuvio Café**, explaining the whole beatnik/Jack Kerouac connection (more on this in the Neo-Bohemians tour). Then zip across the street and into the **Condor Sports Bar**, nowadays a fine, upstanding establishment but once, as you may recall, the site of the first-ever topless club in California—a fact that always seems to satisfy the expectations of small-town folk who like to envision San Francisco as a wild, decadent, anything-goes kind of city. In 1964, dancer Carol Doda made headlines when, with the aid of silicon injections, she

Gold Mountain
644 Broadway
415-296-7733

Pearl City
641 Jackson St.
415-398-8383

Yank Sing
101 Spear St.
415-957-9300, and
49 Stevenson St.
415-541-4949

Harbor Village
4 Embarcadero
Center at Clay St.
415-781-8833

Mayflower Seafood Restaurant
6255 Geary Blvd.
415-387-8338

Golden Gate Fortune Cookie Factory
56 Ross Alley
415-781-3956

Tin Hou Temple
125 Waverly Pl.,
4th Floor

Cafe Niebaum-Coppola
916 Kearny St.
415-291-1700

City Lights Bookstore
261 Columbus Ave.
415-362-8193

Vesuvio Café
255 Columbus Ave.
415-362-8193

Condor Sports Bar
300 Columbus Ave.
415-781-8222

went from a 36B to a 36DD overnight. Doda's titillating topless act included descending on the hydraulically oper-ated white piano that now hangs from the ceiling of the bistro. Her original "topless bathing suit," along with the old marquee sporting the famous blinking nipples, are part of a small shrine in the cocktail lounge dedicated to the club's risque heyday. Newspaper clips along the wall give the place historical grounding; you can score extra points with first-timers by filling in the gory details of the incident involving the stripper found one morning in a very compromising position—naked on top of the piano, sandwiched between the ceiling and the club manager, who'd had a fatal heart attack.

Though not nearly as prurient in their connotation, the salamis that swing from the rafters at **Molinari's Deli** up the street are no less an integral part of North Beach's history, and a must-stop for virgins. Opened in 1896, the deli exudes mangia mangia spirit from every pore. Make your way past the jars of anchovies, artichokes, olive oils, pasta, and tomato sauces, past the glass cases filled with coppa, mozzarella, marinated red peppers and mushrooms, cala-

mari, et cetera, and up to the counter. Grab a hard roll from the box, hand it to the nice Italian man behind the counter, and get him to make you a pepper-salami sandwich with all the trimmings. Carry your precious cargo as directly as possible to **Washington Square Park** for a picnic (you might need to make a stop on the way at **Biordi**, the wonderful Italian pottery and hand-painted ceramics store). After you get comfortable on the lawn, gaze up at the spires of Saints Peter and Paul Church and picture Joe Di Maggio and Marilyn Monroe taking their wedding photos on the steps. Then send your friends on a quick jaunt to the **Liguria** bakery on the northeast corner of the park. Probably they're thinking they couldn't possibly pile anything on top of that sandwich, but the smell of fresh, steaming focaccia will change their minds. The small bakery, with its old-fashioned ovens, was founded on this spot by three brothers from

Genoa in 1911. Still run by members of the family, Liguria does nothing but make three or four kinds of focaccia bread every day. Locals line up around the block for it, and when the shop runs out, they close. (If you can't eat it now, save it for a late-afternoon snack.)

This may sound a little weird, but those **self-cleaning French toilets** are a nifty novelty for those who've never tried them (locals included), and there happens to be one located right on the south border of Washington Square, a perfect pit-stop on your way to Grant Avenue. Deposit a quarter in the slot and watch the magic door slide open. Step inside, do your business, exit swiftly (there's actually a time limit of twenty minutes, so don't get caught with your pants down), and then listen as the little machines inside make all kinds of strange sanitizing noises. You'll have to deposit another quarter to admire the sparkling results of their handiwork.

Upper Grant Avenue has always held a mysterious allure. There's something about the mix of divey bars, impossibly tiny storefronts crammed with assorted bric-a-brac, and cozy European-style cafés that makes you feel like you've discovered something no one else knows about. Though many of the most atmospheric places—Figoni Hardware, Quantity Postcards, the Schlock Shop—have vanished in the mists, I still have a revelation each time I walk down this crooked back street—a faux-leopard-collar jacket in the used-clothing shop; a vintage *Gone with the Wind* poster in **Show Biz**, the movie memorabilia store; great sangria at the **North End Caffè**.

Among the short-fingered handful of other don't-miss stops: **Old Vogue**, which carries fabulous Hawaiian shirts and a huge array of vintage Levi's; **Knitz & Leather** for simple and simply chic handmade leather jackets; and **Macchiarini Design**, a tiny workshop at the end of a long hallway where the Macchiarinis continue to craft stunning African-inspired jewelry into their seventh decade. This family—three generations of artisans—goes far enough back in North Beach history to have a street named after them (the stretch of steps above Columbus Avenue next to Enrico's).

Molinari's Deli
373 Columbus Ave.
415-421-2337

Washington Square Park
between Columbus Ave. and Stockton, Filbert, and Union streets

Biordi
412 Columbus Ave.
415-392-8096

Liguria
1700 Stockton St.
415-421-3786

Self-Cleaning French Toilets
Union and Stockton, Market and Powell, Haight and Stanyan, and Market and Castro streets

Show Biz
1318 Grant Ave.
415-989-6744

North End Caffè
1441 Grant Ave.
415-956-3350

Old Vogue
1412 Grant Ave.
415-392-1522

Knitz & Leather
1429 Grant Ave.
415-391-3480

Macchiarini Design
1529 Grant Ave. Suite B
415-982-2229

Let your friends wander aimlessly along the avenue for as long as they want; just make sure they eventually end up at a sidewalk table at **Caffè Trieste**. Once an arty beatnik hangout (it opened in 1956), Trieste is run by the Giottas, the city's only opera-singing, coffee-making family, who perform popular Italian songs and arias on Saturday afternoons. Get a double latte (fresh-roasted next door and served perfectly—with the dark stuff still separated from the steamed milk in your glass), then settle into a chair and write a missive to Mom, as the strains of "Santa Lucia" waft out the door and the scenesters pore over dog-eared copies of *Dharma Bums*.

Just before sunset, stroll down to the opposite end of Grant Avenue (between Chestnut and Francisco) and look for the staircase leading up to **Jack Early Park**, one of those stumble-upon-it spots that never fails to make newcomers shake their heads in delight and amazement. The "park,"

built by neighborhood resident Jack Early in 1962, is actually not much more than a scenic overlook at the top of a set of zigzag steps flanked by a well-kempt garden. But there's something about the hidden-ness and the hush of the square platform, with its old-fashioned lamppost, that feels secret and special. Lean out over the railing and gaze down onto Fisherman's Wharf, as the barges plow through the bay, and the call of the mournful foghorns and barking sea lions drifts overhead. Behind you, the million-dollar mansions of Telegraph Hill look on approvingly. Request a moment of silence and let the sounds of the city seep into your soul. Then watch your starry-eyed friends for signs of a perfect San Francisco moment.

Filbert Street Steps

Perhaps no single place captures the have-your-cake-and-eat-it-too spirit of San Francisco better than the Filbert Street Steps. Though they sit smack dab in the heart of the city, they exist almost separate from it—an intimate, magical Eden perched against the precariously steep slopes of Telegraph Hill. The cottages that flank the wooden stairs

Caffè Trieste
609 Grant Ave.
415-392-6739

Jack Early Park
off Grant Ave.
between Chestnut
and Francisco

**Filbert Street
Steps**
between Sansome
and Montgomery,
below Coit Tower

Julius' Castle
1541 Montgomery
St. (north of Union)
415-392-2222

along Napier Lane and Darrell Place enjoy the rare privilege of an auto-free environment, yet they boast the most coveted views of the Bay money can buy. Look to the side and you'll feel like you're in a French village—cats lolling beneath vine-covered walls lapping up tin pans of milk, flowerpots spilling over the walkway, watering cans propping open stylishly rusted gates. Look back and you're engulfed by Grace Marchant's beloved terraced garden of baby tears, clambering roses, and bougainvillaea—lush and overgrown, yet all but invisible to the world. Look up and you'll wonder if you're on the right continent: flitting through the treetops are flocks of South American parrots (specifically cherry-headed conures), once caged household pets, now happily undomesticated and breeding in the trees on Telegraph Hill. Look out and the harbor spreads before you, with the East Bay shimmering dreamily in the distance. If you happen to time it just right, and your friends are here around Halloween, take them down the steps in the evening, when the Telegraph Hill dwellers light up dozens of jack-o'-lanterns for the trick-or-treaters.

On your way up or down the steps, be sure to point out significant sites: the art deco apartment house at 1360 Montgomery Street that was the facade used in the Humphrey Bogart/Lauren Bacall flick, *Dark Passage*; the hole on the hill just before you descend to Sansome Street where a house came crashing down a few years ago; the miniature trompe l'oeil doggie park on Montgomery Street just above the steps, with its adorable mural of an alluring poodle and a tempting fire hydrant; and of course **Julius' Castle**, the venerable romantic restaurant with the above-average (and expensive) food, whose views of the bay remain unchallenged in the city.

Doing the Wharf Thing

When you're dealing with San Francisco novices, there are certain visitation requirements, and Fisherman's Wharf is one of them. It doesn't matter that you'd rather spend an afternoon in Turlock. First-timers want to see what all the hype is about, and as host, it's your duty to deliver them to it. So why not make the best of it? The wharf may even surprise you. If you can weed through the sidewalk sketch artists, the piles of "I ESCAPED FROM ALCATRAZ" T-shirts (they've got ones that are so much better now, like "ALCATRAZ TRIATHLON—DIG, DASH, DIVE"), the churro sticks, and the wind-up cable cars, you might even find a few things worth seeing.

Begin at the **Maritime Museum** and spend a few minutes studying the 19th-century renderings and photos of

the old waterfront, when clipper ships graced this C-shaped inner harbor. Then step out onto the back veranda, squint your eyes a little bit, and with the help of the historic ships docked nearby (especially the *Balclutha*, an 1883 square rigger that once sailed around Cape Horn and looks like a giant prop for a swashbuckling pirate flick), you can imagine these waters a hundred years ago. Go down the steps and walk around **Aquatic Park**, making sure to point out the old men in the orange caps (members of the Dolphin Club) swimming in the bay as if it were their own private pool. For some odd reason, not too many people other than Marina district joggers and fishermen seem to venture out onto Municipal Pier at the west end. The long, curving walkway arcs around to the edge of the harbor and into the bay, where you can hobnob with the fishermen and get show-stopping views of the port and Alcatraz. (Caution: if seen at sunset, this vista may very well cause your friends from Buffalo to put a "For Sale" sign on their front lawn.)

Next, head east through **Maritime National Historical Park** and board at least one of the boats. Most opt for the *Balclutha*, because it's the most showy, but the *C.A. Thayer*, an 1895 three-mast lumber schooner, and the hardworking tugboat *Hercules* are equally interesting. In the spring and fall, the *C.A. Thayer* hosts the Festival of the Sea and a music series—a tribute to the nautical life in melodrama and song.

Then make your way past Pier 45, where what's left of the fishing fleet delivers its catch early in the morning, and on to the dreaded **Pier 39**. Honestly—and even your trailer-trash cousins from Middle-of-Nowhere, Florida, will agree—

this is one seriously tacky tourist trap. But if you can stop struggling and accept that, you might actually enjoy yourself. First off, visit the sea lions on the west side docks. People invariably seem to forget that these barking, belching, herring-eating buffoons, now considered one of the numerous attractions on the pier, chose to come here all on their own and not as part of some elaborate fake set-up. It's still amazing to see them lying all over each other, fighting for sunbathing space, and bobbing around the harbor like it was Sea Lion Week at Club Med. Probably the only other things worth checking out at Pier 39, aside from the free juggling and magic acts, which are always worth a few chuckles, the **National Parks Store** (see Green Fiends), and the old **Eagle Café** (see Cheapskates), are the interesting and informative signs chronicling the physical and political history of Pier 39, and, if you're willing to shell out $13, the **Aquarium of the Bay**, a truly fascinating feat of underwater technology.

The history markers—photo/text vignettes that describe, among other things, the machinations of financing this massive venture, dredging the harbor, and finessing City Hall politicos back in the '70s when unions were all-powerful—offer a fascinating look at the waterfront, and may take some of the pain out of standing in line later to eat shrimp at Bubba Gump's.

The aquarium offers a pretty cool "underwater" view of the bay. You ride a people-mover through two enormous acrylic tubes while fish swim all around you. It's like a live version of *The Little Mermaid* (see Nieces/Nephews for details).

From the outside, **Lou's Pier 47** down the street seems like it might be one of those bars that push expensive cocktails and cheesy disco dancing (à la Houlihan's), but it's not. The second-story bar is one of the few places where you can hear live music—specifically blues—all day, every day. Admittedly, some of the bands are reminiscent of those you hear at high school reunions, but others are local favorites and genuine talents (hey—a gig's a gig). Either way, it's a nice little break from the madding crowd.

Maritime Museum
near Hyde St. Pier,
900 Beach St.
415-561-7100

Aquatic Park
Beach St. between
Larkin and Van Ness

Maritime National Historical Park
next to Aquatic
Park at Larkin St.,
495 Jefferson St.
415-447-5000

Pier 39
Embarcadero east
of Fisherman's
Wharf
415-981-7437

National Parks Store
Pier 39
415-433-7221

Eagle Café
Pier 39
415-433-3689

Aquarium of the Bay
Pier 39
415-623-5300

Lou's Pier 47
300 Jefferson St.
415-771-5687

From Lou's head west and walk through **The Cannery** (Lark in the Morning, a store that sells musical instruments from around the world, is perhaps the only reason to slow down here anymore) on your way to the **Buena Vista Café** for Irish coffee. Sit at the bar (not a table) and watch the deft bartenders line 'em in a long row and pour 'em— creamy and perfect. The cocktail was not invented here, but it was the late *San Francisco Chronicle* columnist Stanton Delaplane who brought the recipe back from Dublin in 1952, and a Buena Vista bartender who re-created it for the first time stateside.

Next, chowtime. When a-million-and-one tourists head to a seafood restaurant on Fisherman's Wharf, locals naturally assume it sucks and run in the opposite direction. It's a

matter of personal pride. But you've gotta ask yourself, What keeps bringing these people back? The hype? The enormous cocktails? A lack of imagination? Maybe, just maybe, there's some merit in the maré. I think that's definitely true of Alioto's and maybe even of Scoma's. For first-timers, the fish-receiving station at **Scoma's** is a big bonus, a chance to see the wharf actually at work. The building boasts big windows where you can watch the daily catch being hoisted from fishing boats onto big tables, where it's cleaned, filleted, declawed, et cetera. The famous crab comes in November through May, salmon season is May through September, and you don't have to get up at dawn to catch all the action. Local fisherman are notoriously irregular with their deliveries; it all depends on which way (and how hard) the wind is blowing. The restaurant is tucked in at the end of Pier 45, on a surprisingly quiet stretch of the wharf, fronting a small arm of the harbor. Maybe its hidden location is one of the keys to Scoma's unflagging popularity—who knows? Wharf restaurateurs have been trying to figure out for years what makes this the highest grossing restaurant in California. On any given day, the menu offers maybe a dozen kinds of fresh fish and shellfish, including (when in season) swordfish, ahi tuna, halibut, snapper, salmon, sole, sand dabs, oysters, and scallops. This is also a great place to eat if your virgins have kids. Besides the fish-handling station, a huge child-pleaser, Scoma's has place mats kids can color and a special children's menu that offers nonfishy food. (Two caveats: expect to pay top tourist dollar; don't expect anything the caliber of Aqua or Farallon.)

For sheer historical value, you owe first-timers a lunch or dinner at **Alioto's**, where practically everyone is named Nunzio (descendants of the original Sicilian family who opened this place as a walkaway fish stand back in the 1920s still run the ship), and where authentic San Francisco cioppino, the Italian shellfish stew made with zesty red sauce, was first popularized. If you've never been to Alioto's, you're in for a surprise: the food is pretty good, especially if you stick to the Sicilian dishes. And every few years, Alioto's takes Viagra or gets a new sous chef and the menu really sparkles with top-notch seafood risotto, seafood sausage stuffed with lobster and other delicacies, and their famous cioppino—a hearty, messy, chock-full-o-fresh-Dungeness bowl of San Francisco goodness.

Finish off the evening with a ride on the cable car back to downtown. At night, when the crowds have died down, your virgin friends can truly appreciate the concept of riding "halfway to the stars" as Tony Bennett described it.

Other Mandatory Stops

You can take 'em or leave 'em, but the first-timers love 'em. In brief:

Walking across the Golden Gate Bridge—As the fog buffets you around like a cat toy and the sailboats disappear into the mist, sing a rousing version of "San Francisco, open your Golden Gate . . ." or "California Here I Come."

Cocktails at sunset at the Cliff House—Go ahead, get sappy. Applaud when the sun dips below the horizon. That's why you come here. A hipper alternative is English ale at the **Beach Chalet** overlooking the schools of hot, young surfers.

Beach Blanket Babylon—There's a reason this is the longest-running musical revue in history. It's funny, it's lively, it's clever, it's got ridiculously gargantuan hats. And where else are you ever going to see a chorus line of men in

The Cannery
2801 Leavenworth
415-928-0289

Buena Vista Café
2765 Hyde St.
415-474-5044

Scoma's
Pier 47 (Jones St.)
415-771-4383

Alioto's
8 Fisherman's Wharf
415-673-0183

Cliff House
1090 Point Lobos Ave.
415-386-3330

Beach Chalet
1000 Great Highway
415-386-8439

Beach Blanket Babylon
678 Green St.
415-421-4222

togas, sandals, and bald caps singing "I'm a Yankee Doodle Ghandi?"

Driving Highway 1—Doesn't matter how many times you've done it, every time you come over the crest near Devil's Slide it takes your breath away. The precipitously winding road that skirts those sheer cliffs, the sun-bleached beaches, and the wild green surf is nothing short of miraculous. Rent a convertible and do it right.

Alcatraz Island—The best tour for your tourist buck. Spend the extra $2 and get the audio narration of the cellhouse, which features tales of The Rock told by former guards and inmates. Sit in the solitary confinement cell. Stare out at the city from the ferry docks and imagine the

tantalizing agony of being so close to San Francisco and never being able to set foot on her shores.

Sam Woh Restaurant—The food, she stinks. But like the **House of Nanking** (where the food's better, but the lines are longer), dining here is a San Francisco tradition. In the old days, when the impossibly narrow, rickety restaurant was run by hilarious dictator Edsel Ford Fong, you couldn't beat the place for atmosphere. These days it's tamer, but you still have to walk through the kitchen and up the staircase to get to the dining rooms, the sink is still in the middle of the room (remember to wash your hands), and if chow fun noodles are your bag, you can still get big, sloppy platefuls of 'em here.

Wine Tasting—Okay, admit it. You love doing this as much as they do. But not when you have to sit bumper-to-bumper with a bunch of drunks on Highway 29. So do yourself and your novice friends a favor and bypass Napa Valley for the verdant vineyards of the Russian River region, where tastings are free and picnic grounds are plentiful. Head up Highway 101 past Santa Rosa to River Road and follow it to the string of picturesque wineries along Westside Road, in particular **Davis Bynum**, **Rochioli**, **Hop Kiln**, and **Rabbit Ridge**. Rochioli makes lip-smackin' pinot noir and has lovely picnic tables that overlook vineyards; the Hop Kiln tasting room next door is housed inside a historic stone building that was once used to dry hops for beer making. Rabbit Ridge and Davis Bynum are equally pretty, and they make wonderful, well-priced wines.

GOING TO EXTREMES

I like to call this the "-est" tour. It's the one where you get in the car and take your friends who hail from the flatlands down the steepest streets and crookedest streets, and up to the highest summits for the supremest views of the city. Virgins love it because it's the San Francisco they see in all those movie car-chase scenes. You love it because you get to pretend you're Karl Malden in a forgotten episode of "Streets of San Francisco."

Steepest Streets—There are two: Filbert between Hyde and Leavenworth, and Hill Street above Church near 22nd Street. Milk it for all its worth. Drive very slowly to the top. Inch the nose of the car over the crest. To the untrained eye, it seems like you're about to drop off the edge of the earth. Wait for the gasps and white knuckles on the back of the seat, then plunge over the edge while laughing maniacally.

Crookedest Streets—Wait in line and do the requisite serpentine ride down **Lombard Street**. Let the kids hang out the sunroof. Take the photo looking down Hyde Street. Then hang a right at the bottom of the hill and go three blocks to Union Street and take them for a walk down **Macondray Lane**. The tiny, tucked-away street, with its rickety wooden walkway and apartments hidden amid overgrown vines, was the model for the fictional Barbary Lane of Armistead Maupin's *Tales of the City* books.

Afterward, go to the back of Potrero Hill and show them the real "crookedest street in the world"—minus all the hype and tourists. The end of **Vermont Street** packs more thrilling twists and turns into its eight switchbacks than Lombard; plus the views are almost as good, and you get the added bonus of landing in the Mission district, home of the best burritos this side of Tijuana.

High Points—Though the city was built around seven main peaks, there are actually 43 hills in San Francisco, each of them with something to say about the lay of the land.

Alcatraz Island
Blue and Gold Ferry
Service, Pier 41,
Fisherman's Wharf
415-773-1188

**Sam Woh
Restaurant**
813 Washington St.
415-982-0596

**House of
Nanking**
919 Kearny St.
415-421-1429

Davis Bynum
8075 Westside
Road, Healdsburg
707-433-5852

Rochioli
6192 Westside
Road, Healdsburg
707-433-6491

Hop Kiln
6050 Westside
Road, Healdsburg
707-433-6491

Rabbit Ridge
3291 Westside
Road, Healdsburg
707-431-7128

Lombard Street
between Hyde and
Leavenworth streets

Macondray Lane
off Leavenworth at
Union St.

Vermont Street
between 20th, 21st,
Kansas and San
Bruno streets

Twin Peaks—The granddaddy of inspiration points offers a view of the city and environs to the east, north, and south. The only problem with this overlook is the freezing, blowing fog that often engulfs it and obscures views. If that's the case, drive down to the perch just below it, either on Diamond Heights Boulevard just as it rounds the bend to

Safeway, or at the top of Upper Market Street, where the tip of the Pyramid and the lights of the Bay Bridge are just a little more tangible.

20th and Church Streets (Dolores Park)—Sit at a bench at the top of the park and downtown jumps out at you like a children's pop-up book.

Tank Hill—Go up Stanyan Street to the very tippy-top and hang a left at Belgrave Park. Hike up the dirt path. Be prepared to gasp. To the left, the Golden Gate Bridge, the Pacific, Golden Gate Park, and Saint Ignatius; to the right, downtown, the Pyramid, the Bay Bridge, and the East Bay.

19th and Texas Streets—The best point on Potrero Hill from which to survey the downtown landscape. Ironically, the house on the corner was the main setting for the movie *Pacific Heights*.

Marin Headlands—This is the postcard view of San Francisco. Nothing beats watching the fog roll in through the Golden Gate. Take the first turnoff after the bridge onto Conzelman Road.

NIGHT

There are so many restaurants that do California cuisine (or some variation on the theme), that when the uninitiated ask, "Where's the best place?" you invariably look at them stupidly and say, "Um, I know this great Thai restaurant. . . ." What they want, of course, is the stuff they've been reading about in *Zagat's* and *Gourmet* magazine. Here's where you should take them:

Chez Panisse—The restaurant that invented California cuisine some 30 years ago still makes exquisite food—

homey, flavorful, simple, and using the freshest fish, game, and produce from local, mostly organic farms and ranches. I once had a summer tomato salad with goat cheese there that made me weep with joy. Reservations are not optional at the downstairs restaurant, which serves a nightly four-course, prix fixe menu for (at last check) $75 on weekends, not including tax, wine, and a 15 percent gratuity that's automatically tacked on to the bill. It ain't cheap, and even with your month-in-advance reservations you may have to wait a few minutes (people love to linger), but it's worth it.

If the price isn't right, or you didn't have time to plan in advance, the upstairs casual café is a good second choice, pulling its Mediterranean-inspired menu from the same refrigerators, but offering a wide range of à la carte items at prices that average about $20 for an entree. They don't take dinner reservations Fridays and Saturdays (you may go through a bottle of wine waiting at the bar), but they do take a limited number of same-day reservations Monday through Thursday. Also, Mondays at the downstairs restaurant are a relative bargain: $50 for a three-course dinner.

Globe—This lively little spot in Jackson Square, which serves until 1 a.m., is where chefs head after they finish their shifts. The meat-heavy menu doesn't mean you should overlook dishes such as baked mussels, shrimp, and scallops served on a plate with indentations that coddles the shellfish in their own individual garlic-butter bath. Another great touch: salads and soups served in giant handmade pottery dishes and mixing bowls.

Cafe Kati—Kirk Webber creates dishes that are as beautiful as they are tasty—sculptural creations, really—with curlicue vegetables, towers of spun sugar, and hieroglyphic drizzles. Diminutive Cafe Kati was one of the first wave of "fusion" restaurants that married the flavors of India, Thailand, the Pacific Islands, and China to California homegrown meats and vegetables.

Tadich Grill—What can you say about this Gold Rush classic, the oldest restaurant in San Francisco (circa 1849) that hasn't already been said? Take your friends here for the history, the curtained booths, the conversations at the long wooden counter, the grumpy old waiters in white. Take

Chez Panisse
1517 Shattuck Ave.,
Berkeley
510-548-5525

Globe
290 Pacific Ave.
415-391-4132

Cafe Kati
1963 Sutter St.
415-775-7313

Tadich Grill
240 California St.
415-391-1849

yourself here for all the aforementioned, plus the sole meuniere and the sand dabs.

LuLu—It's hard to beat this cavernous room for its lively see-and-be-seen scene. Plus, the menu reads like the dictionary definition of California cuisine: wood-fired rosemary chicken, skillet-roasted mussels, thin-crusted pizzettas, garlic-and-olive-oil mashed potatoes, and pasta dishes overflowing with vegetables straight from the organic garden. Who cares if you can't hear yourself think?

Zuni Cafe—Judy Rogers's original house of Cal-Med cuisine was doing wood-fired meats long before LuLu was even a blip on the screen. The crowd is Hayes Valley meets Pacific Heights; the decor is neo-industrial meets New Mexico; the food is sublime. Lots of attitude and good smells. All in all, pure San Francisco.

The Spinnaker—Not for the seafood, which is above average at best, but for everything else: the location on a pier directly over Sausalito harbor, the view (to end all views) of the San Francisco skyline, and the path that takes you from the front door along what is perhaps the West Coast's most picturesque waterfront parkway. Watch the twinkling lights dance in the Bay and your friends won't be the only ones lost in Neverland.

WHERE TO STAY

Though I generally prefer to stay in offbeat, cozy hotels, San Francisco virgins will probably get the most from a larger, showier place in one of the tourist centers.

The **Argonaut Hotel**, opened in 2003, is the first real luxury hotel to park itself directly on Fisherman's Wharf. A link in the Kimpton chain of classy boutique properties, the hotel is housed in a historic brick building, just steps from Ghirardelli Square, the Cannery, and Maritime Park. As you might expect, a nautical theme runs throughout the place— porthole windows, rich royal blue and gold décor, wooden plank floors, a steamer trunk for a front desk—giving it a salty, wharfy feel that first-timers will appreciate. They'll probably love even more the fitness center, the flat-screen TV in their room, free high-speed Internet access, and the nightly wine reception.

Then there are the Nob Hill grande dames—the **Mark Hopkins**, the **Fairmont**, and the **Huntington**. Of these, the Huntington is the most personable (it's still family-owned), though not as constantly renovated as the other two. The Mark really feels like a grande dame, with its venerable skyroom lounge and its sweeping driveway entrance. The Fairmont, with a recent overhaul under its belt that has brought it back to its original Julia Morgan glory (minus all the red velvet and gold tassels), may just edge out the Mark for sheer spectacle. Along with the fabulously kitschy Tonga Room, the Corinthian marble columns, the gilded-relief ceilings, and its stint as poster-girl for the TV show "Hotel," the Fairmont boasts the distinction of being the place where Tony Bennett first sang "I Left My Heart in San Francisco." Hard to top that.

On the modern end of the scale, the theater-district **Hotel Monaco** shows off San Francisco's stylish side in the best light—a larger-than-life art nouveau poster for the golden age of travel. This is the place to send first-time visitors who prefer to tiptoe on the edge of trendiness rather than sink waist-deep in tradition. With its soaring whimsical sculptures and murals, bold colors and patterns, and just enough kooky touches—pet goldfish for your room, nightly tarot card readings—to put a San Francisco stamp on things, the Monaco could almost be a sightseeing destination in and of itself. The hotel scores extra points for its house restaurant, Grand Café, which feels like an American brasserie set in a Paris train station circa 1929 and has one of the best après-theater bars in town.

LuLu
816 Folsom St.
415-495-5775

Zuni Cafe
1658 Market St.
415-552-2522

The Spinnaker
100 Spinnaker Drive, Sausalito
415-332-1500

The Argonaut Hotel
495 Jefferson St.
415-563-2800

Mark Hopkins Hotel
1 Nob Hill /
999 California St.
415-392-3434

The Fairmont Hotel
California and Mason streets
415-772-5000

The Huntington Hotel
1075 California St.
415-474-5400

Hotel Monaco
501 Geary St.
415-292-0100

tour 3 Parents

Parents. Can't live with 'em, can't take their credit cards with you when you move out. But no matter how many times you've woken up surrounded by pizza boxes and dirty laundry and smiled with

contentment when you realized that it was just the cat using your plant as a litter box and not your mom's clicking tongue, you still want to impress them when they come to visit. It doesn't matter if they only live as far away as Palo Alto, because this is your town now—your neighborhood, your friends, your beat-up futon, your stack of unpaid parking tickets—and for once you get to be the one with all the presents under the tree.

A couple of things to keep in mind: most parents want the *Sunset* magazine version of San Francisco, not the underground guide, no matter how young and hip and "with it" they pretend to be. They want

The Magic Flute
3673 Sacramento St.
415-922-1225

the San Francisco where people are polite and pick up their trash, where there are brochures and interesting historical markers to read, and where there are plenty of conveniences (read: necessities) such as clean bathrooms and, of course, parking. Second, you'll want to find a good place to put them up that is not your apartment. Frankly, you don't want your parents getting too familiar with the contents of your bathroom cabinets or the strange messages on your answering machine. Most importantly, if they're staying for longer than a weekend, you're going to need a break so you can get back in touch with your real personality. Otherwise, you might find yourself locked in the bedroom with the music turned up loud, and all those years of hard-won independence will be down the toilet.

Lastly, try to throw your parents a bone at least once during their stay: wear the damn birthday shirt, let your dad map out the best route even though you've been there a hundred times, tell them how much your friends like them. You've got nothing to lose but some emotional baggage.

MORNING

All parental visits begin with brunch; a few sure-fire hits:

The Magic Flute—It's not the beloved Tuba Gardens, but it's the next best thing, owned by the same people, and directly across the street from where the garden/gazebo restaurant that hosted a-million-and-two intergenerational Sunday outings used to be. The Magic Flute captures much of that spirit, with flower boxes, white tablecloths, sponge-painted walls, alfresco dining on an enclosed patio under umbrellas, and a brunch menu that includes benedicts, omelets, and Belgian waffles.

The Terrace Room—Even if you've taken an oath never to do anything this bourgeois, make an exception for brunch at the Ritz. Besides scoring major points with the 'rents, you'll probably be surprised (and maybe just a tad disappointed) at how much you yourself get into it. This is the Zsa Zsa Gabor of Sunday brunches—a seriously classy (and pricey) affair served on a sunken rooftop terrace amid an Alice in Wonderland rose and hedge garden. The unbelievably lavish buffet begins with a bottomless champagne glass, then segues into fresh-chilled prawns and oysters on the half shell, a complete caviar bar, smoked meats and fish of every imaginable variety, lamb carved off the rack, a half-dozen hot entrees, and a table featuring nothing but muffins, breads, and other baked goods. Just figuring out which courses you haven't tried can be an all-day event, so it's a good thing they provide entertainment (a jazz combo performs all day). But wait. Don't pop the top button yet. There's more. Inside the dining room is a dessert spread that would make Willy Wonka blush.

Ella's—This is the place to go to reassure your parents that not all your associates are low-life, futon-surfing slackers. The wildly popular brunch spot on the edge of

Presidio Heights attracts the bubbly foam of young champagne society, along with assorted stroller-pushing couples and Pacific Heights/Western Addition stragglers who wait in long lines for made-from-scratch buttermilk pancakes and irresistible sticky buns.

Beach Chalet and Park Chalet—The Cliff House is traditional, but the menu, like the building, is showing its age (both are in the midst of an overhaul, but that's for another edition), and Louis's repertoire is perhaps just a tad too down-and-diner. The Beach Chalet or its downstairs sister, the Park Chalet, however, are definitely on your parents' wavelength. Aim for an ocean-view or a garden-side table, order the banana bread French toast with banana rum sauce, and watch them ooh and aah.

Clement Street Bar and Grill—"Like attracts like,"
they say, so it's not all that surprising that most of the folks
who eat here tend to look like somebody's parents. This is a
really "nice" place, with all that that implies. Noisy without
being raucous, hanging-plant homey, but with classy dark-
wood paneling, white tablecloths, and a fireplace. The menu
is a happy balance of foods you eat at home and stuff you
eat only at fancy brunch restaurants: bagel and lox platters,
crab cakes Benedict, sourdough French toast, baskets of
warm muffins and fresh breads, and the requisite spicy
Bloody Marys and strong coffee.

NOON

For some strange reason, after parents reach a certain age,
they become obsessed with parking. It's a time in their lives
when you can expect more than 40 percent of any conversation to include such phrases as: What's the parking situation
there? Do the meters take dimes and nickels? Is there a
parking lot? How much does it cost? Is that a safe neighborhood to park in? Do you have to parallel park or can you go
nose in? They become experts at discerning the color of
curbs from great distances and, in certain extreme cases,
gear entire outings around the fact that they've found a free,
all-day parking spot.

San Francisco is not exactly a parking friendly town—
and certainly it's a huge adjustment for parents who are used
to the embarrassment of parking riches in the suburbs (take a
spot—take three). Couple this with the fact that gas stations
in the city are disappearing faster than Starbucks are proliferating, and you have a parental nightmare. There are several
things you can do to allay their fears:

1. If they insist on driving the Cadillac here, scope out a
   parking spot ahead of time (or give up yours), deposit
   the car, and take alternate means of transportation the
   rest of the time.
2. If they're flying in, pick them up from the airport
   before they've had a chance to peruse the car rental
   agencies.

Terrace Room
Ritz-Carlton,
600 Stockton St.
415-296-7465

Ella's
500 Presidio Ave.
415-441-5669

**Beach Chalet &
Park Chalet**
1000 Great Hwy. at
Ocean Beach
415-386-8439

**Clement Street
Bar and Grill**
708 Clement St.
415-386-2200

3. Before you go out to a restaurant, research the street parking situation. If it's bad, make sure there's valet parking or a nearby parking garage. Do not circle for hours like you usually do, praying to the God of Parking Karma. This is guaranteed to drive parents into a paranoid frenzy from which they may never recover.

Parking It in the Park

At some point you're going to have to make the requisite visit to Golden Gate Park; knowing a few trade secrets and doing your homework on park history will go a long way to soothing any ruffled feathers over that whole tuition money/ Jamaica vacation snafu.

For those who've experienced the agony of trying to find a parking spot in the park on a Sunday that isn't in a different time zone, here's a lifesaver: You can park at **Stow Lake** on Sunday—for free (at least for the time being). And unbelievably, there always seem to be plenty of spots. Even better, you are no more than a 10-minute walk to the Arboretum, Japanese Tea Garden, rose gardens, and de Young Museum. Stop, stop. You can thank me later.

Most of us think of the **Strybing Arboretum** as a nice garden in which to throw down a picnic blanket and feed the enthusiastic (read: rabid) squirrels. But now that the folks have become cult-like devotees of the 24-hour Gardening Network, it might behoove you to dig a little

below the sod. Did you know, for instance, that the arboretum has more than 7,000 varieties of plants, with species from places as far-flung as the Asiatic cloud forests, South Africa, and eastern Australia? Did you know there's a succulent garden and a fragrance garden for the sight impaired? Did you know docents offer free tours of the garden daily at 1:30 p.m. and that there are gardeners on hand to help you answer troublesome perennial-planting questions? Didja? Didja?

There's something about a little bronze plaque in honor of fallen war heroes or a sports legend of yesteryear that is categorically irresistible to people of the parental persuasion. The park, as it happens, is filled with statues and monuments that honor such figures, but they are cleverly hidden in the most inconspicuous locations. "Uncle" John McLaren, who tended the park as superintendent for more than 50 years, did not care for statues. In fact, he hated them so much, it is rumored that he took the one sculptor Earl Cummings created of McLaren himself and hid it in the stables, where it was not discovered until after his death in 1943. Though it may seem troublesome at first, finding statues in the park can be a great way to tour the park and have an ersatz scavenger hunt at the same time. The pursuit takes you through some of the park's prettiest glens and groves (McLaren, it is said, planted certain gardens just to hide unsightly statuary). My favorites include General Henry W. Halleck, for its obscurity of both location and identity. Lincoln's Civil War Chief of Staff and framer of the California constitution (put that in your Trivial Pursuit box and smoke it!) is tucked between the tennis courts and John F. Kennedy Drive. And my nomination in the Why Him? Category goes to the statue of Irish Patriot Robert Emmet, who stands at the edge of the Academy of Sciences, his bewildered countenance suggesting he is as confused about his presence here are we are. You can find maps to the monuments at the Japanese Tea Garden, McLaren Lodge, and the Fine Arts museums.

Making Nice-Nice with Mom

When faced with an impending visit from mom, and the inevitable dilemma of how to make up for all the Mother's Day/birthday cards you forgot to send over the years, kids-in-the-know head to **Shelldance Nursery**. Located on a bluff overlooking the ocean in Pacifica, this amazing orchid conservatory, part of the Golden Gate National Recreation Area, is worth a visit for the scenery alone. The owners are gardeners and land stewards who helped save the nursery from being flattened for a freeway. Since then, they've made it a mission to cultivate and preserve dozens of varieties of rare orchids, including one that has survived four generations of

Stow Lake
50 Stow Lake Dr.,
take the 9th Ave.
entrance to the second driveway past
the Tea Garden

Strybing Arboretum
9th Ave. and Tea
Garden Dr.
415-564-3239

Shelldance Orchid Nursery
2000 Highway 1,
Pacifica
650-355-4845

one family. Plants are for sale and come with easy-to-tend instructions (hint, hint), and there's also a nice gift shop and art gallery for browsing.

If you're already doing the flowers, why not seal up the inheritance with chocolate? After all, you live in a place that overflows with vats of blue-ribbon purveyors. My top choices:

Who knew? **XOX Truffles**, voted top American truffle by publications ranging from *Chocolatier Magazine* and *Food & Wine* to the *New York Times* and the Food Network's *Rosengarten Report,* are made right under our noses in North Beach! Aside from an assortment of exotic flavors—cocoa-powder-dusted crème de framboise to white-chocolate with dark chocolate centers; French roast-flavored to six varieties of vegan soy truffles—Chef Jean-Marc Gorce makes each creamy wonder a perfect pop-in-your-mouth size, just right for moms who invariably want "just a bite" (usually of whatever you're having).

No one does discs like **Joseph Schmidt**. The deceptively flat little chocolate "Slicks," stuffed with everything from dark lemon to peanut butter, pack as much punch as truffles three times their size. Purveyor to all the finer stores, Schmidt crafts all his creations in a Mission District warehouse but also keeps a tidy little shop on 16th Street below Church, where you will find Slicks and truffles, as well as his fantastical trademark chocolate sculptures: bowls, tulips, champagne bottles, golf balls, flowering trees, butterflies, and other objects of his confection.

The name **Scharffenberger** has become a household word to confection and pastry chefs the world over—synonymous with 100-percent pure, dark, artisanal chocolate. Getting mom a bar from the store is okay, but you'll make her month if you reserve a spot on a factory tour, offered three times daily at the small Berkeley plant. Watching the machines swirling vats of gooey chocolate promises to deliver on every Willy Wonka fantasy you—er, *she*—ever had. Samples are given out at the end.

XOX Truffles
754 Columbus Ave.
415-421-4814

Joseph Schmidt
3489 16th St.
415-861-8682

Scharffenberger Chocolate
914 Heinz Ave.,
Berkeley
510-981-4050

Lake Merced
Lake Merced Blvd.
and John Muir Dr.

Angler's Lodge and Casting Pools
Golden Gate Park,
JFK Dr. at 36th Ave.

Big Four
Huntington Hotel,
1075 California St.
415-771-1140

Ritz-Carlton
600 Stockton St.
415-296-7465

Anchor Steam Brewing Company
1705 Mariposa St.
415-863-8350

Bonding with Dad

Fishing with Dad is a time-honored ritual that is part of nearly every father-son bonding movie ever made. Does it work? Who knows, but it's worth a try. Rent a boat and go trout fishing in **Lake Merced**, which isn't exactly Montana's Big Blackfoot, but it's well stocked, and if you catch one that's been tagged, you get prize money for it.

If that sounds too strenuous, you can just practice the art of the four-count fly cast at the **Angler's Lodge and Casting Pools** in Golden Gate Park. Talk about the weather, the war years, the time you sneaked back into the house at five in the morning (oops).

Afterward, take Dad to dinner at the **Big Four** and drinks at the **Ritz-Carlton**. The former, inside the Huntington Hotel, is a place steeped in the cigar smoke of San Francisco's four original Old Boys—railroad barons Collis Huntington, Charles Crocker, Mark Hopkins, and Leland Stanford. Over a smoked wild-boar chop or rack of lamb, as embers glow in the etched-glass panels and you bask in a cradle of dark oak and hunter green that bespeaks Old Money, work up the courage to ask him for that loan.

Later, you can continue to loosen the purse-strings with a couple of single-malt scotches at the bar in the Ritz's main dining room. The clubby enclave, diminutive though it may be, boasts one of the country's largest collections of single-malt scotches.

The Drinking of the Beer is another father-son tradition that must not be overlooked. At ballgames, in front of the TV, or at the local tap, nothing says "Don't worry, I haven't turned into a freak" better than the sound of a hissing bottle cap. And if you can combine The Drinking of the Beer with a historic landmark and an only-in-San-Francisco experience, you're gonna win some kind of normality award. Aside from making damn good ale, the **Anchor Steam Brewing Company** offers an interesting perspective on a time when San Francisco boasted more breweries than coffeehouses. Tours are offered by appointment only, and you'll need to book a reservation about three to four weeks ahead, but you'll learn tons about our famous homebrew, and samples of Anchor's many fine ales await you at the end of the tour. Savor the flavor as you discuss the real reason why it's called "steam" beer (hint: there's actually no steam process involved).

A Family Outing

Commune with the spirits of San Francisco's founding fathers at the **Neptune Society Columbarium**, one of the city's truly hidden gems and a great way to show your parents that you still respect your elders. The gorgeous 1898 belle époque building, with its soaring stained-glass dome and windows (one of which is thought to be the work of

Louis Comfort Tiffany), houses the ashes of some of San Francisco's foremost citizens. It stands alone now in all its neoclassical glory, tucked behind the Coronet Theater, where once it marked the gateway to the Odd Fellows cemetery. All the bodies were moved out of San Francisco long ago, but the columbarium remained and was eventually restored to its turn-of-the-century splendor. Amid the urns of alabaster, copper, and more unusual shapes and substances (there's a silver martini shaker, a tree stump, a baseball, and even a Johnny Walker bottle) lie the remains of the Folgers of coffee fame, the Magnins, Kaisers, Eddys, Shattucks, Hayeses, and Brannans. Definitely take a guided tour from caretaker, ad hoc historian, and storyteller extraordinaire Emmitt Watson (you'll need an appointment), who's spent the last decade making sure our city elders are kept in the style to which they were accustomed.

Getting Out of Town

Day trips play a key role in maintaining good parent-child equilibrium. And Sonoma is perhaps the best of the day-tripping options for a number of reasons:

1. It involves getting out of your neighborhood and reducing the number of times your mother shakes

her head at the local crazies and says, "So this is how you live?"

2. It involves a moderate but not-too-long scenic drive through pastoral Marin County.

3. It's quaint and charming and has lots of nice shops (for your mom), and it's full of juicy war stories about early California (for your dad).

4. If all else fails, you can drink a couple of bottles of good wine—and the fact that you can never please your parents won't seem quite so tragic.

Once you arrive, park at the town plaza and head directly to the **Sonoma Cheese Factory** or **Vella Cheese** to pick up your first round of picnic supplies. At the Cheese Factory, work your way around the sample bins while you decide which variety you want. I prefer my cheese a bit stinkier (they carry a limited selection of more pungent flavors like Cambozola and Schloss), but the housemade hot pepper or pesto Jack should pack enough of a wallop to satisfy most tastes.

Around the corner, Vella Cheese has been crafting artisanal Jacks since 1931. The old stone building, once a brewery, houses the factory and retail room for these family cheesemakers, who limit their output to several varieties of Jack, a couple of cheddars, asiago, mezzo secco, and toma. If you do nothing else, be sure to try the dry Jack, a favorite of cheeseheads for miles around.

Next, take your cheese, your bread, your garlic-stuffed olives, and your petulant little chardonnay directly to a picnic table in the park, and nosh. Remember to save a few breadcrumbs for the ducks. Afterward, while your mom goes nuts in the arty knick-knack stores, steer your dad to **Mission San Francisco Solano de Sonoma**, where he can indulge in tales of the Bear Flag Revolt of 1846. A few doors down from the mission is the **Old Swiss Hotel**, which, if you're within twenty miles, is a must-detour on any parental tour. The old adobe building was built in 1850 as a wing to the large residence of General Vallejo's brother Salvador. It's been the Swiss Hotel and restaurant (owned by the Marioni family) since 1926. First stop: the bar, a small, cozy, dark-

Neptune Society Columbarium
1 Lorraine Court, off Anza and Stanyan streets
415-752-7892
Tours are by appointment Monday through Friday; call
415-221-0794

Sonoma Cheese Factory
2 Spain St. on Sonoma Plaza
707-996-1931

Vella Cheese
315 Second St. East, Sonoma
707-938-3232

Mission San Francisco Solano de Sonoma
114 East Spain St, Sonoma
707-938-1519

Old Swiss Hotel
18 West Spain St., Sonoma
707-938-2884

wood affair that spills out onto sidewalk tables, with bartenders who've been there longer than some of the scotch. The thing to order is the Glariffee, a very tasty, cold Irish coffee created by owners Ted and Helen Dunlap (née Marioni) with a recipe so secret, not even the bartenders know how to make it. Helen still lives in a house at the very back of the property and concocts a batch of Glariffees every day. The recipe is stashed in a safe-deposit box and upon Helen's death will be passed down to one of her nieces. While you sip, make sure to point out the wonderful old photos along the wall, which offer a merchant-by-merchant tour of Sonoma in the '20s and '30s.

The restaurant here is extremely parent-friendly, too, with a big garden patio, red-checkered tablecloths, and hearty Italian fare that includes housemade seafood ravioli with lobster-basil cream sauce and roasted rosemary chicken, plus gourmet pizzas from a wood-fired oven. If you have a few too many of those Glariffees, this is also a nice place to park for the night (rates are in the $120-$200 range, depending on the season).

Should you decide to throw a few wineries into the mix while you're up here, these are the spots to hit:

Buena Vista—Where that wild Hungarian Agoston Haraszthy planted the first zinfandel grapes in California. The old stone building is beautiful (there's a guided history tour of the property every day at 2 p.m.), and there's a nice gift shop inside. During the summer months, Buena Vista

hosts a Shakespeare festival on Sunday evenings—the perfect fare to accompany a picnic supper.

Bartholomew Park—Owned by the folks who brought you the Gundlach-Bundschu winery, this one is part of a lovely hillside park that overlooks the valley. Inside, in addition to some tasty reds, there's a small-but-fascinating wine museum, with artifacts such as Haraszthy's hand-written letters and dishy historical trivia about the building, which once served as a hospital for women of ill repute.

Ravenswood—Great setting, even greater wine, especially the Alexander Valley zinfandel and the merlot. Parents (and okay, kids too) usually get a kick out of the winery's slogan: Nulla Vinum Flaccidum (No Wimpy Wines), which is available on everything from bumper stickers to T-shirts; their summer BBQs make this a potential one-stop shop.

Chateau St. Jean—Located off Highway 12 a short drive out from town, this place looks like it could double for the summer estate of Louis XIV. Yards of sybaritic green lawn, a sun-dappled fountain and fish pond, and a breezy collection of white wines put this on the top ten list for moms.

Though it's closer to home, you can achieve a similar equilibrium on a visit to **Muir Woods National Monument**, **Muir Beach**, and the **Pelican Inn**. If your parents are convinced that San Francisco is merely Sodom and Gomorrah with a few extra hills thrown in, this trip will make them see the light. First, stop at Muir Woods, where one minute spent at the base of any of the 200-foot-high, 1,000-year-old redwoods will save you months of explaining why you got arrested at a "Save the Headwaters Forest" rally. Then proceed to Muir Beach to watch the surf crashing against the craggy rocks and contemplate the vast expanse of Big Blue. You'll see their eyes moisten at the sheer aching beauty of it all (I'm welling up just thinking about it). Have a catch with your dad; stroll along the shoreline picking up shells with your mom. Tell them about your hopes and fears and bad love affairs, because they're not going to be around forever, and there isn't anyone else in your life who's genetically programmed to understand you the way they are.

At the end of the day, walk up the road to the Pelican Inn for a pint and some bangers and cottage pie. The cozy Elizabethan-style country inn, restaurant, and pub, with its rough-hewn, dark wood beams, brick fireplace, honeysuckle vines, and Tudor bar, is a popular watering hole for seasiders and hikers, and a nice bit of Olde England in the midst of earthy Marin. The bar serves ales, sherries, ports, wine, cider, and even real mead. If you get warm and sleepy, book a room and spend the night beneath a down comforter in an old-fashioned canopied bed, next to a decanter of sherry (rates are $200-$240 including English breakfast).

Buena Vista Winery
18000 Old Winery Rd., Sonoma
707-938-1266

Bartholomew Park
1000 Vineyard Ln., Sonoma
707-938-1266

Ravenswood
18701 Gehricke Rd., Sonoma
707-938-1960

Chateau St. Jean
8555 Sonoma Hwy., Sonoma
707-833-4134

Muir Woods National Monument
off Highway 1 near Mill Valley
415-388-2595

Muir Beach
End of Pacific Way off the Panoramic Highway

Pelican Inn
10 Pacific Way, Muir Beach
415-383-6000

You don't need me to tell you about taking the **Tiburon Ferry**. The question is not whether to go, but where to sit once you get there. After you've walked around the shoreline taking pictures of the San Francisco skyline and nosed in all the trinket and expensive doodad shops, you'll need to pick a restaurant with an outdoor deck. For parents, Sam's is probably too young and inebriated; Guaymas might be too spicy and ethnic (unless they love margaritas); but **Sweden House** might just hit the spot. The sweet little café serves homey favorites such as fried-egg croissants and chicken salad, along with a plethora of house-baked Swiss and Swedish pastries like Florentines and éclair. And it's got a deck with a view of the bay and city skyline just like the big boys.

NIGHT

So maybe before dinner or after the show, the parents like to tip back a few martinis or a sidecar and reminisce about what it was like when they were young. **Absinthe** sets the perfect scene for such an occasion – all red velvet and retro, it feels classy, without toppling over into the realm of fuddy-duddy. The folks will no doubt be wow-ed (and you might

be, too) when they order up a barely remembered Old School cocktail (Pisco Punch, anyone?) and the bartender doesn't bat an eye.

If they love the oldies (and you know they do), take them to the **Plush Room** for a little Cole Porter and Gershwin in an atmosphere of decidedly plush velvet and stained glass. A relatively small cabaret, it attracts big names in the torch singing business, among them Michael Feinstein, Andrea Marcovicci (she got her start here), Weslia Whitfield, Patty Lupone, and Paula West. This might actually be a good place to send Mom and Dad for a romantic evening alone while you order out Chinese and watch "The Daily Show."

A visit to a fancy rooftop cocktail lounge with a sweeping panoramic view of the city should be on every parental itinerary at least once. It almost doesn't matter which one. For nostalgia, the **Top of the Mark** is your best bet, a starlit room that hosted the last dance for many a sailor shipping out to sea during World War II. These days the room plays the old standards for a new wave of swing dancers.

Picking a dinner restaurant can be tricky. You might not want to overwhelm them with one of those raging of-the-moment places that still have a wait at 11 p.m. On the other hand, you might not want to underwhelm them with a place so obscure or on-the-fringe that they feel ill at ease.

A few restaurants tread a happy middle ground, among them **Harris' Restaurant**, the city's classiest old-time steak house, replete with plush, king-size booths, potted palms, and a long menu of prime-cut, dry-aged red meats from the Harris Ranch. Of course you get baked potatoes with sour cream and bacon bits; naturally there's Caesar salad and fried zucchini.

If the folks have plans to see a Broadway musical while they're in town, the only pre- or post-Golden Gate Theatre dinner spot to consider is **Original Joe's**. Joe's is a 70-year-old bastion of civility in a sea of urban seaminess. Never mind the liquor bottles and crackheads that you'll have to step over to get to the front door. Once they're tucked into a burgundy vinyl booth, the 80-year-old tuxedoed waiter bringing them a Manhattan and a 20-ounce porterhouse or a heaping plate of fried calamari, all will be forgiven.

The Waterfront offers you and your elders the best of all worlds. If you're treating (what a concept!), you can spring for hors d'oeuvres on the heated patio; if they're footing the bill, head upstairs for a seriously swanky white-tablecloth experience. Either way, you get crab cakes, wood-oven roasted fish, Mediterranean-style specialties, and foot-of-the-bay views to die for.

WHERE TO STAY

The historic **Hotel Drisco** in Pacific Heights may be the city's best-kept secret—luxurious without being pompous or ridiculously overpriced, comfortable but not worn (it was

Tiburon Ferry
Ferry Building,
Embarcadero at
Market St.
415-705-5555

Sweden House
35 Main St., Tiburon
415-435-9767

Absinthe
398 Hayes St.
415-551-1590

The Plush Room
940 Sutter St.
415-885-2800

Top of the Mark
Mark Hopkins
Hotel,
1 Nob Hill /
999 California St.
415-392-3434

Harris' Restaurant
2100 Van Ness Ave.
415-673-1888

Original Joe's
144 Taylor St.
415-775-4877

The Waterfront
Pier 7, The
Embarcadero
415-391-2696

Hotel Drisco
2901 Pacific Ave.
415-346-2880

JUST LOOKING, THANKS

When I was younger, one of my favorite mother-daughter activities was walking around on Sundays pretending we were house hunting so we could look inside the big, expensive homes for sale in the ritzy neighborhood that bordered our own. We'd sigh with envy over the astounding views, the master bathrooms with gold sinks and Jacuzzi tubs, the Miele dishwashers, Wolff ranges, hand-painted Italian tile, and Oriental rugs. We'd make silent gagging gestures at the bearskin rugs, the rooms encased in white marble, and the collections of LeRoy Neiman paintings.

Even if this isn't your family tradition, it's a great way to get your cheap architectural thrills while seeing how San Francisco's better half lives. Don't waste time on small potatoes; head directly to Pacific Heights, Presidio Terrace, or Sea Cliff, where the most modest of mansions hits the market at several million. Homes are generally open for public viewing from 2 to 4 p.m. on Sundays; they're listed in the real estate section of the *Chronicle*.

completely made over a few years back), courteous but never stuffy—and it boasts all the amenities a mom or dad could want: bathrobes and slippers, in-room VCR and CD player, breakfast buffet and wine hour, newspaper delivered to your door each morning, and free use of the nearby Presidio YMCA. All this for (more or less) $175 a night.

Modest neighborhood inns are another good compromise between your house and a hotel that's clear across town. The **Stanyan Park Hotel**, on Stanyan and Waller streets across from Golden Gate Park, is a homey, informal place with an air of suburban refinement. The rooms are spotlessly clean but not fancy, and the hotel serves a nice continental breakfast in the downstairs dining room.

If you live in the vicinity of the Mission or Noe Valley, check the folks into the **Hidden Cottage Bed and Breakfast**. Longtime city residents Dave and Ginger Cannata have transformed the top floor of their house at 25th and Noe into a charming, airy aerie that feels like home away from home. The room comes complete with hardwood floors, VCR (they'll rent you movies), its own fenced-in sundeck, and a private backyard entrance. Mom will love the enormous bathroom and the yards of closet space. In the morning croissants, muffins, and coffee come delivered in a basket to your door.

Stanyan Park Hotel
750 Stanyan St.
415-751-1000

Hidden Cottage Bed and Breakfast
1186 Noe St.
415-282-4492

Ethniks

I often say—sometimes to no one in particular—that in San Francisco, it's possible to travel around the world without ever crossing a county line. We put the glow in the global melting pot, the verse in diversity, the ethn in . . . well, you get the picture.

Here in this foreign fondue, where great soul food is crafted by native Chinese and the best

Swedish massage is given by a tiny Filipino lady named Brenda, I am always reminded of the words of the immortal Buckaroo Banzai, who sagely intoned that, "No matter where you go...there you are."

Round a corner in Little Italy and suddenly you've stepped into Little Hong Kong; turn your head in the Financial District and you're transported to an outdoor café in Paris; shout "Erin Go Bragh" along the Richmond District's Irish Mile and someone from a Russian tea room will answer "Nasdrovia!"

While I've always believed that the Bay Area has a shop, restaurant, festival, parade, hoedown, ritual, or yurt to represent just about every tiny cultural outpost and U.N. nation-state on earth, I've never actually put my rupies where my boca is. So I figured it was time to set aside my irrational fear of chicken feet and test out my theory, preferably with some visiting melting potheads in tow—those wide-eyed, small-town folks who hunger for an exotic experience, who yearn to discover the cultures of a far-off continent, who long to hear a language that doesn't include the phrase, "You want fries with that?"

Washington Square Park
Union St. and
Columbus Ave.

Caffè Greco
23 Columbus Ave.
415-397-6261

North Beach History Museum
U.S. Bank, 1435
Stockton St.
415-626-7070

MORNING

Start your global trek early in the a.m. in North Beach, where eastern and western civilizations are caught in the multicultural crosshairs. At 6 a.m. in **Washington Square Park**, surrounded by the smells of baking Italian pastries and focaccia, Asian seniors perform their tai chi ritual—an exercise regimen that looks like a slow-motion pantomime ballet. The sight of rows of tiny, old Chinese men and women never fails to elicit giggles, followed by curiosity, and then the urge to try it and see if it's as easy as it looks (it's not).

Then on to breakfast, Italian-style, which must include espresso at **Caffè Greco**, where what's left of North Beach's paisanos and homesick expats sit and sip and talk politics in Itanglish—Italian with a bunch of English colloquialisms thrown in for emphasis. If they're feeling adventurous or hung over, try the caffe freddo sambuca, a shot of cold espresso with sambuca liqueur; if they're wimps, an Americano with cream and sugar.

To see how it used to be in North Beach's Italian heyday, walk over to the **North Beach Historical Museum** (inside U.S. Bank, on the upstairs mezzanine level). Along the wall are photos of the old neighborhood and its habitués: Joe DiMaggio in the '30s, the Buon Gusto Sausage Factory, the beach that gave North Beach its name (long since filled in and paved over), and the North Point docks, where immigrants from all points east and west made their way into the New World. Next door, **A. Cavalli & Co.** is one of remaining vestiges of "old" North Beach—in fact, it's the oldest (1880) bookstore in San Francisco. Shelves are stacked with all manner of Italian-language books—novels, cookbooks, and classics—as well as more than 100 Italian daily newspapers and popular magazines.

After you've soaked up the continental vibe, head east (culturally and geographically) for Chinese brunch, a.k.a.

dim sum, and for a truly ethnic experience, immerse yourself in a place where the only English they understand is point and nod.

Two of my favorites for authenticity are **Pearl City** and **Dol Ho**, which offer, among other things, the aforementioned chicken feet, along with cartfuls of traditional steamed, roasted, and fried snacks such as shanghai buns, siu mai (pork-and-vegetable dumplings), and har gau (steamed shrimp dumplings). Be forewarned: your friends may initially be put off by the aesthetics of these places—the storefronts won't exactly win any cleanliness awards—but once inside they'll be so caught up with the exotica of smells and sights that a little bit of grease and crumbs won't matter.

In a town that grew up hip-deep in Irish Catholics, it never fails to blow my mind that the oldest Catholic cathedral west of the Rockies sits here, at the edge of Chinatown. Stately **Old St. Mary's Cathedral**, built in 1854, rests on a foundation of granite brought over from China, but the façade and interiors attest to the power of the western sphere of influence. Don't miss the display of historic photos in the entrance, the free lunchtime concerts, and the clock tower with its somber warning to young men (who found themselves led into temptation by the brothels that once stood across the street), "Son, observe the time and fly from evil." If you happen to hit it just right, you may be serenaded by the adorable little girls from St. Mary's school who,

on special occasions and festival days, dress in bright
Mandarin coats and satin pants and march down Grant
Avenue playing glockenspiels.

The line between east and west gets even blurrier a few
blocks over on Waverly Place at the **Clarion Music Center**,
an unassuming little storefront where you'll find one of the
country's most diverse and exotic collections of musical
instruments. Along the wall are huqins (a sort of Chinese
violin), Australian Didjeridoos, Moroccan zornas (ancient
snake-charming instruments), and all manner of strange-
looking contraptions that you'd be hard-pressed to figure
out which end to blow into.

Finish up the morning with a tour of **Portsmouth
Square**, San Francisco's literal and figurative Ground Zero.
While it might not seem all that impressive on the surface
(unless you're impressed by ancient Chinese men playing
speed checkers and mah jong, which I am, but that's another
story), perhaps nowhere else in the city exemplifies the colli-
sion of cultures that San Francisco is built upon better than
this spot. The city's oldest public square, it was once the
center of the fledgling village of Yerba Buena, a Mexican
trading post. Then in 1846, at the onset of the Mexican-
American War, the Stars and Stripes was raised over the
square, establishing it as an American township. Fast forward
to May 12, 1848, when Sam Brannan ran into the square
shouting something about "gold in them thar hills," promptly
launching the most massive migration (and immigration) in
American history, and you begin to appreciate the ethnic
implications of this square. At this point, if your friends aren't
checking their compass, you're doing something wrong.

NOON

Take your favorite globetrotter and your appetite and hit the
cosmopolitan streets (passport optional).

The New French Quarter

Francophiles have always gathered in the restaurants on tiny
Belden Place and Claude Lane in the Financial District for

A. Cavalli & Co.
1441 Stockton St.
415-421-4219

Pearl City
641 Jackson St.
415-398-8383

Dol Ho
808 Pacific Ave.
415-392-2828

Old St. Mary's Cathedral
660 California St.
415-288-3800

Clarion Music Center
816 Sacramento St.
415-391-1317

Portsmouth Square
Kearny St.,
between Clay and
Sacramento

their fix of all-things-French, including one of the most raucous Bastille Day celebrations this side of the Eiffel Tower. Of late, however, the French Quarter has sprouted an offspring in a corridor of Polk Street on Russian Hill, an area with sidewalk cafés and folksy bonhomie that feels perhaps a bit more Provence than Paris.

At the north end there's **La Place du Soleil**, a tiny shop filled with hand-decorated vintage postcards, baby booties,

lacy linens, and baubles. Down the street, **Nest** proffers pate knives and pickle forks with decorative enamel handles and sheer cotton pajamas that look French, even if they aren't. A little farther, **La Tulipe Noire** is an eclectic mélange of antiques, dolls, chandeliers, old milk jugs and umbrellas.

On the gastronomic side, there's the magnifique **La Boulange de Polk**, where you can share an apple chausson or a tartine (open-faced grilled sandwich) at a sidewalk table and listen to the waiters conversing in rapid-fire French. You'll pay a few more francs at **Le Petit Robert** and **La Folie**, but you'd be hard-pressed to find more authentic, upscale Gallic cuisine and ambience anywhere else in town. If you hanker for the good ol' French colonial days, go across the street to **Aux Delices**, where you can sample Vietnamese specialties (spring rolls, shrimp soups) mixed with Franco classics such as onion soup and canard a l'orange in a quaint, white-tablecloth setting.

Lastly, for a completely unwatered-down taste of French culture, step through the blue wrought-iron gates of **Alliance Française**, about a long baguette's-length away on Polk and Bush streets. Inside the "official center for French language and culture," with its underground bistro and upstairs courtyard café, its French film screenings, food and wine tastings, lectures, and exhibits, you are transported to the side streets of Paris. The accents are real, the subtitles are English, and everywhere you turn, it is assumed you speak and read French, unless you indicate otherwise. The crème fraîche on the vichyssoise is Alliance's restaurant, Curbside Bistro, awash in dark wood, mirrors, sun-splashed yellow walls and chalkboards filled with illegible scribble—atmosphere so thick you won't even miss the clouds of Galoise smoke. Settle into some paté de lapin maison (rabbit paté), feuilleté d'escargot (snails in puff pastry), or Le Bouchon special maison (a warm, dark chocolate/raspberry cake with a liquid center) and dream of the City of Lights, even if you've never been there.

South of the Border

There is no ethnicity more amply represented in the Bay Area than Latin American. In fact, it can be easily argued that California culture is really just Latino and Chicano culture plus a Krispy Kreme donut stand. With a history wrapped up in its origins as a Mexican territory, and centuries of immigration from Central and South America that have endowed us with a population so diverse as to rival those native lands, picking one or two places to represent it all seems dismissive at best and trivializing at worst. But what the hey—you have to start somewhere. I often begin at the **Mexican Museum**, which by the time of this printing will be ensconced in a big, new home in the Yerba Buena district designed by famed Mexican architect Ricardo Legorreta. Judging from the previews, this multifaceted museum should provide a good grounding in Latino artistic traditions in the Americas. From here, head south into the Mission District, the spiritual heart of San Francisco Latino culture. Stop in at **Galeria de la Raza/Studio 24** and spend an hour in the small but powerful gallery, which showcases activist and edgy Chicano and Latino art; then go next door and shop for inexpensive art gifts: jewelry, hand-painted novena candles, ceramics, wrestler masks, and Day of the Dead sugar skulls.

Next, get a sense of the amazing mural artistry that decorates more than 200 walls around the Mission up the street at **Precita Eyes Center**. This gallery and workshop is headquarters for the Mural Arts Center and offers regular tours of area murals, as well as information and exhibits.

Afterward, follow your nose across the street to **Panaderia La Mexicana**, a wonderful Mexican pastry shop

La Place du Soleil
2356 Polk St.
415-771-4252

Nest
2340 Polk St.
415-292-6198

La Tulipe Noire
2418 Polk St.
415-922-2000

La Boulange de Polk
2310 Polk St.
415-345-1107

Le Petit Robert
2300 Polk St.
415-922-8100

La Folie
2316 Polk St.
415-776-5577

Aux Delices
2327 Polk St.
415-928-4977

Alliance Française
1345 Bush St.
415-775-7755

Mexican Museum
Mission St., between 3rd and 4th streets
415-202-9700

Galeria de la Raza
2857 24th St.
415-826-8009

Precita Eyes Center
2981 24th St.
415-285-2287

Panaderia La Mexicana
2804 24th St.
415-648-2633

and bakery, and snack on heavenly pan dulce shaped like seashells, sugar-dusted custard-filled Mexican beignets, and all variety of buttery jam-topped cookies.

Then make your way up 24th Street to the **Mission Cultural Center for Latino Arts,** which hosts exhibitions,

film screenings, lectures, music and spoken-word performances, and classes relating to Latino culture.

Finish up with lunch at one of the numerous outposts for regional Central or South American cuisine, whose offerings range from traditional platos to showcases for cocina nuevo Latino.

Some of my favorites include **Limon** for modern Peruvian cuisine (the ceviche made with halibut, squid, shrimp, and mussels is legendary, and the fresh fruit ice-cream is flown in directly from Peru); **Alma,** chef Johnny Alamilla's exceptional take on nuevo Latino cooking; and **Panchita's 3** for Salvadorean and Mexican specialties, including dreamy pupusas, seafood soups, and thick, dark mole dishes.

And of course, no trip to the Mission would be complete without a stop at a burrito joint. The choices are numerous and the products almost always satisfying, but if I had to pick, I'd head to **Pancho Villa** for any of the grilled-meat options, **Mariachi's** for non-meat eaters (a dozen kinds of vegetarian burritos and lard-free refried beans), **Casa Sanchez** if you want to douse your burrito in supremely fresh and delicious homemade red or green salsa, **Taqueria Cancun** if you prefer sliced avocado to guacamole, and **La Taqueria** if you prefer zesty, lumpy, tangy guacamole to sliced avocado.

Asian Persuasion

Yes, there's Chinatown for all your Hong Kong-style needs; and there's Clement Street for Chinatown 2: The Sequel. But if you're looking for a more geographically well-rounded, *haute culture* tour of the city's Asian offerings, take your ethnically challenged friends to the new Asian Art Museum, followed by a tour of the Heart of the City Farmer's Market and lunch at a Vietnamese pho house on Larkin Street.

The **Asian Art Museum** is a wonder of tech-modern architecture seamlessly blended with the Beaux Arts aesthetics that are at the building's core (it used to house the Main Library). Inside the galleries, antiquities hail from almost every corner of that continent: Japan to Indonesia, Thailand to Uzbekistan, Korea to Tibet. Don't miss the collection of Chinese jade, the Korean lacquerware, and the Indonesian wayangs (shadow puppets).

One of the best finds in the museum (aside from the glass-enclosed balconies at the top of the escalators that make it seem as if you are free-floating over the city) is Café Asia, where you can sample at least a half-dozen Asian cuisines in one sitting. Start with Thai chicken and rice noodles in coconut-infused broth, move on to a Japanese bento box or Korean barbecued beef sandwich, and cap it off with coconut tapioca pudding and a paper-thin sesame wafer cookie.

Next door, in (appropriately) United Nations Plaza, the **Heart of the City Farmer's Market** is where all the ingredients for a truly multicultural stew come together—and without peacekeeping forces: Vietnamese farmers sell lemongrass and galanga alongside third-generation butterbean growers from the Central Valley; Chinese vendors offer live chickens right off the truck; and booth after booth overflows with exotic-looking eggplants, wood-ear and straw mushrooms, fresh mahi mahi, and jicama—all of it at prices that make the Ferry Plaza market look like an overpriced candy store for WASPs.

Afterward, walk up to Larkin Street and stop in for a lunch of pho (noodle soup) at **Turtle Tower** or **Vietnam II**. More timid types should go for pho ga (poached chicken); daring ethniks should go native with the combo beef bowl, a carnivorous cornucopia of flank steak, brisket, tripe, and meatballs simmered in savory broth made with pork bones, onions, ginger, and star anise.

Mission Cultural Center for Latino Arts
2868 Mission St.
415-821-1155

Limon
3316 17th St.
415-252-0918

Alma
1101 Valencia St.
415-401-8959

Panchita's 3
3115 22nd St.
415-821-6660

Pancho Villa
3071 16th St.
415-864-8840

Mariachi's
508 Valencia St.
415-621-4358

Casa Sanchez
2778 24th St.
415-282-2400

Taqueria Cancun
2288 Mission St.
415-252-9560

La Taqueria
2889 Mission St.
415-285-7117

Asian Art Museum
200 Larkin St.
415-581-3500

Heart of the City Farmer's Market
Market St., between 7th and 8th streets
415-558-9455

Turtle Tower
631 Larkin St.
415-409-3333

Vietnam II
701 Larkin St.
415-885-1274

NIGHT

Did I also mention we put the "sub" in subculture? Around the Bay Area, small pocket communities crop up hither and

thither like tiny schools of fish caught in an international eddy. There's a Hmong community (from Southeast Asia) in the Tenderloin, a Samoan enclave in the Crocker/Amazon district, and pockets of displaced Armenians in the Inner Richmond and Ingleside districts. Little Eritrea has found its way to a small stretch of Divisadero Street, and in the bakeries and tea rooms around Geary and Balboa streets, as well as in the fascinating Russian

Center in lower Pacific Heights, a spirited population of Soviet expats continues to thrive.

Russian Roulette

The **Russian Center** is by far the most intriguing spot to experience Russky culture. For more than 50 years, this Victorian building on Sutter and Divisadero has housed a tiny, jam-packed museum, library, and archive chronicling Russian accomplishments in the New World: artifacts, medals, flags and decorative objects that once belonged to the court of Tzar Nicholas II; costumes from legendary Russian dancers; paintings and photos of notable Russians (the identity of whom, unless you read Cyrillic, will probably remain a mystery much like the whereabouts of Anastasia).

The center is also home base for a number of Russian dance and arts companies, including the center's own opera company, and it hosts regular Friday night "Vecherinkas," socials with live music, dancing, snacks, and naturally, vodka tasting.

Across town in the inner-Richmond, **Cinderella Bakery** is the place to take your homesick Russian grandmother for a piroshki, a glass of kvas, and a convivial shmooze with others of her generation (see Grandparents); if you're looking for something stronger, the sometimes deserted **Russian Renaissance** room offers traditional dishes such as stuffed cabbage and vareniki (savory dumplings filled with potato, meat, and mushrooms), along with an extensive and creative vodka menu (try the Buffalo Grass). On weekend evenings, the place fills up with locals who dance and sing to Russian folk music.

A block over, **Katia's Russian Tea Room** is a sort of a community center that fronts as a restaurant run by Katia Troosh and her family. Here you can get your fix of pel' meni (beef or pork dumplings) and blini (fried crepes with sweet and savory fillings) and eavesdrop on local gossip, matchmaking efforts, and the current state of Russian politics.

When Irish (Black) Eyes Are Smiling

With its plethora of Irish bars, Irish celebrations, and Irish cops and construction workers, San Francisco is practically Ireland West. But to really get to the beating heart of Irish culture in this town, you have to experience Amateur Boxing Night at the **United Irish Cultural Center** out by the zoo. The center, which also presents big-screen TV rugby nights and concerts by Ireland's hottest musical imports, hosts a pugilistic party a few times a year. It's a chance to come out and see old San Francisco at its feistiest, when the Sunset District boys, the cops, the supervisors and mayoral candidates, the priests, and the parishioners all come together to curse and holler and slap each other on the back as the boy named O'Conner TKO's the challenger.

Around the World in 80 Meals

Perhaps nowhere else in the country is the question, "What are you in the mood for?" such a loaded one. By the time you finish listing all the possibilities, your friends will have collapsed from starvation. A few of the most interesting and obscure:

Little Nepal—The best part about this tiny Nepalese restaurant, aside from superb tandoori, is that a meal here actually feels like you've gone to some place approximating Nepal. From the waitperson who wears traditional dress, bows when you enter, and greets you with the customary salutation "Namaste," to the prayer flags and small shrines that adorn the walls and ledges and the Tibetan flute music

Russian Center
2450 Sutter St.
415-921-7631

Cinderella Bakery
436 Balboa St.
415-751-9690

Russian Renaissance
5241 Geary Blvd.
415-752-8558

Katia's Russian Tea Room
600 Fifth Ave.
415-668-9292

United Irish Cultural Center
2700 45th Ave.
415-661-2700

Little Nepal
925 Cortland Ave.
415-643-3881

that plays softly in the background, you may find yourself contemplating a trek on Everest before the evening is over.

Lhasa Moon—Just across the border, this restaurant, a darling of critics, serves the food of free Tibet, with offerings that include churul (pungent cheese and minced beef soup) and gutse rithuk (Tibetan hand-rolled pasta cooked in a country lamb stew).

Albona Ristorante Istriano—The Istrian Peninsula, a tiny strip of Croatia (formerly Italy) just below Trieste on the Adriatic Sea, is not so small that it isn't represented here in Melting Pot, USA. This lovely, somewhat elegant restaurant features food that melds Italian and central European culinary sensibilities—braised rabbit with onions and juniper berries, pork cutlet roulade with prosciutto and sauerkraut. The staff will make you feel like you're one of their long lost cousins (the one not vying for part of the inheritance) and will suggest their favorite dishes, make sure your water and wine glasses are always full, and tell stories about the homeland. The restaurant's location, halfway between Fisherman's Wharf and North Beach, is another bonus: it somehow manages to avoid the crowd and parking hassles of both.

The Helmand—With all that's been going on in this part of the world, it behooves you, enlightened Bay Arean that you are, to bridge the cultural divide by taking your flag-waving, bhurka-mocking friends to the city's solitary offering to Afghanistan, the Helmand, where owner Mahmoud Karzai will ply you with specialities of his homeland, such as baby pumpkin ravioli with leek sauce, while he wins you over with his gracious manner and tempting desserts. Do it for yourself. Do it for diplomacy. Do it or the terrorists win.

GLOBAL GRAB BAG

Bombay Creamery and Sari Village (552 Valencia St., 415-431-1103)—Bangles, bindis, toe rings, and saris are sold on one side; on the other is a small deli/café that serves such delicacies as rose and almond saffron ice cream.

Yum (1750 Market St., 415-626-9866)—An emporium for the global gourmand, the spice collection is as intriguing for the number of powdered extractions I'd never heard of as for its unique packaging (in tidy little green-metal canisters). But the most amazing thing here is the array of soda pops from around the world; among the finds is original-recipe Dr. Pepper that tastes just like childhood in a tiny green-glass bottle.

The African Outlet (524 Octavia St., 415-864-3576)—A tiny shop crammed to the doorjambs with African fabrics, tribal artifacts, masks, textiles, beads, and jewelry. Getting in is tough; getting out empty-handed even tougher.

A la Turca—Turkish cuisine is scarce in these parts, but several people who know have said this little, no-frills restaurant is the closest thing to home cooking they've found on the West Coast. Try a Black Sea pie, made with spinach and feta, and variations that include ground beef, chicken, mushrooms, pineapple, roasted onion, and tomatoes.

Bissap Baobab—I think this may in fact be the only Senegalese restaurant in the city, and for that alone it's worth trying. No huge surprises, most dishes are stew-type concoctions flavored with cumin, chilies, ginger and the like; more unusual is a whisky drink called fleur, blended with ginger and tamarind, that will knock you back to Senegal.

Old Krakow—My friends and I jokingly call this place Old Crackhouse, but that has nothing whatsoever to do with the food or the atmosphere (really, it has nothing to do with anything—we're just starved for entertainment). My Polish father would have approved of this place, rife with all the belly-filling specialties of the Old Country: borscht, duck rolada, stuffed cabbage, and herring salad.

Mandalay—Though it might sound weird, one of the best things at this Burmese restaurant (north of Thailand, east of Bangladesh) is the tea leaves salad. My advice: don't tell them what's in it, just order it. After they've had a few bites of this delicious, crunchy, nutty house specialty, they won't care.

Tita's Hale 'Aina—This Castro district Hawaiian restaurant is part eatery, part cultural center, serving up inexpensive and plentiful platters of pupus, Kalua pig and cabbage, and Cocomac prawns along with live traditional music on the last Friday of every month.

Mix and Match

Like the old Reese's Peanut Butter Cup commercials where two people—one holding chocolate, the other holding peanut butter—are walking down the street and crash into each other, creating a surprising new taste sensation, so was San Francisco Fusion cuisine born. With all this cross-pollination, it was inevitable—but who knew it would taste so good?

Lhasa Moon
2420 Lombard St.
415-674-9898

Albona Ristorante Istriano
545 Francisco St.
415-441-1040

The Helmand
430 Broadway
415-362-0641

A la Turca
869 Geary St.
415-345-1011

Bissap Baobab
2323 Mission St.
415-826-9287

Old Krakow
385 West Portal Ave.
415-564-4848

Mandalay
4348 California St.
415-386-3895

Tita's Hale 'Aina
3870 17th St.
415-626-2477

Restaurant LaMoone—One of myriad Asian/fusion restaurants, this one boasts some truly original combinations, among them dry-aged rib-eye tataki with wasabi mashed potatoes (seared rare, almost like tartare), tofu Napoleon with coconut cream, and calamari with plum-orange dipping sauce.

Anzu—On the one side, you got yer prime-aged Midwestern steak; on the other, you got a sushi bar presided

over by a master sushi chef. Throw in a sake martini and you've got the ultimate surf 'n' turf.

The House—One of the first and still perhaps the foremost fusion restaurant in the city, House is appropriately on the outskirts of North Beach, where chow mein morphs into fettucine. The menu borrows from Japanese, Chinese, and Californian traditions, offering such hybrids as ginger-soy glazed sea bass with garlicky noodles and ribeye in teriyaki sauce.

Zante's—The pizza is average, the Indian food a step above that, but the Indian pizza rocks—a slab of naan-like dough onto which is piled spicy spinach puree, tandoori and tikka masala chicken, and bits of cauliflower, eggplant, and diced lamb.

Ethnic Events

It's arguable that just about every event in San Francisco could be called ethnic; these are a few of the most internationally flavored:

World Music Festival—This annual gathering of traditional music specialists, held in September, has in the past included Russian and Afghan folk groups, classical music from Northern India, the Peking Opera, and Arabic choral music—a testament to San Francisco's powers of international cooperation.

San Francisco International Arts Festival—This recently established festival, also held through September, showcases a diverse array of musicians, filmmakers, dancers, and theater performers from all over the world. It's a rare confluence that can have throat singers of Central Asia on a bill with the emerging artists of hip-hop theater.

Ethnic Dance Festival—San Francisco's rich and vibrant dance scene is never more evident than at this annual festival held on three weekends in June. Some two dozen groups from every corner of the globe—Polynesia to Senegal, India to Mexico to Scotland—perform dances from their native traditions. It's a colorful, musical, toe-tapping spectacle.

WHERE TO STAY

Admittedly **Globe Youth Hostel** is not the place for those who value creature comforts and privacy, but if a true cross-section of world (mostly European) culture is what you had in mind, this South of Market hostel lives up to its name. Languages and world music flow fast and freely throughout the corridors and community/socializing rooms.

In the downtown area, the **Cornell Hotel de France** is a cozy, modest three-star hotel (a bit worn around the edges, no premium bath products) that feels like an inn somewhere on the outskirts of Paris—from the accents of owners and Orleans natives Claude and Micheline Lambert and the collection of prints by Modigliani and Lautrec, to Rameau, the family dog, who lolls insouciantly in the guest lounge. The hotel's downstairs restaurant, Jeanne d'Arc, is a favorite among local Euro expatriates, with a menu so French (Coquilles St. Jacques & Crevettes de Compostelle, Magret de canard du val de Loire) you'll feel like an ugly American when you ask for a translation. Definitely the place to be on Bastille Day.

Restaurant La Moone
4072 18th St.
415-355-1999

Anzu
in the Hotel Nikko,
222 Mason St.
415-394-1111

The House
1230 Grant Ave.
415-986-8612

Zante's
3489 Mission St.
415-821-3949

World Music Festival
236 West Portal Ave., #164
415-553-6272

SF International Arts Festival
415-978-2787

Ethnic Dance Festival
Fort Mason Center,
Landmark Bldg. D
415-474-3914

Globe Youth Hostel
10 Hallam Pl.
415-431-0450

Cornell Hotel de France
715 Bush St.
800-232-8698

tour 5   Tourist Incognito

There's always one in the crowd—the guy who's seen it all, the gal who's been there, done that. They are the Anti-Tourists, also known as the Tourist Incognito. For these folks, going to an actual tourist attraction and being among the eager, unwashed, camera-toting map-wielding masses would be the equivalent of going to the prom with their dad.

And yet, ironically, this is precisely why they're here. And so it falls to you to reconcile these contradictory impulses. To give them the tourist experience without giving them the I-Just-Escaped-From-Alcatraz, Clang-Clang-Clang-Went-The-Trolley TOURIST EXPERIENCE. (Note: your options do not include putting a bag over their heads and hitting the Wharf.)

MORNING-NOON

After a low-key cup of coffee at the neighborhood java stand, pull the bucket hats down low and strap on a pair of reflector Ray Bans for the only official city tour in which you can participate fully and yet remain virtually anonymous. The **Barbary Coast Trail** is a self-guided 3.8-mile walk that wends its way through Union Square, Chinatown, North Beach, and Fisherman's Wharf, offering a bookful of fascinating historical tidbits and anecdotes about the wild and saucy days of Frisco town, the Gold Rush, the earthquake, and other landmark eras. The trail, marked by unobtrusive bronze medallions embedded in the sidewalk, begins at the Old U.S. Mint on 5th Street and follows a path past 20 significant sites, culminating at Hyde Street Pier.

You can reassure tourist phobes that along the way there will be no megaphones, no buses, no docents holding up flags, no gaggle of camera-wielding grandmas. They can pretend to be looking at the scuffs on your shoes while they surreptitiously follow the markers, glancing every now and again at a discreet pocket guide that they can get to accompany the tour. (Even better, tour originator Daniel Bacon will soon come out with an audio version, available for rent at the Friends of Recreation and Parks store in Union Square, that will make concealment all the more simple: slip in an ear piece and you can pretend you're listening to the ballgame.) The pocket guide and a more complete book that includes maps and detailed history, are available at Borders, the Rand McNally bookstore, and the California Historical Society around the corner from the Old Mint.

If you finish at Hyde Street Pier and still have some time on your hands, slip past the showy sailing vessels down at Aquatic Park and duck into Pier 45 where the **Liberty Ship** *Jeremiah O'Brien* is docked. The steaming cargo vessel is a true unsung war hero, having crossed the English Channel 11 times to bring supplies to the troops during the D-Day invasion. In 1994, after painstaking restoration by a crew of mostly volunteers (some of whom

Barbary Coast Trail
begin at the Old U.S. Mint, 5th and Mission streets, www.sfhistory.org/bct

Liberty Ship Jeremiah O'Brien
Pier 45, end of Taylor St.
415-544-0100

actually served on the *O'Brien*), the ship returned to the beaches of Normandy for the 50th anniversary of D-Day—the only big ship of the original armada to sail back under its own steam. The *Jeremiah O'Brien* is open to the public daily for self-guided tours, and unlike the boats at Hyde Street Pier, visitors can explore the entire ship top to bottom unimpeded by helpful sea hands who call you matey and ask you to swab the decks. If they're feeling bold, visit on the third weekend of the month when they fire up the huge steam engines, or on one of the dates (approximately four times a year) when you can actually take the *O'Brien* on a spin around the Bay.

Afterward, if you want to give them a waterfront dining experience that doesn't involve chowder in a sourdough bread bowl, hightail it off the wharf and head to **Pier 23**, which has survived its line-out-the-door frat-party days to emerge once again as a fabulous waterfront spot where white collar and blue collar co-mingle for fresh cracked crab, peel-and-eat shrimp, steamed clams, and the best dockside patio this side of the Ramp. Order a bucket of Coronas, watch the Giants game, and blend in with the crowd.

Roads Less Traveled

Anti-tourists want to go to the Halloween party but they don't want to wear the costume. Here are some ways to have your apple and bob for it, too:

Happily, the most famous street in San Francisco has an obscure, uncelebrated, more authentic cousin across town.

Vermont Street twists down the backside of Potrero Hill with tighter switchbacks and at a steeper pitch than Lombard, offering a thrill ride unencumbered by traffic jams and wayward pedestrians. Admittedly, Vermont's plain-old asphalt isn't as aesthetically pleasing as Lombard's cheerful red bricks, but at the end of the road you can take solace in a platter of postmodern sushi at **Blowfish Sushi to Die For** or Cuban-style garlic plantains and yucca at the locals-only **El Nuevo Frutilandia**—two things you won't find in the vicinity of Lombard.

In Chinatown, dodge the throngs along Grant Avenue and head straight to **Stockton Street**, where your friends can get a whiff of the real, working Chinatown. Between Broadway and Columbus, residents get down to business, perusing the markets for live chickens before purchasing the plucked versions; dickering over buckets of water eels, mahi mahi, and turtles; and elbowing each other to find bargains on bok choy and bamboo shoots. It's a crowded, noisy, aromatic experience, and there's nary a pair of white shorts in sight, even though it's barely two blocks from the main drag.

Afterward, sidestep the hordes lining up for lunch at the over-hyped House of Nanking and duck into sleepy **Chef Jia's**, located right next door. For decades, this hardworking little Hunan/Mandarin hideout has served up sizzling platters of wok-fried garlic chicken and honey-chili eggplant, and steaming bowls of hot and sour soup that run circles around Nanking. Did I mention that it's cheaper, too? And cleaner? And that the service is less surly?

Two paths lead from one of the city's other famous landmarks, Coit Tower, but for some reason, the majority always choose to descend the Filbert Steps. All the better for your low-profile friends, who will find the charms of the northern **Greenwich Steps** equal to those on the south side—with an added bonus of free admission to the city's wild parrot aviary. From the driveway atop Telegraph Hill, take the first set of brick steps that begins a few yards below the parking circular. From here you'll descend along the edge of Pioneer Park, past houses and cottage gardens that will give you the worst case of real estate envy you've ever had. Secret and secluded, the homes tucked against this lush hillside are the living embodiment of the San Francisco found in fairytales and romantic Hollywood movies. When you get to the area right around 300 Greenwich, start listening for the chirps of South American parrots, a large flock of which has carved out its own bit of baja in these trees. Then soak up the keyhole views of the bay and Treasure Island before you make the final descent to Sansome Street.

Believe it or not, even the tourist-infested cable car has an often overlooked branch that may just be free enough of Doris Day lookalikes to suit your friends. The **California**

Pier 23
at the Embarcadero
415-362-5125

Vermont Street
between 20th St.
and Potrero Ave.

Blowfish Sushi To Die For
2170 Bryant St.
415-285-3848

El Nuevo Frutilandia
3977 24th St.
415-648-2958

Chef Jia's
925 Kearny St.
415-398-1626

Street Cable Car is like the attention-starved middle child of the cable car family, attracting mostly worker bees in the late afternoon, who rarely look up from their newspapers and almost never hang off the running boards. Best bet if your friends harbor a secret desire to do just that (and you know they do), is to catch the cable car at the Embarcadero around 5 p.m.; by the time you hit the backside of Russian Hill it will likely be so crowded with commuters they'll *have* to stand up and hang off a pole.

Secret Viewfinder

It doesn't have the sex appeal of Telegraph Hill or even Twin Peaks, but that won't matter a lick once you get a load of the views from **Grand View Park**, a spectacular windswept knob

that is rarely visited, save for the odd retiree out walking his dog or the errant triathlete in training. Hidden in a purely residential nook of the Inner Sunset at the top of a set of steep stairs (a double whammy for the untourist who is also a fitness freak), the park boasts absolutely showstopping panoramas of downtown and the Bay Bridge on one side and the vast expanse of the Pacific on the other. If your friends happen to be anti-social environmentalists (a strangely common occurrence) you can compensate for the lack of atmosphere by telling them that this park is one of the last remaining habitats for the endangered Franciscan wallflower and the bush monkey flower.

NIGHT

What better way to avoid recognition as an interloper than at a bar or restaurant without a name?

The infamous **No Name Bar** is a Beat-era institution smack dab in the middle of Sausalito's Bridgeway Boulevard. Its lack of identity seems to render it invisible to the teeming masses disembarking from ferryboats parked across the street. Step inside and you'll be greeted by a local crowd sipping beer and listening to live jazz and blues at the well-worn wooden bar. You know this is a place that's "keeping it real" when the guy next to you picks up a horn and starts jamming with the band.

If the sun setting below the city skyline beckons and you want to get an up-close-and-personal look, but not aboard a tourist barge, walk down Bridgeway to **Sea Trek**, where you can rent a kayak for a guided moonlight paddle around Richardson Bay and float past houseboats and harbor seals all the way to Angel Island. Sunset trips are open to all levels of experience (they give you a short lesson before you go), and if you get peckish, you can even book a dinner trek that includes a stop at the **Sausalito Taco Shop** for tasty ceviche and agave margaritas.

Undercover Alcatraz

With only one mode of transportation going to the island, seeing Alcatraz without jumping on the bandwagon is tricky. Tricky, but not impossible. Your best bet is an **Alcatraz Night Tour**, which, besides being a whole lot spookier than the afternoon excursions, attracts a lot fewer people. Only one or two of these tours are offered a night, and tickets are limited, ensuring that anyone seeking alone time, either inside a prison cell or out, will get it. Be forewarned though: even antisocial types have been known to have a change of attitude after watching the sun set or the fog blow in from the forlorn edge of the prison walls.

Lonely at the Top

No visit to San Francisco would be truly complete without an evening spent sipping a cocktail from a window-side seat overlooking the lights of the city. Of course, trying to avoid the martini mobs at places like Top of the Mark or Harry Denton's Starlight Room is about as easy as avoiding the fog in July. But if you don't mind clinking glasses with a few geezers, take your pals to the Skyroom Lounge on the 12th floor of the **Marines Memorial Club** (see also Grandparents

California Street Cable Car
415-544-0100

Grand View Park
Take Kirkham St. to the staircase between 14th and 15th Ave. Follow 14th to Noriega. The staircase on your right leads to the park.

No Name Bar
757 Bridgeway, Sausalito
415-332-1392

Sea Trek
Schoonmaker Marina, 85 Libertyship Way, Sausalito
415-332-8494

Sausalito Taco Shop
1115 Bridgeway, Sausalito
415-331-5595

Alcatraz Night Tours
Blue and Gold Fleet, Pier 41
415-705-5555

Marines Memorial Club
609 Sutter St.
415-673-6672

tour). Amazingly, this bar and restaurant atop a historic 1926 building (originally the first women's club west of the Mississippi), is virtually undiscovered by locals and visitors alike. No, it's not terribly glamorous, but there's no cover, the views are just as sparkling, and drinks are about half the price you'd pay at the Carnelian Room.

WHERE TO STAY

Though its restaurant, the Fifth Floor, is well-known among foodies, the **Hotel Palomar** is one of the best-kept secrets in town—a stylish four-star boutique hotel in the heart of downtown, right around the corner from the San Francisco Shopping Centre, so discreet that many people walk right past it. A modest awning marks the entrance (there's an even more covert doorway out back for the fashion and entertainment moguls who frequently hole up here), but the actual hotel doesn't start until you get to the fifth floor, and even when you get there, you'll find yourself wondering if this is the lobby or some hipster's living room you accidentally stumbled into. It's really both, a lounge relaxing enough that guests feel no compunction about kicking off their shoes and hosting impromptu dinner parties. Happily for them, the bar adjacent to the Fifth Floor, a restaurant with a notoriously long waiting list, serves the full dinner menu and purportedly has the largest selection of French wines in North America.

The **Palace Hotel** has all the history, grandeur, and opulence of the showier Nob Hill grande dames, but not the location, and consequently not nearly as much hype. The landmark hotel, host to the likes of Oscar Wilde, Rudyard Kipling, Enrico

ALTERNATIVE WINE COUNTRY

Nothing kills a good wine buzz faster than sitting in traffic on Highway 29. Good news is you don't need to run with the pack to enjoy beautiful vineyards and great vintages:

Bonny Doon Vineyards (2 Pine Flat Rd., Santa Cruz, 831-425-4518)— Sporting names like Cardinal Zin and Le Cigare Volant, self-described grape nut Randall Grahm creates wines as wonderful and unconventional as his personality. An afternoon at the rustic, woody tasting room in the hills above Santa Cruz is the antidote to the Napa crush.

Wente Vineyards (5050 Arroyo Rd., Livermore, 925-456-2405)—It's not as alluring perhaps as the other wine regions, but Livermore Valley has its charms. Wente is the granddaddy— its Spanish-style white-stucco-and-red-tile tasting room is at the center of a large spread that includes a restaurant, golf course, and amphitheater where big-name pop stars play in the summer. All in all, a pleasant place to while away a weekend.

Caruso, Lillie Langtry, and just about every president from McKinley to FDR, keeps a surprisingly low profile, ideal for your crowd-averse friends, who might have to dodge the occasional history buff (City Guides tour here on Saturdays), but on weekdays can enjoy the resplendent Garden Court and Pied Piper Bar in relative solitude.

Hotel Palomar
12 Fourth St.
415-348-1111

Palace Hotel
2 New Montgomery
415-512-1111

tour 6   Green Fiends

As Kermit likes to say, it's not easy being green. But it's a whole lot easier here in organic-produce-no-GMOs-nuke-free land than in places where tofu translates as some kind of foot fungus.

Green people come in various degrees of intensity. There are the types who won't order anything

with meat, but won't ask if the soup's made with chicken stock, and might pick the meat parts out of your burrito and feel just fine about eating the rest of it. Then there are those (such as myself) who won't wear fur but don't have a big problem with leather shoes, who support the Rainforest Action Network and the Sierra Club but draw the line at eschewing toilet paper in favor of pine needles while backpacking. And of course, we all know someone (or someone who knows someone) who is the most extreme vegan—

Ferry Plaza Farmer's Market
Embarcadero at foot of Market St.
800-949-3276

Pier 7
Embarcadero, just west of the Ferry Building

the vegetarian equivalent of an orthodox Jew—for whom even dishes that have once touched animal byproducts are verboten. Fortunately, there are places in the Bay Area that will please the ecologically insistent as well as the environmentally nonchalant.

MORNING

Herbivores and carnivores will find common ground and good eats Saturday mornings at the **Ferry Plaza Farmer's Market**. To get the best selection of morel mushrooms and baby fennel, you really need to get there by 10 a.m. or even earlier, so drag your butt out of bed with your overly energetic houseguests (who aren't bogged down by undigested pieces of beef), force some sustainably farmed French roast down your throat, and catch a streetcar heading downtown, pointing out sights along Market Street as you go. What sets this farmer's market apart from the one on Alemany or the one in the Civic Center—for tourists—is mainly location. A positively decadent array of fresh-from-the-vine edibles, artisanal cheeses, hot-from-the-oven breads, still-flopping fish, and gourmet goodies ranging from small-press olive oils to handcrafted chocolates spread out on stands and stalls inside the newly christened market hall, as ferryboats dance on the bay and the old clock tower beckons travelers into port. The contrast between green growing things and modern industry is fascinating; and the overflowing carts and food displays are almost like exhibits at some kind of produce museum. Try to catch the weekly shop-with-the-chefs tour (10:30 a.m.), when the likes of Brad Ogden (One Market, Lark Creek Inn) or Reed Hearon (Rose Pistola) show you how to pick and cook veggies like a pro.

Afterward, walk down the Embarcadero to **Pier 7**, an old fishing pier that was restored a while back with vintage-style street lamps and a wooden-plank promenade. Stroll to the end, find a comfortable bench, and watch the fishermen cast into the swell as the barges roll by.

You'll have to get up even earlier to get the pick of the crop at the **Flower Market** on Sixth and Brannan. Not all visitors are willing to wake up with the sun for the perfect  bouquet of American Beauties (especially if they're on vacation), but if yours are, both you and they will be rewarded with a magnificent, fragrant flower show. Though this is primarily a wholesale market for florists, many growers sell to the public. Afterward, settle in for a surprisingly upscale breakfast at the Flower Market café—mostly traditional meaty fare, but of course, there are a few vegetarian options.

If you haven't worked up an appetite for granola yet, skip the café and trek over to the Presidio to walk the **Ecology Trail**, a short loop that takes you past coastal bluffs, forested hills, and wooded groves, where you'll observe a large variety of endangered and rare plant life. A booklet, available in the visitor center at the Main Post, provides descriptions of natural highlights along the way.

Breakfast

Most vegetarian cuisine seems to fall comfortably into the breakfast category—fruits, grains, wholesome muffins, tofu scrambles, etc. And while there's certainly no shortage of bacon, sausage, and corned-beef hash on diner menus, almost every restaurant in the city also has an assortment of vegetarian options.

The granddaddy of vegetarian brunches is of course **Greens** at Fort Mason, and no visiting herbivore (or her host) should miss the experience. This sacred cow of no-meat restaurants proved that vegetarian dining didn't have to consist of birdseed and tofu (and isn't necessarily low-cal). Started by the Zen Center, it still gets much of its produce from Green Gulch Farms across the bay (see below). The food under chef/author Annie Somerville is outstanding—zucchini pancakes with Gruyère, deep-dish veggie pie under a parmesan-mashed potato crust, luscious portobello mushroom sandwiches, spinach and Gorgonzola salads—and the views are astounding. As the waves lap at the docks outside the picture windows, sit on one of the recycled burlwood benches and watch the sun dance off the whitecaps.

After you've digested (and it may take a few turns around the block), make your way to Building E, home of the nonprofit Oceanic Society, where you can sign up for a sea excursion to the **Farallon Islands** for the next day. If your friends are here anywhere between December and April, they might get to see a gray whale or two as the creatures make their way south during their annual migration. The all-day boat tours are led by naturalists and marine mammal experts, and even if you don't see any whales, you'll get to witness the wildlife of the open ocean—pelicans, sea lions, the occasional stray windsurfer.

Challenging the bagel for most quickly proliferating trend in non-meat breakfast food is the crepe. New creperies have popped up everywhere in the last few years, each with more inventive fillings than the last (and many pushing crepes as dinner). In the Richmond District, **Café de la Terrasse** wins the prize for most ecumenical, with sweet and savory options that are not only vegetarian, but organic, kosher, and served with a side of Internet (the owner, who's from Brittany, opened the creperie on the site of his former cybercafé).

The **Crepe Vine** on Irving and **Crepes on Cole** both offer a wide selection with all the standard stuffings—fruits, cheeses, veggies, purees—as well as some with more unusual fillings bound to appeal to veg-heads (i.e., tofu with vegetables in peanut sauce). Portions are huge at both places. The Mission's wonderful **Ti Couz**, which set the standard for authentic Breton crepes in this town, features sweet and savory selections made with either buckwheat or white flour and filled with anything from ham and cheese (for nonveggies) to Nutella or mushrooms in sauce.

In Noe Valley, **Miss Millie's** has garnered a large city following for tasty, nonstandard veggie fare—a combo of creative and satisfying cuisine that doesn't leave you hankering for a side of bacon. For brunch, the order is definitely either lemon-ricotta pancakes with blueberry compote

Flower Market
698 Brannan St.
415-392-7944

Ecology Trail
in the Presidio,
starts near YMCA/
Main Post

Greens
Fort Mason,
Building A,
Marina Blvd. at
Buchanan
415-771-6222

Farallon Island Excursions
Fort Mason,
Building E
415-474-3386

Cafe De La Terrasse
5217 Geary Blvd.
415-379-9588

The Crepe Vine
624 Irving St.
415-681-5858

Crepes on Cole
100 Carl St.
415-664-1800

Ti Couz
3108 16th St.
415-252-7373

Miss Millie's
4123 24th St.
415-285-5598

or any egg dish or tofu scramble that comes with "hash browns," loosely and wonderfully interpreted here with roasted beets, yams, and other root vegetables instead of potatoes.

Overflowing plates and wonderful side salads and homefries may help to explain the long lines outside **Savor** down the street. This family friendly café gets extra bonus points for a full selection of house-baked breads, including jalapeño and blue corn, and for its sunny patio out back.

Green Gulch Farms

Where else in the world can you combine organic grocery shopping with meditation, soul-searching, lunch, and an afternoon of sunbathing, hiking, and sightseeing along one of the most pristine stretches of beach in the Bay Area?

Green Gulch Farms outside Mill Valley is first and foremost a Zen center, where you can take instruction in meditation, Buddhist philosophy, and the ritual uses of Japanese tea. One of the ways the center supports itself is by cultivating the loveliest, most delectable-looking organic produce

I've ever seen—much of it sold to San Francisco's high-end restaurants. Below the meditation buildings, nestled in a wreath of tall trees, lie rows of baby lettuces and leafy vegetables, acres of herbs and edible flowers, and overflowing pots of native plants. The center welcomes lay people all week, but Sunday is the best public day. If you're open to new experiences, arrive early in the morning for the meditation program and lecture, followed by tea and lunch. After 11 a.m., there's a public produce and plant sale. Buy your dinner fixings, then take a leisurely walk through the gardens down to **Muir Beach**. After a little sun and sand, hike up the hill for an awe-inspiring overview of the California coastline. If your eco-friends are truly inspired, they can spend the night. The center's guest house, built with hand-planed and hand-pegged timber, has twelve rooms, each with its own balcony and traditional Japanese futon-style furnishings. Accommodations include meals and snacks (all vegetarian, but not vegan), which you eat with the residents. If you're not a religious type, that's okay too. No participation in any of the center's Zen life is required (having respect for those who are participating goes without saying).

If your friends happen to be here around New Year's, find out when Green Gulch is holding its lotus lantern boat ceremony—a Buddhist tradition that celebrates peace in the new year. Participants make little boats out of folded paper, place candles inside them, and as the sun goes down, set them afloat on the center's pond. There's also singing, poetry reading, and a tea ceremony.

While you're over on this side of the Rainbow Tunnel, make a detour to the **Marine Mammal Center** in Fort Cronkite near Rodeo Lagoon, where marine biologists nurse ailing and orphaned California sea lions and seals back to health. These folks are the original Bay Watch team, running to the rescue of beached whales, sea lions, dolphins, and other stranded mammals. At the facility you can see pups being bottle-fed, talk to careworkers about the whale population, and learn about the bad things in our ocean that lead to marine mammal fatalities. (This also a great place to take kids.)

NOON

A successful outing with eco-friends should probably involve something in nature, though that doesn't necessarily mean you've got to cross a bridge to find it. **The San Francisco League of Urban Gardeners** (SLUG) oversees about 50 public gardens in San Francisco, many of which are tucked into hidden spots—on hillsides, flanking staircases, behind office buildings. Though some of the prettiest ones can be difficult to find and/or get in to, they're worth the effort—if only to appreciate the ability of inner-city folk to carve out a little green sanctuary in the concrete jungle.

Saint Mary's Urban Youth Farm, just up from the Alemany Farmer's Market, is a demonstration garden farm that provides internships for kids from the projects. You'll find everything here that you would at a Sonoma orchard, except on a smaller scale and with a bit more freeway noise.

Savor
3913 24th St.
415-282-0344

Green Gulch Farms
1601 Shoreline Highway, take the Stinson Beach/Mill Valley exit off Highway 101
415-383-3134

Muir Beach
off Highway 1, near Mill Valley

Marine Mammal Center
Fort Cronkite near Rodeo Lagoon in the Marin Headlands
415-289-7325

San Francisco League of Urban Gardeners
2088 Oakdale Ave.
415-285-7584

Saint Mary's Urban Youth Farm
Alemany near Bayshore, next to Farmer's Market

The farm is open Saturdays from 9 a.m. to 4 p.m., and if you're one of those people who can't go near a green space without pulling a few weeds, volunteer gardeners are welcome.

Bernal Heights is a haven for urban gardens and a great offbeat neighborhood to spend an afternoon nosing around in. Start off with a depth charge (a shot of espresso in a big cup of regular coffee) on the sylvan patio of **Progressive Grounds**, the artsy coffeehouse on hip Cortland Avenue (for more on Cortland Avenue, see Gender Blenders). Then walk west down Cortland to the **Good Prospect Community Garden**, a tidy, landscaped patch of hillside that flanks both sides of a stairway with pretty flowers, vines, and shrubs. Sit on the steps and drink in the sun-soaked, organic, earthy aromas.

Next, veer north to Eugenia Street, climb the hidden stairway past adorable Victorians and clapboard cottages,

and then catch a second set of even more hidden steps on Elsie Street, until you reach the top of Bernal Heights. On the south side of Bernal Heights Boulevard are the **Bernal Community Gardens**, a neighborhood-tended green that looks out over the southern hills. But the real payoff is the short hike to the bald top of **Bernal Hill**, which affords fantastic views stretching all the way to Mount Diablo on one side and the Golden Gate on the other. (My friend Richard likes to take guests up here to watch the official "Rolling In of the Fog," since Bernal Heights stays clear of those misty fingers long after the Richmond is in pea soup.)

Other noteworthy gardens:

Alice Street Community Gardens—This small green oasis in the middle of SoMa, cultivated by a dedicated group of Filipino seniors and disabled people, grows everything from vegetables to English roses. There are nice tables and wooden benches for impromptu picnics, and an eye-catching eight-story mural depicting Phillipine heroes throughout history gives the garden the feel of an ethnic village.

Potrero Hill Community Garden—Flanking Vermont Street (the real "crookedest street in the world") this garden affords a fabulous vista of downtown and beyond.

Sutro Gardens—A self-guided historical walking tour, picnic tables, sweeping views of Seal Rocks and the Pacific, and the remains of Adolph Sutro's house are some of the highlights of this picturesque green park located on that knoll above the Cliff House. Walk around to the back side of the park and you'll discover a gem of a hanging garden, terraced down the hillside and filled with seasonal flowers and blooming shrubs.

Arkansas Friendship Garden—A group of South Africans started this garden, and the result is part tropics, part chaos. The uppermost portion is planted with banana trees, and there's a greenhouse with an entrance that's so tangled in overgrowth, it literally creates a green room.

Dearborn Community Garden—This prim and proper garden sits directly behind the Pepsi-Cola bottling plant on a tiny alleyway in the Mission. Bees are also raised here.

Ping Yuen Garden—The only access to this remarkable garden is through the hallways of the Ping Yuen housing project, one of the oldest Chinatown projects. If you can find a way in, the contrast between beauty and blight will amaze you.

Hooker Alley Community Garden—This side of Nob Hill is about as gray and urban as it gets, so it's thrilling to find that somewhere, somehow, vegetation has managed to thrive. The youngest gardener in this narrow strip of greenery and flowers is an octogenarian.

Michelangelo Community Garden—This garden within a garden is located on a steep hillside above North Beach and the wharf. The flowers are tended with loving care by people who have been doing it forever (there's a waiting list of more than a year for plots). Benches offer a nice, relaxing pastoral perch.

Garden for the Environment—This demonstration garden keeps growing and growing and growing, now taking up about half the block on 7th Avenue between Lawton and

Progressive Grounds
400 Cortland Ave.
415-282-6233

Good Prospect Community Garden
Cortland Ave. at Prospect St.

Bernal Community Gardens
Bernal Heights Blvd., above Ellsworth

Bernal Hill
end of Folsom or Alabama streets

Alice Street Community Gardens
bordered by 4th, 3rd, Folsom and Harrison

Potrero Hill Community Garden
McKinley Park, San Bruno at 20th

Sutro Gardens
above the ruins of the Sutro Baths, off Point Lobos Ave.

Arkansas Friendship Garden
22nd St. between Arkansas and Connecticut

Dearborn Community Garden
Dearborn St. between 17th, 18th, Guerrero, and Valencia

Ping Yuen Garden
Pacific Ave. near Grant Ave.

Hooker Alley Community Garden
Mason St. between Pine and Bush

Michelangelo Community Garden
Greenwich St. between Jones and Leavenworth

Garden for the Environment
7th Ave. and Lawton

Judah. For green thumbs thinking about moving out this way, it's a chance to see a huge variety of plants that you thought would never grow here, blooming like there's no tomorrow. You can also pick up lots of literature about green outings and events around town.

If you hit it just right, SLUG hosts an Open Gardens tour in early June, when community gardens around town open their gates to the public; some of them offer free samples and treats. You can grab a list from SLUG headquarters and stroll the primrose paths at your leisure or take a guided bus or bike tour.

Though lunch doesn't seem to be a big meal in the veggie world, often falling into the category of a nosh, you won't find a bigger and better nosh than at the **Whole Foods Markets** on Franklin Street and 4th and Harrison. The national natural foods chain is truly overwhelming, even for San Franciscans who are used to great food markets. At the Franklin Street location, yards and yards of robust butter lettuces, baby carrots, and golden tomatoes all reside under photo profiles of the farmers who grew them. There are acres of bulk foods (including twenty different kinds of granola), a full bakery which makes some of the best sourdough rye bread I've ever had, a deli and take-out counter that serves better food than many restaurants (gourmet vegetarian wraps, green papaya salad, Moroccan chicken couscous, jerked sweet potatoes), a fresh housemade pasta bar, and—if all this overstimulation wears you out—there's a Peet's Coffee outlet. I've never thought of a grocery store as an entertainment venue, but Whole Foods opens up vast new possibilities.

Eco-Shopping

Shopping in the green world used to conjure images of clothes made out of tree bark, chairs made of old tires, shampoos that didn't make suds, and—of course—Birkenstocks. It certainly never smacked of high style . . . until Birkenstocks and clogs became de rigueur and aromatherapy became a household word. If Nature Boy or Girl doesn't have a haute hemp boutique where he or she comes from, spend an afternoon trying these on for size.

PlanetWeavers—The ethnic, gifty, and just downright curious items at this Haight Street emporium are good for the earth as well as the soul. African drums, Buddha statues, didgeridoos, Indonesian masks, bonsai kits, aromatherapy products, and mounted tropical insects (grown and harvested by rainforest peoples on environmentally safe captive-breeding farms) are just a small sampling of the inventory.

The City Store—A great place for nostalgic locals and authentic souvenir-hunting visitors, these tiny outlets (one in City Hall, the other in the entrance to the Musée Mécanique at Pier 45) are repositories for recycled San Francisco artifacts from various city departments. Run in part by homeless and formerly homeless residents in coop-eration with the city of San Francisco, the store offers perfect adornments for your solar-powered, compost-fueled, hemp-insulated habitat: old street and road signs such as Haight and (for those who remember the days before it became Cesar Chavez) Army Street, the famous Forty-Nine Mile Drive markers, parking meters (from the days when they still took pennies), original 1922 Lombard Street bricks, fire hydrants and other police and fire department cast-offs, cable-car cable, and posters from memorable city events gone by.

Pier 39 seems like the least likely place to take green types in search of souvenirs, but tucked away on the second level, between trashy trinket shops and food-on-a-stick stands, the National Parks Store sells everything pertaining to and picturing our country's national parks. This is the store where you can get a book about the Presidio, framed graphic posters of Half Dome, or redwood tree educational stacking blocks. The smaller parks store outlet at the Crissy Field Warming Hut (there's another one in the Embarcadero Center) not only sells eco-friendly products, the building itself is a model of environmental sustainability. Walls are insulated with recycled denim-cotton, the cabinets are formaldehyde-free, the floor planks and furniture are salvaged wood. Naturally, all sales go to support the national parks.

Whole Foods
1765 California St.
415-674-0500, and
399 4th St.
415-618-0066

PlanetWeavers
1573 Haight St.
415-864-4415

The City Store
inside City Hall, Van Ness and Hayes St., and at Pier 45, Fisherman's Wharf
415-554-4000

National Parks Store
Pier 39
415-433-7221

San Francisco Zoo—People who refuse to eat animals are also not likely to find the offerings at the zoo (the ones on view, not on the café menu) entirely palatable. But besides offering such consciousness-raising products as endangered-species stuffed animals, this is one of the only places in town with a café that serves exclusively shade-grown coffee (the forests where shade beans are grown provide a vital habitat for migratory songbirds). Of course, if the animal cruelty issues surrounding captive animals bother anyone in your group, skip the zoo and go pick up trash down at Ocean Beach.

Zonal Gallery—Designed on the premise that when old bed frames and iron gates get real rusty, they should be sent to the art gallery, not the scrap heap, the walls here are covered with a fascinating array of recycled art and furnishings, as well as paintings and crafts.

East Bay Eco-Tripping

Being the center of all things PC, it's only natural that Berkeley should also have an abundance of earth-easy places. Begin a leisurely Saturday afternoon on 4th Street, at the confluence of earthy stream and yuppie creek. Make a mandatory stop at **Earthsake**, which features natural bedding and home furnishings, lotions and body products,

and organic cotton baby clothing by Ecosport and Earthlings. Then head across the way to the **Discovery Channel Store**, a huge warehouse of educational, scientific, and nature-related products from globes to polished stones to giant telescopes.

At the end of Fourth Street is **Restoration Hardware**, where you can ogle turn-of-the-century-style lanterns, latches, and lightswitch plates (even though they're new, they look old). Better yet, drive north on San Pablo Avenue to **Ohmega Salvage**, where you can find the real thing—crackly Italian tiles, neoclassical pediments, moldering Greek statuary, Tiffany lamps, gilded mirrors, door knockers, skeleton keys, and tons of antique fixtures, all salvaged from the wrecking ball.

Then head over to 10th Street for fancy garden accouterments and clothing made with sustainable rainforest products at **Smith and Hawken**. Your friends may only know this outfit through its catalogs, and they'll be thrilled at the prospect of getting those Asiatic lily bulbs for half off (the Berkeley location features a retail shop and a discount outlet store).

By now, hopefully, you're hungry, but just because you're a veggie doesn't mean you don't crave fast food like every other red-blooded American. Some creative meatless types in Berkeley keyed into this very collegiate state of mind (hey, living in harmony with nature doesn't mean you can't recognize a good marketing concept when it smacks you in the tempeh) and opened **Smart Alec's**, an "intelligent fast food" eatery on Telegraph Avenue. Order the gourmet, high-protein, cholesterol-free veggie burger; some air-baked French fries, and a fruit smoothie, and feel good about yourself.

Worth a visit to pay homage, if not to forage, is **Smokey Joe's Café** down Shattuck Avenue. The 30-year-old diner claims to be the first vegetarian restaurant in the country, and if the vintage political posters on the wall are any indication, they may just have a case. Plus, you can't beat their motto: "Where the Elite Meet to Eat No Meat."

NIGHT

Well, I've resisted saying it up to this point but . . . only in San Francisco. I'm talking about haute vegan restaurants. Only a city such as this one can take a cuisine that consists of legumes, tofu, and leafy greens and turn it into a fashionable, money-making enterprise. Your earthy friends will be truly amazed at the quality and inventiveness of some of the menus. Among the crop:

Ananda Fuara—The location at 9th and Market streets isn't exactly prime tourist territory, but for creative global veggie fare, many swear by this place. The menu runs the

San Francisco Zoo
Great Highway at Sloat Blvd.
415-753-7080

Zonal Gallery
568 Hayes St.
415-255-9307

Earthsake
1772 4th St.,
Berkeley
510-559-8440

Discovery Channel Store
740 Hearst Ave.,
Berkeley
510-841-1279

Restoration Hardware
1731 4th St.,
Berkeley
510-526-6424

Ohmega Salvage
2407 San Pablo Ave., Berkeley
510-843-7368

Smith and Hawken
1330 10th St.,
Berkeley
510-527-1076

Smart Alec's
2355 Telegraph Ave.,
Berkeley
510-704-4000

Smokey Joe's Café
1620 Shattuck Ave.,
Berkeley
(no telephone)

Ananda Fuara
1298 Market St.
415-621-1994

FALLING OFF THE WAGON

I've never known a vegetarian who didn't have a secret hankering for a big juicy burger now and again. What better time than vacation to indulge your guilty pleasure? Best bets:

Bullshead, 840 Ulloa Street, 415-665-4350

Joe's Cable Car, 4320 Mission Street, 415-334-6699

Bill's Place, 2315 Clement Street, 415-221-5262

Slow Club, 2501 Mariposa Street, 415-241-9390

Burger Joint (where you can fool yourself into thinking you're going to order a garden/veggie burger, then mumble beef in the waitress's ear), 807 Valencia Street, 415-824-3494.

gamut from dal to breakfast burritos, falafel to Indian curry, ravioli to pizza. Many contend that their no-meat meatloaf with mashed potatoes and mushrooms is better than the real thing.

Millennium—Now ensconced in uptown digs next to the Savoy Hotel, Millennium serves vegetarian cuisine for the 21st century. It's the place to take orthodox vegans for a really nice meal. The dining room is classy and warm, and even though the menu is strict, the wait-staff doesn't have a holier-than-thou atti-tude. Among the creative and surprisingly flavorful fusion dishes is a plantain torte, the Millennium steak, and an Asian-style Napolean. The all-organic wine list (a first in the state, if not the country) allows you to drink guilt-free, and don't miss the desserts, especially if chocolate-tofu mousse is on the menu.

Herbivore—This trendy-looking Valencia Street restau-rant (they recently opened a second location on Divisadero Street) serves totally vegan "California" cuisine—seitan

sandwiches, gnocchi with pesto, garden burgers, no-dairy lasagne, Kung Pao tofu, and red curry dishes.

Lucky Creation—Most Chinese restaurants have a good selection of vege-tarian dishes, or meat dishes they try to disguise as vegetarian. Lucky Creation in Chinatown does the opposite. The all-veg menu reads like a meat-lover's dream—

pork, chicken, beef—but they're all cleverly disguised bean-curd and wheat-gluten creations, which amazingly approximate the texture and mouth-feel of their real meat counterparts. Don't miss the fried sesame-seed walnuts with sweet and sour sauce, which I haven't seen on a menu since

Red Crane closed, or the imitation barbecued pork, or any of the clay pot dishes.

Urban Forage—The phenomenon of raw cuisine—unprocessed, uncooked, animal-free food—seemed to be on the rise for a while but then never quite took off (can't imagine why). Urban Forage is trying to revive the trend with a menu of "live" foods, such as marinated Portobello mushroom with walnut-fennel pate topped with spinach and miso-tahini sauce, and a hummus wrap made with cauliflower hummus, sauerkraut, and grated carrots inside a collard-green and lettuce-leaf tortilla. Liking or not liking the food is almost irrelevant. Take your green friends here for the totally San Francisco experience—guaranteed they don't have anything like this back home.

Panhandle Pizza—I happened on this tiny pizzeria on a research jaunt one afternoon and have been a fanatic fan ever since. From the corn meal–olive oil crusts to toppings that include fire-roasted red peppers, scallions, smoked mozzarella, artichokes, roasted garlic cloves, marinated shrimp and chicken, and the very nonveggie but awesome Aidell's andouille sausage, this place kicks pizza butt. Five of the nine house specials are vegetarian, and you can substitute soy cheese for mozzarella (or request a cheeseless).

Juicy Lucy's—Self-described as ovo, lacto, vegan, and macrobiotic-friendly, this groovy juice bar in North Beach also offers tamari-baked tofu sandwiches, cookies, and other yummy smoothie accompaniments.

Maggie Mudd—The cheery, day-glo ice-creamery offers some of the city's best housemade gelato, but its crowning achievement is the selection of soy creams—rich, decadent, and completely dairy-free. Try the chocolate peanut butter or the coffee almond fudge.

XOX Truffles—This little North Beach confectioner puts out truffles that are consistently rated the top in the U.S. by people who rate such things (like *Gourmet Magazine*). The good news for greenies: alongside a selection of traditional flavors are a few soy/vegan varieties, including the transcendent dark chocolate a l'orange.

Millennium
580 Geary St.
415-345-3900

Herbivore
Valencia at 21st St.
415-826-5657

Lucky Creation
854 Washington St.
415-989-0818

Urban Forage
254 Fillmore St.
415-255-6701

Panhandle Pizza
2077 Hayes St.
415-750-0400

Juicy Lucy's
703 Columbus Ave.
415-786-1285

Maggie Mudd
903 Cortland Ave.
415-641-5291

XOX Truffles
754 Columbus Ave.
415-421-4814

If you're lucky enough to have a harmonic convergence of visiting greenies and **Earth Day** (the weekend closest to April 22), you can take your pick of fun, eco-friendly activities. The official festival (with live music, crafts, et cetera) usually takes place around Fort Mason. The March for the National Parks, a fund-raising walk led by rangers, runs through the Presidio and Crissy Field on the same day.

Green City Project (415-285-6556), a nonprofit clearinghouse for eco-organizations who need volunteers as well as a sponsor of year-round earth-friendly activities such as habitat restorations and watershed tours. A calendar of events is available at the Garden for the Environment, 7th and Lawton avenues.

The beach is always a good bet for nature lovers, but if you can combine it with **Coastal Cleanup Day** in September, you get the ultimate California surf, sun, sand, and do-gooder experience. Call the California Coastal Commission, 415-904-5200, for information.

WHERE TO STAY

Despite its decidedly ungranola decor, the **Hotel Triton** hits organic paydirt with its EcoRooms, 24 guest rooms equipped with environmentally sensitive and responsible products, including biodegradable and hypoallergenic soaps and shampoos, energy-efficient lighting, water-saving showers and toilets, recycling receptacles, organic-cotton bed and bath linens, and a portable air-filtration unit. The rooms are even cleaned with earth-friendly products.

A similar mindset holds true at the **Hotel Cosmo**, a retro-sleek hotel with an arty bent and a great neighborhood bar that's popular with musicians and entertainment-industry types. Compost and bottle bins encourage guests to recycle newspapers, pizza boxes, and soda cans, and rooms come with natural-cotton linens and soaps.

The Mosser, a block from Yerba Buena Center, is the perfect spot for your earthy friend who's also short on cash—these two oddly seem to go hand in hand. Don't be snowed by the minimalist-modernist touches (wireless Web-TV, space-age in-wall CD players). The apple on your bed is organic, and a portion of your room fee is donated to support international reforestation projects (the owner is an avowed environmentalist).

Hotel Triton
342 Grant Ave.
415-394-0500

Hotel Cosmo
761 Post St.
415-673-6040

The Mosser
54 Fourth St.
415-986-4400

tour 7 Artsy Aunties

You know her, you love her. She's in all the Woody
Allen movies. She's your slightly eccentric, wild-
haired, flowy-skirt-wearing aunt—the one who
always gave you those "interesting" Christmas presents. You loved her the best of all the relatives
because she was fun, and kinda kooky, and knew

stuff about rock music, and let you have
puffs of her cigarette when your mom
wasn't looking. Her apartment (she'd never
do anything so bourgeois as own a house)
was always a marvelous clutter of lamps
draped in fringed Chinese shawls, incense,
dried roses, and old record players spinning
Piaf or Jacques Brel or bootleg Dylan.

In my case, my avant-garde aunt was actually an uncle from England. A playboy of the
western world, he seemed to live a terribly glamorous
life that was always just on the gray side of shady.
And when he came to visit, we went to new places

and tried unusual things that we never would have done on our own. While at first we were always a little skeptical, we invariably ended up enjoying ourselves immensely.

MORNING

No enlightened aunt worth her weight in empowerment will want to miss a trip to "Feminist Avenue," a.k.a. Valencia Street. Though the anchors of the area, Old Wives' Tales bookstore and the late, great lesbian bar Amelia's, are both gone now, there's still a strong female vibe in the neighborhood. Begin at the **Women's Building** on Eighteenth Street, a center run by and for women. Join a Rhythm In Motion class; find out where to catch an all-women's comedy night or a lecture by Camille Paglia; and be sure to stroll around the outside, which is swathed in a mural tapestry called the "Maestrapeace"—a multicultural, multigenerational collaborative effort by seven women artists that chronicles the contributions of women throughout the world.

Next stroll down to **Osento**, the women-only spa located in a funky old Victorian house on Valencia Street, for a soak in the communal hot tub, a sauna, a dip in the outdoor cold plunge, and a massage. This low-key spot has been a gathering and relaxing place for women for twenty years, and though most of the clientele is lesbian, it is by no means exclusive.

Then head over to **Botanica Yoruba**, where your aunt can replenish her stock of incense, patchouli oil, Novena candles, and assorted witchcraft accouterments; and to the **Cut Loose** outlet for a natural-cotton shift or an unstructured long jacket (all washable of course—dry cleaning is so unenlightened). Most of the inventory is end-of-season and overruns, but the sale prices are worth breaking the "no white after Labor Day" rule.

A visit to Valencia Street would not be complete without a stop at **Good Vibrations**, the sex emporium. Unlike porn shops or most mail-order catalogs, Good Vibrations is a place that constantly reinforces the notion that sex is not a dirty

Women's Building
3543 18th St.
415-431-1180

Osento
955 Valencia St.
415-974-8980

Botanica Yoruba
998 Valencia St.
415-826-4967

Cut Loose
1218 Valencia St.
415-282-0695

Good Vibrations
1210 Valencia St.
415-974-8980

little secret. There are no dark rooms, no sectioned-off bookshelves, no items wrapped up in brown butcher paper. Sex toys of every shape, color, variety, and flavor line the walls, and the no-nonsense staff is only too happy to explain their uses. The selection of erotic and self-help literature is extensive, and there's a full calendar of events ranging from the silly to the sensual to the serious. At first you may find yourself looking around to see if anyone's watching you surreptitiously thumb through *The Good Girl's Guide to Bad Girl Sex*—they're not. Before you know it, you'll be shamelessly perusing the display of antique vibrators. This is the most erotic fun you can have in town without a cover charge.

NOON

New Age mysticism is hardly fringe anymore, but chances are you don't have your charts or chakra read on a regular basis, because somehow it still seems a little bit "out there." Your wacky auntie is the perfect excuse to pass the buck and indulge in a little inner-self-analysis and psychic exploration. Spend an afternoon down in Hayes Valley, where the razing of the Central Freeway has opened up a whole new world of spiritual and artistic freedom.

The **Psychic Eye Book Shop** is a fascinating emporium of metaphysical merchandise—sort of a Walmart for all your New Age needs. Wander through the aisles of tarot cards, Egyptian cat icons, miniature cymbals, Tibetan singing bowls, incense, herbs, candles, talismans, Chinese health balls, crystals and stones, self-discovery books, and meditation tapes. Then have your palm, your chakras, or your astrology chart read by any number of on-site astrologers and psychics; most services cost about $10.

Afterward, fight the good fight (or just get everyone to settle down with a soothing cup of herbal tea) at **Momi Toby's Revolution Café & Art Bar**, which still feels quietly revolutionary, if the revolution was being waged with tuna casserole and jazz. Of all the boutiques and cafés in rapidly gentrifying Hayes Valley, this one still seems to hold to its underground artistic/political roots: flyers for exhibits paper the walls along with emerging artist offerings, rolled and well-thumbed newspapers litter the tables, the café sits over a frequently in-use photography darkroom, and the regular mixed-age clientele—when not hip-deep in political round-table debate or listening to live jazz—can usually be found actually reading (gasp!).

Pottery and Crafts

Every avant-garde aunt has a wild, artistic streak. And even though she may have evolved through her raku pottery and beaded lampshade phase, she's always on the lookout for unique handmade crafts or that sensuous figurative work. Take her directly to **La Tienda**, the retail shop in the Mexican Museum at Fort Mason (it's moving to a fabulous and expansive new home in the Yerba Buena district in 2005), where you'll find crafts from all over Latin America, including painted masks, Day of the Dead figurines, tree of life dioramas, tin ornaments, wall hangings, and embroidered textiles. There's a similar selection a few buildings over at the **Museum of Craft & Folk Art**, supplemented with African carvings, Turkish rugs, baskets, handwoven clothing, and furniture. In the Mission, **Galeria de la Raza** is a local institution. On one side, an art gallery features revolving exhibits by Chicanos and Chicano-Americans; on the other a small shop offers a colorful array of folk art, painted furniture, figurines, paintings, shrines, and books on Latin American culture.

If she's here in December, find time to attend the **Celebration of Craftswomen**, an annual sale and celebration of fine crafts by women from all over the country. Items range from handmade quilts to jewelry and ceramics. In October, the main event is **Open Studios**, when artists all over town open up their private domains and sell directly to the public. On each of four weekends, different neighborhoods are showcased, including the underdiscovered artist enclave at Hunter's Point Naval Shipyard. To get an idea of who does what, go to the Open Studios exhibit at **Somar Gallery**, where each artist has a representative piece on display. Then pick up a map of the studios and go nuts.

Psychic Eye Book Shop
301 Fell St.
415-863-9997

Momi Toby's Revolution Café & Art Bar
528 Laguna St.
415-626-1508

La Tienda
Mission and 3rd streets
415-202-9703

Museum of Craft & Folk Art
Fort Mason, Building A, Marina Blvd. at Buchanan
415-775-0990

Galeria de la Raza
2857 24th St.
415-826-8009

Celebration of Craftswomen
Fort Mason
415-383-3470

Open Studios
415-861-9838,
www.artspan.org

Somar Gallery
934 Brannan St.
415-552-2131

If your aunt wants to get into the act, take her to the **Sharon Art Studio**, that curious, stone, castle-like building atop the knoll next to the carousel in Golden Gate Park. This lovely little aerie offers drop-in drawing, brush painting, and stained-glass making classes for all skill levels.

Take your sketchpad and spend an afternoon capturing the bucolic splendor of Sharon Meadow on canvas while the flower children dance around the drumming circle and little kids roll like barrels down Hippie Hill.

Terra Mia in Noe Valley, the paint-your-own-pottery place, is a popular spot with budding artists under four feet tall and the moms who bring them there. If you can tune out the constant chant of "Please don't touch that," you can while away an afternoon or evening designing everything from dish sets to toothbrush holders and enormous pasta bowls. The studio provides the bisque-ware as well as the glazes, brushes, stencils, etc. You simply paint. When you're done, you hand it over, and they'll fire it within a couple of days.

Dressing the Part

Every flowy-frock-wearing aunt needs to restock her wardrobe once in a while, and Indonesia or Guatemala is an awfully long way to go for a batik or something in natural cotton. For simple-yet-elegant tunics, drapey raw-cotton dresses, and ensembles you might wear to a wedding on Mount Tam, head to **Alaya** on 9th Avenue. The small boutique usually has just the right look for someone not interested in anything form-fitting, midriff-baring, or spandex-infused.

Joshua Simon on 24th Street offers a slightly more youthful look with an ethnic bent. This is a great place for scarves and shawls, exotic-print tops, crinkly gathered-waist skirts, and 100-percent-cotton leggings and tees. Sort of chic, modern-day Earth Mother wear.

A pioneer of washable rayon and velvet, **CP Shades** (sadly, now only in Berkeley) makes gathered-waist pants, long baggy vests, and loose button-down jackets look positively glamorous. Your aunt will be so smitten with the brocade-trimmed velvet jackets and pant sets—funky, loose, and as comfortable as a pair of pajamas—she won't mind the fossil-fuel consumption.

Aunties who align themselves more with Diane von Furstenberg than Stevie Nicks will die and go to heaven at **Cris** on Russian Hill. The consignment boutique is filled with the likes of vintage Versace, Gucci, Prada, and yes, even Pucci. The gently worn, pre-owned selection will fit right in with your aunt's views on recycling, and the prices won't insult her pocketbook.

For the finishing touches, spend an afternoon in **Life Henna Lounge** on Lower Haight Street, where you can get an elaborate henna tattoo, along with custom-blended soaps, incense, and the latest offerings in temple decor.

Grace Cathedral

Some aunties might find a visit to a sanctum of organized religion terribly "establishment," but Grace Cathedral is such an unconventional hybrid of traditional belief systems and New Age spiritual searching that you'll be instantly forgiven. At the east entrance, just past the magnificent Ghiberti bronze-relief doors (which are cast from the same mold as those that hang in the Florence Baptistry), is the Labyrinth—a mystical maze of meditation. Carved in a geometric swirling pattern in the floor of the cathedral, the labyrinth is a replica of the one at Chartres Cathedral, which was laid in stone in 1200. According to the brochure, those who participate in this ancient rite are supposed to find inner peace and "become attuned to the potential of the spiritual self." Labyrinth walkers are asked to remove their shoes, clear their minds and hearts, and follow the path at the pace their "bodies want to go." On the way in, the idea is to free your mind of thoughts and emotions; at the center, stop, meditate, "and receive what there is to receive"; on the way out, become empowered with "the energy, vision, and courage to meet the demands of the 21st century." (For those who want to try this in a less formal, more inconspicuous setting, there's a labyrinth outside, too, just to the north of the front doors.)

Sharon Art Studio
Golden Gate Park,
Sharon Meadow,
near Stanyan St.
entrance

Terra Mia
1314 Castro St.
415-642-9911

Alaya
1256 9th Ave.
415-731-2681

Joshua Simon
3915 24th St.
415-821-1068

CP Shades
1829 4th St.,
Berkeley
510-204-9022

Cris
2056 Polk St.
415-474-1191

Life Henna Lounge
604-A Haight St.
415-252-9312

Grace Cathedral
1100 California St.
415-749-6310

Day-tripping

The town of Freestone, appropriately located on the Bohemian Highway between Sebastopol and Bodega Bay, is really not much more than a picturesque bend in the road punctuated by a couple of beautiful, historic Victorian houses, a serene nursery, and—oddly enough—**Osmosis**, America's only enzyme baths. Why the founders picked Freestone is a mystery, but for more than a dozen years, avid spa-goers and curiosity seekers have been flocking here to enjoy the benefits of a soak in a giant vat of heated cedar fiber, rice bran, and some 600 enzymes. The Japanese apparently originated this treatment, which is supposed to break down toxins, relieve stress, and soften the skin. If you and Auntie have already gotten up the nerve to try this, go ahead and do the works. Begin with a cup of enzyme tea, to be drunk while sitting on a futon on a small veranda over-

looking a tranquil Japanese garden. Next immerse in the enzyme bath, followed by a shower and either a half-hour blanket wrap accompanied by "Metamusic" (designed to balance the left- and right-brain hemispheres) or a 75-minute massage. Throw in a couple of extra bucks, and you can have it in an outdoor pagoda.

Afterward, amble across the street to the **Wishing Well Nursery**, which seems to be part garden, part quail habitat, and part art gallery. As you wander through rows of fuchsias, begonias, and roses, fuzzy little chicks scurry underfoot. In the back of the garden are a giant urn and a choir of Greek maidens—crafted by Bernard Maybeck, who built the Palace of Fine Arts, they are relics of the 1915 Panama-Pacific Exposition. They were discovered by the owners in a field in Petaluma. Inside the house is a small shop-*cum*-art gallery filled with vintage and vintage-looking curios—dried roses, cameos, flowerpots, trinkets, sachets, and so on.

On the way back to town, take Highway 116 through Sebastopol, otherwise known as Antiques Avenue. A dozen or so collective antiques markets and shops line the road, some with genuine antiques, others with interesting collectibles that are not terribly old. Stop and pick up an iron door knocker, a Russian avant-garde poster, a turn-of-the-century lunchbox, or an old church pew.

NIGHT

If she wasn't an *artiste*, surely she was a *danseur*, an ephemeral wood nymph in the mold of Isadora Duncan. Take her to a performance at the **Yerba Buena Center for the Arts** theater, where innovative dance groups such as Paul Taylor, Alonzo King's LINES Ballet, Smuin Ballets, and Joe Goode Performance Group regularly appear.

Or head over to the York Theater in the Mission, where you can take in a little thought-provoking drama while supporting the women's movement at **Brava! For Women in the Arts**. The multicultural theater group stages works by women playwrights.

Afterward, grab a bite at **El Nuevo Frutilandia**, where she can empathize with Cuban exiles about the failings of Communism over a plate of yucca root in garlic sauce.

Far Out, Man

The Audium, one of those quirky '70s things that refused to go the way of Roots shoes and peacock feathers, is the kind of happening that groovy aunts will delight in. The "concerts" have actually been going on since the '60s, when composer Stan Shaff and equipment designer Doug McEachern, both musicians interested in "new musical vocabularies," began performing at SF State and other venues. The permanent theater on Bush Street was built in 1975 and designed specifically for "spatial composition" and sound movement. Shaff mans the foyer, takes the tickets, then leads you into a theater where chairs are positioned in concentric circles, surrounded on all sides by hundreds of speakers. The lights lower until you're immersed in pitch blackness, and then, from a console on one side, Shaff begins to weave taped sounds in an intricate aural sculpture. Ambient sounds both familiar and strange—snatches of music, conversations, marching bands, parade noise, drums, rushing water—wash over, under, and around you at

Osmosis
209 Bohemian
Highway, Freestone,
707-823-8231

Wishing Well Nursery
306 Bohemian
Highway, Freestone,
707-874-0312

Yerba Buena Center for the Arts
corner of Mission
and 3rd streets
415-978-2787

Brava! For Women in the Arts
2781 24th St.
415-641-7657

El Nuevo Frutilandia
3077 24th St.
415-648-2958

The Audium
1616 Bush St.
415-771-1616

various tempos and levels of intensity. Somewhere midway into it you find yourself losing sense of time and place. When you return to the here and now, you might have an overwhelming urge to call your parents, eat Hostess HoHos, or pull out the Beatles' *White Album*. Trust your instincts.

Afterwards, ruminate over a pot of monkey-picked Iron Goddess of Mercy tea at **Samovar Tea Lounge** in the lower Castro. The elixir, which promises to "penetrate your issues, and dissolve them…offering transcendence via the tealeaf," can be sipped while reclining on cushions and nibbling on grilled ginger tofu, miso shrimp, or lapsang tuna. And if the conditions of the tea plantation workers nag at her conscience, set your aunt's mind at ease: the café patronizes economically and environmentally sustainable family tea estates and local farms.

All this spiritual delving is bound to bring on a serious appetite. At **Kan Zaman** in the Haight you can ponder what it all means over plates of Mediterranean mezze (hummus, tabbouleh, baba ghanoush and other Middle Eastern appetizers) while reclining on pillows, grooving to the hypnotic sway of belly dancers, and smoking apple- or honey-scented tobacco through a giant hookah pipe. If you find yourself going off on a fantastical reverie like the caterpillar in Alice in Wonderland, so much the better.

Finish off your weekend at **Kabuki Springs and Spa**, a Japanese-style spa. Begin in the communal hot pool for a

sister bonding session (there are separate days for men and women), and spend a half hour or so jumping from the cold plunge into the hot pool and back. Next a steam, followed by a cool shower, followed by a stint in the dry sauna, another plunge in the cold pool, and finally a Japanese-style seated bath. For the finale, try the exotic Javanese Lulur body treatment, a traditional Indonesian ritual that involves massage with jasmine frangipani-scented flower oil, lulur—a turmeric and rice scrub—and yogurt. You'll both be wet noodles by the time you're done, so it's only fitting that you go around the corner to **Mifune**, Japantown's great (cheap) little noodle house, for a bowl of ramen or udon.

WHERE TO STAY

Artistic types of all kinds will feel at home at the **Art Center Bed and Breakfast**, a low-key (there's no sign out front) inn carved out of an 1857 French provincial–style apartment building in the heart of Cow Hollow. The 80-something owner, Helvi Wamsley, an artist who will offer pointers for amateur painters, is always eager to engage in salon discussions on art and culture. Wamsley's art pervades the inn, which features five units—two small studios with fireplaces, two large suites with private street entrances, and a three-room apartment. In back is a sunny skylit garden room—the perfect place to paint that still life. Full breakfast is served.

The **Victorian Inn on the Park** itself is not particularly avant garde, but it's located along the Panhandle, in a quiet, mostly residential neighborhood that's destined for hipness any minute. Set between the Western Addition and Haight-Ashbury, the blocks around the inn are starting to bud with groovy new cafés and restaurants. This B&B is housed in an absolutely gorgeous (and enormous) historic 1897 Victorian that was once the residence of a wealthy SF family. It was restored about 15 years ago to its turn-of-the-century splendor, though modern amenities (including private bathrooms) were added for guests' convenience. There's a continental breakfast in the morning, and sherry or wine is served evenings, in front of the fire in the front parlor.

Though they don't necessarily broadcast it, the **Hotel Juliana** is a mostly women-run hotel that caters to female clientele (and their canine companions), with touches such as "in case you forgot" items in the mini-bar, a selection of women's magazines in the rooms, a nightly wine reception, and an on-call manicurist and massage therapist. Tucked away in that mid-downtown zone between the Financial District and Nob Hill, this classy little boutique hotel is neither too upscale nor too down-home—just right for the auntie who's outgrown the crash pad but isn't ready for the shmancy grande dame.

Samovar Tea Lounge
498 Sanchez St.
415-626-4700

Kan Zaman
1793 Haight St.
415-751-9656

Kabuki Springs and Spa
1750 Geary Blvd.
415-922-6000

Mifune
1737 Post St.
415-922-0337

Art Center Bed and Breakfast
1902 Filbert St.
415-567-1526

Victorian Inn on the Park
301 Lyon St.
415-931-1830

Hotel Juliana
590 Bush St.
866-325-9457

Nieces, Nephews, and Other Antsy Adolescents

tour 8

Being a kid in San Francisco can be both a liberating and a confining experience. Back when I was growing up, while my suburban counterparts rode their bikes in circles around the orchards, I was riding the bus down to the Castro Theatre to watch Gene Kelly musicals and having herb tea with my friends at the Owl and the Monkey. Then again, I never saw a drive-in movie until I was in college.

Certainly, there's plenty for the average adolescent or pre-adolescent to do in San Francisco, but sometimes doing it with parents (or worse, parents' friends) can be downright excruciating. Compromise is the key. Find places that are fun for both adults and kids, or places where adults can do one thing and kids can do another. And on those days when you can't find a middle ground, and you are subject to the inevitable rolling of the eyes and jutting of the chin, keep in mind that "because I say so" goes a lot further when you're footing the bill.

MORNING–NOON

Perhaps the best kid thing (and maybe even the best grown-up thing) to happen in San Francisco since the last edition of this book is the redevelopment of **Crissy Field**, a small miracle of nature and savvy urban planning that gave the former Miss Gravely Spit and her congenial runner-up, Miss Windsurfer Parking Lot, an extreme makeover that happily was not just skin-deep. The main promenade is now a legitimate walking/biking/jogging path that flanks the city's most stunning stretch of beachfront: Golden Gate Bridge arcing gracefully to the west, Aquatic Park ships to the east, and in front of you, Alcatraz and a colorful cavalcade of sailboats, ferries, and windsurfers dancing just out of arm's reach.

Start with a slow amble from the east parking lot along the path to the sheltered lagoon, where if it's a reasonably warm day, kids can puddle around in the inlet pools or chase waves while you kick back on the thick tundra grass. If you've planned ahead, there's a plethora of picnic tables and barbecue grills where you can settle in for a snack, and if you haven't, you'll be thrilled to know you no longer have to traipse into the Marina for sustenance. The lunch gap has been amply filled by cafés at both ends of the park. The larger one in the Crissy Field Center offers soups, salads, gourmet sandwiches (no, seriously; we're talking turkey and grilled Portobello mushroom on Grace focaccia), espresso drinks, and the like; the delightful Warming Hut at the west end features similar fare but on a limited scale. Both use organic ingredients and products that come from sustainable farms, and both are attached to small gift shops where kids and parents can browse through books, puzzles, stuffed animals, posters, local artisan wares, and other fun souvenirs.

On your way to the warming hut, be sure to stop in at the **Gulf of the Farallones National Marine Sanctuary**

Crissy Field
entrance at Marina
Blvd. near Lyon St.,
Warming Hut
415-561-3042

**Gulf of the
Farallones
Marine
Sanctuary**
Crissy Field
415-561-6625

visitor center, a wonderful free mini-museum where kids can dig through sand to find sea creatures, listen to the sounds of shore birds, and explore a touch-tank filled with anemones, urchins, hermit crabs, and starfish.

From here, it will be nearly impossible to avoid the allure of the Golden Gate Bridge and **Fort Point**. Go the extra mile just to stand at edge of the railing and get sprayed (or at high tide, completely soaked) as the waves crash against the rocks. Then turn around and get an up-close-and-personal look at the massive steel girders that hold up the bridge. One look at the structure's underside and you won't question its status as one of the Seven Engineering Wonders of the World.

Daredevils can get an even closer (almost unnerving) view of the Golden Gate's underbelly from the top of the fortress wall inside Fort Point. The hollowed-out fortification that once served as the city's first line of defense against a hostile sea invasion has never battled anything more than fierce winds, but that won't matter to your friends' 10-year-old son, especially after he gets to poke his head inside a cannon, or sit inside an army barracks, or track hostile seagulls through a spyglass.

Ferry Tales

For most kids (and even for most adults), taking a ferry anywhere constitutes an outing. But taking one to the most notorious prison in American history is payday. If your friends have a mind to take a tour while they're here—especially if the kids are along—**Alcatraz Island** is the one to take. It's

got history, it's got Hollywood sex appeal, it's got ghosts, a boat ride, and Al Capone.

Start out at Fisherman's Wharf with a walkaway crab or shrimp cocktail and then visit at least one of the following kitschy Wharf attractions before heading over to Pier 41 to catch a ferry:

See You in San Francisco—Through the miracle of digital photography, kids (keep telling yourself you're only doing this for the kids and you might just start to believe it) can get giant pictures of themselves climbing and standing on top of the Golden Gate Bridge and other local landmarks. Dang if these things don't look real! (Plus, in this age of homeland security, it's the closest you'll get to setting foot on anything besides the bridge's designated walkway.)

Ripley's Believe It or Not Museum—This collection of freaky natural and manmade phenomena is just ridiculous enough to be oddly compelling. Kids, of course, find displays such as the two-headed calf, the shrunken torso, and an 8-foot cable car made entirely from matchsticks beyond fascinating. (Parents who don't want to do this type of thing too often should wait at the entrance: the African fertility statues inside take credit for 935 pregnancies to date.)

A street vendor painting—Hey, it may not be a Picasso, but at least it's original. My personal favorites are the guy who paints designs on condom wrappers and the elderly gentleman who will write your name in colorful Chinese pictographs; both usually ply their trade along Jefferson Street.

Now you're ready to hop the **Blue and Gold Ferry** to The Rock, where you can take a ranger-led or a self-guided tour of the old cell house. (Do the audio tour—it's narrated by former Alcatraz guards and inmates, who talk about life behind bars in a way no outsider ever could.) Along the way you'll get to see where such notorious criminals as Capone and the Birdman of Alcatraz did time, and even sit inside a cell. (A note to the uninitiated: these tours are very popular; call ahead for reservations, especially in the summer months. And wear warm clothes. It can get damn cold out there.)

For older kids, the other common ferry destinations— Larkspur, Sausalito, Tiburon—don't hold much appeal beyond the actual boat ride. But lots of people overlook the black sheep of the ferry family—the **Alameda/Oakland Ferry**, which leaves from the Ferry Building and Pier 41 approximately every two hours and zips you across the bay on an airfoil to **Jack London Square**, a warmer, funkier version of Fisherman's Wharf. Kids will have fun following the wolf tracks through the square to learn about the Oakland waterfront's most famous author. The historical markers lead to the Jack London statue and museum and

Fort Point
415-556-1693

Blue and Gold Ferry to Alcatraz Island
Pier 41 on the Embarcadero
415-773-1188

See You in San Francisco
Anchorage Shopping Center, 2800 Leavenworth St.
415-441-3686

Ripley's Believe It Or Not Museum
175 Jefferson St.
415-771-6188

Alameda/ Oakland Ferry
departs from the Ferry Building and Pier 39
510-522-3300

Jack London Square
on the Embarcadero in Oakland

eventually end up at the Potomac, President Franklin D. Roosevelt's yacht, once known as the "floating White House." The yacht offers tours and cruises. In the surrounding complex, there's a small Museum of Children's Art; an enormous Barnes and Noble bookstore (one of the largest bookstores in Northern California); great family restaurants, including the Old Spaghetti Factory, Pizzeria Uno, and Scott's Seafood, which sits directly on the water looking out over the bay; and, in the summer, concerts performed dockside. The first Saturday of every month there's an antiques and collectibles show along Water Street; and every Sunday there's an open-air farmer's market from 10 a.m. to 2 p.m. (For adults, the best thing in Jack London Square—and maybe in all of Oakland—is Yoshi's jazz club, which attracts the biggest names in the business. See the Romantically Inclined tour).

Graves, Ghosts, and Ghouls

So maybe it's a little morbid to take kids to a cemetery for entertainment, but probably no more so than going to a ghost town or watching *Night of the Living Dead*. Besides, how often do you get a chance to see Wyatt Earp's grave?

The legendary gunslinger and sheriff who made Tombstone, Arizona, and the OK Corral the stuff of Hollywood movies is laid to rest at the **Hills of Eternity**, a Jewish cemetery on El Camino Real. Earp died in 1929 and was buried in the family plot of his wife, former actress Josephine Marcus (she was Jewish), from whom he was rarely, if ever, separated. Also buried at Hills of Eternity is blue jeans inventor Levi Strauss.

While you're in the neighborhood, you should also take a little lesson in San Francisco history over at **Cypress Lawn Cemetery**, where half the city's hoi polloi are buried, including publisher William Randolph Hearst, firebrand and tower namesake Lillie Hitchcock Coit, cable car inventor Andrew Hallidie, and arts patron Charles de Young. The cemetery, built in 1892, offers tours of the mausoleums,

some of which (like the Flood Family's) are enormous architectural monuments. Also of note are the chapel's stained-
glass windows, designed by Louis Comfort Tiffany.

Good Sports

Okay, okay, so you've already thought about taking in a
Giants or A's game. SBC Park is your choice for balls-into-
the-bay drama; the Oakland Coliseum is a better bet for
good seating, lots more sunshine, and, according to my
friend Rosie, the best fish sandwiches (served on Black
Muslim Bakery bread) ever to grace a ballpark. But what if
it's the off-season, or the team's on the road? Then what?
Head to **Big Rec Field**, the baseball diamond in Golden Gate
Park at 7th and Lincoln, where you can catch a semi-pro
game almost any weekend. First though, go to 9th Avenue
and pick up some supplies—a hoagie or a hot dog from
Submarine Center No. 2, or maybe a burrito from **Gordo
Taqueria**. Then settle in on the bleachers for a few innings
of serious hardball. If the game isn't as intriguing to grown-
ups as to aspiring shortstops, adults can wander off to the
solitude of the Shakespeare Garden or sign up for a few sets
of tennis at one of the twenty or so courts located right
behind the field.

It may be sensory overload for you, but for kids whose
idea of team sports means sharing a Game Boy, **Metreon**
center is an electronic slice of heaven. Start at the bottom
and work your way up: at Sony Playstation you can try out
the latest video games in a surround-sound large-screen
virtual-reality theater, then sample MP3s and laser discs
and shake your groove thing on a video dance pad at
Digital Solutions. Upstairs there's a game room with interactive boxing, NBA basketball, air hockey, interactive digital
games, and (my favorite) Hyperbowl—a virtual reality
bowling alley that lets you roll a ball through the streets of
San Francisco. If your synapses aren't completely fritzed by
this time, there's also a giant IMAX movie theater with a
screen so enormous it practically swallows you whole (the
under-the-ocean 3D movie will have you dodging sharks
and trying to come up for air).

Hills of Eternity
El Camino Real,
Colma
650-756-3633

**Cypress Lawn
Cemetery**
El Camino Real,
Colma
650-755-0580

Big Rec Field
7th Ave. and Lincoln
Way

**Submarine
Center No. 2**
corner of 9th Ave.
and Lincoln Wy.
415-731-0400

Gordo Taqueria
1233 9th Ave.
415-566-6011

Metreon
4th and Mission
streets
800-METREON

For a more family-participatory experience, cross over the Howard Street bridge onto the Rooftop at Yerba Buena Gardens and spend the afternoon ice skating or bowling. Amazing, given their location in the middle of downtown, these state-of-the-art recreational facilities seem often overlooked—rarely if ever boasting a line or a crowd. Across the courtyard lies the wonderful **Zeum**, a hands-on high-tech creative arts center for kids eight to eighteen, where you can draw and produce your own cartoon or star in your own karaoke music video.

Shopping

Teenage girls love to shop. There's no denying it. So suck it up, put on your best face, and pretend you're impressed by four-inch platform tennis shoes. (Hello—we had platform tennies with live goldfish in them, remember?)

Urban Outfitters—Trendy urban clothing, home furnishings, and pop culture merchandise for the generation that falls somewhere between X and Y.

Abercrombie & Fitch—More powerful than the Gap, racier than a speeding pair of Diesels, this store sets the

fashion bar for high school girls—a relentless trend machine that (sadly) never really ventures much beyond variations on the worn, faded t-shirt.

Buffalo Exchange—One of the best (and cheapest) of the used-clothing emporiums, mainly because of the constant influx of new merchandise. The selection usually includes old Levi's, '50s housedresses, bowling shirts, tight polyester blouses, leather jackets, and a good smattering of last year's Gap-wear.

Original Levi's Store—Granted, Levi's don't hold the same appeal to this generation of teenagers as the last, but at the ginormous Union Square store they've thrown in the added allure of Original Spin, an in-store shop where you get to create your own custom jeans or have your khakis modified to your specifications—button fly, low-rise, tinted, scraped, stone-washed, you name it.

Virgin Megastore—The prices at Tower are cheaper, but they don't have the multimedia entertainment value of Virgin: video walls, listening stations, lots of in-store appearances by hot new artists, a huge selection of CD-ROMs, a café, a bookstore—oh, and about a million compact discs.

Though shopping isn't usually a passion for adolescent boys, there are a couple of places that might get them to take off the headphones for a few minutes. For Harry Potterheads, **The Booksmith** on Haight Street not only stocks the latest J.K. Rowling tomes but often carries a variety of Potter ephemera—wands, hats, games, calendars, etc., usually prior to and just after the next installment. They also have a number of signed editions by other boy favorites: Lemony Snicket, Eoin Colfer, et al.

For fans (fanatics?) of Magic the Gathering, Yu-Gi-Oh, and Spiderman comics, **Cards and Comics Central** on Geary will make your day (and probably wreck your parents' week). An emporium of comics, action figures, trading cards, posters, and game accouterments, they also host weekly card tournaments for serious players.

More multimedia entertainment center than retail outlet, **Niketown** offers all the latest in "swoosh" gear—logo jackets, sweatshirts, caps, duffel bags, and of course, "The Shoes"—but the boys come here almost more to see the video walls and the displays of Michael Jordan, LeBron James, etc.

NIGHT

Admittedly, evening activities and teens can be the stuff of parental nightmares. A few adolescent-approved entertainment options that don't require fake IDs:

Tactile Dome at the Exploratorium

Amazingly, this sensory funhouse (conceived by August Coppola—Francis Ford's brother, Nicolas Cage's father, and erstwhile SF State professor) has been in operation for more than twenty years, and it's still going strong. That's probably because adults love it just as much as kids do. Maybe more.

Zeum
Rooftop at Yerba Buena Gardens, 4th St. between Mission and Howard
415-777-2800

Urban Outfitters
80 Powell St.
415-989-1515

Abercrombie & Fitch
865 Market St.
415-284-9276

Buffalo Exchange
1555 Haight St.
415-431-7733

Original Levi's Store
Union Square, Stockton and Post streets
415-501-0100

Virgin Megastore
2 Stockton St. at Market
415-397-4525

The Booksmith
1644 Haight St.
415-863-8688

Cards and Comics Central
5424 Geary Blvd.
415-668-3544

Niketown
278 Post St.
415-392-6453

Tactile Dome at the Exploratorium
Lyon St. and Marina Blvd.
415-561-03362

This is a great thing to do at night, preferably before dinner, because all that crawling around can work up a serious appetite and being upside down and sideways with a belly full of pizza may not be such a great idea. The dome is designed to help you expand and explore your sense of touch. It's completely black inside, a factor which has been known to frighten some younger children (the supervising "dome guy" has speakers in each room with which he monitors everyone, and he'll come and get you out if you're

feeling scared or claustrophobic). You enter in groups of two or three and are instructed to feel your way around each room for openings and interesting tactile experiences—identifiable household objects, unusual shapes and textures (if you find the keys, you may proclaim yourself a Dome Master). Sometimes you crawl; sometimes you walk; sometimes you slide or bounce. Be open to losing your sense of direction and distance and to allowing your other faculties to compensate for sight. It's a major giggle fest that gets more fun each time through.

Basketball

The **Pro-City Summer Basketball League** is hands-down one of the coolest and best ways to entertain teenage boys (and their dads). Every summer from June through August, college basketball players and pros play games at Kezar Pavilion. Besides getting to watch your favorite hot college players sharpen their skills, you might get to see three-pointers made by the likes of Rex Walters, Jason Kidd, Gary Payton, Joe Smith, and other pros. Games are played Monday through Thursday nights at 8 p.m. and—the best part—it's free.

Minor Setbacks

Teenagers are at that painful age when they're listening to a lot of rock/rap music, but they're not old enough to get into nightclubs to see their favorite bands. **Bottom of the Hill** gets between the rock and that hard place. This under-

**Pro-City
Summer
Basketball
League**
Kezar Pavilion,
Stanyan and Waller
streets
415-695-5009

**Bottom of the
Hill**
1233 17th St.
415-621-4455

**924 Gilman
Street**
Berkeley
510-525-9926

Rainforest Café
145 Jefferson St.
415-440-5610

Buca di Beppo
855 Howard St.
415-543-7673

ground, shabby-chic Potrero Hill club showcases up-and-coming local bands and on Sundays becomes teenager heaven with a music line-up that welcomes all ages. On select Sundays spring to fall, they also offer a fabulous (and fabulously cheap) barbecue feed. The cookout starts at about 4 p.m.; the bands or DJs about 5:30 p.m. Grab some chicken and potato salad, sit on the back patio, and bond over power pop.

For serious thrash, garage band, punk, and other sweaty, head-banging music in a safe and sane atmosphere, there's **924 Gilman Street** in Berkeley, an all ages, no alcohol, cooperative nightclub whose motto is "Doing it for the kids, not to the kids." The club features bands with appropriately antisocial names, but it has a policy of not booking homophobic, ageist, sexist, or racist groups. The $5 cover is supplemented by a $2 membership fee for first-timers (good for one year). It's a place where parents can comfortably send kids into the mosh pit without having to worry that they've stumbled into a lion's den.

Kid-Approved Restaurants

Yes, you can drag an eight-year-old to Fleur de Lys, but frankly why ruin the experience (for the diners at the next table). There are plenty of places where a kid can be a kid, and where adults won't wish they'd brought a tranquilizer gun (for themselves).

Rainforest Café—The closest San Francisco comes to a genuine Disneyland-style attraction, the whole place is set up like a tropical jungle with vines and trees and waterfalls. Snakes lunge down from the ceiling, elephants and gorillas swing their trunks and beat their chests, a giant acrylic tank thrashes with live fish of every color and stripe—oh, and you can eat here, too (the food, believe it or not, is pretty good and fairly healthy, though as you might expect, over-priced).

Buca di Beppo—You don't come here because you actually want them to eat the monstrous servings of spaghetti topped with meatballs the size of 8 Balls. You come because there's something inherently entertaining about the sight of a bowl of pasta that could feed the Jolly Green Giant—and because, well, the food is rather tasty in that New York Mama Mia kind of way. This chain has elevated bad taste to a high art, with over-the-top '50s-tacky décor (think photos of women in strapless dresses scarfing plates of pasta with their hands behind their backs, choir boys picking their noses, and gilded statues of David) and a soundtrack that begins and ends with "That's Amore." Large parties should request the Pope's table, featuring a lazy Susan with a swiveling bust of the Pope.

Mel's—The original '50s American Graffiti diner actually stood on the very same Geary Street spot where the

modern-day version now resides. It was brought back to life with an eye to all the old details— tableside jukeboxes, a long soda counter, American flags, gum-snapping waitresses, patent-leather booths, blue-plate specials such as meatloaf and open-face turkey sandwiches, and huge milkshakes.

Max's—The South of Market diner is a hybrid between Mel's and a Jewish deli, with good food served in huge portions (along with a heaping pile of tongue-in-cheek attitude). Best bets include Reuben sandwiches, chicken pot pie, Chinese chicken or Cobb salad, and anything in the cake or pie department. Make sure to read the menus front to back; they're a scream, especially Max's rules, which promise a meal on the house if a waitperson ever asks you, "Is everything all right?"

Johnny Rockets—Less of a diner than a glorified soda fountain, this local chain serves all the usual nostalgic fare— hamburgers, fries, shakes—and it's open late.

Isobune—A great place to introduce youngsters to the undersea wonders of sushi. Chefs stand on an island behind a moat, rolling and slicing their seaweed-wrapped rice creations. Then they place the finished products on little floating plates that circle around the sushi bar like boats in the harbor. Diners pick up selections that look appealing. The entertainment value of the sushi boats often distracts kids—and some adults—from the fact that they may be eating eel or sea urchin.

Benihana—If salmon roe won't fly, this old haunt is just next door. Inexplicably, it has somehow retained its popularity where other gimmicky chains have failed (witness Chuck E. Cheese). That's probably because the gimmick still works. Zany, wisecracking chefs, trained in the art of cleaver juggling, kamikaze slicing and dicing, and shrimp-to-plate tossing, make cooked-to-order surf 'n' turf at your table. Though the jokes are a little stale, the high jinks are still pretty fresh, and the food is surprisingly decent.

House of Prime Rib—I'm not sure why, but meat-eating teens really seem to like this bar and grill out of the 1970s mold, with its big booths and big slabs of prime rib carved tableside. Growing boys can even get seconds.

Barney's Hamburgers—I recommend this place to vegetarians eating with nonvegetarians; it's also a great place to go with teens, many of whom seem to adopt the vegetarian lifestyle in their high school years. The menu features a variety of beef burgers with all sorts of toppings, plus a big selection of chicken sandwiches, tofu burgers, and garden burgers—oat patties mixed with shredded carrots, zucchini, cheese, and other natural goodies. Great curly fries.

Bill's Place—A San Francisco institution since 1959, this family-owned restaurant features more than twenty-five kinds of burgers, many of them named after local celebrities. The burgers are big and juicy, and the prices are incredibly reasonable.

North Beach Pizza—There are so many places to eat in North Beach, you could write an entire book on just that, but not many of them are appealing to kids as well as adults. North Beach Pizza scores on both accounts. Probably the most popular pizza delivery restaurant in the city, the two eat-in locations on Grant Avenue (one at Union, the other at Vallejo) are loud, boisterous, steamy, and fun, especially late at night. It's the kind of place that makes you feel like you're part of the locals scene. Don't even think about ordering anything but pizza.

The Gold Spike—Family-style Italian restaurants, once all the rage, are getting harder and harder to find these days, but you can still get the full six courses (including spumoni

Mel's
2165 Lombard St.
415-921-3039

Max's
311 3rd St.
415-546-0168

Johnny Rockets
2201 Chestnut St.
415-931-6258;
81 Jefferson St.
415-693-9120; and
1946 Fillmore St.
415-776-9878

Isobune
1737 Post St.
415-563-1030

Benihana
1737 Post St.
415-563-4844

House of Prime Rib
1906 Van Ness Ave.
415-885-4605

Barney's Hamburgers
3344 Steiner St.,
415-563-0307; and
4138 24th St.,
415-282-7770

Bill's Place
2315 Clement St.
415-221-5262

North Beach Pizza
1499 Grant Ave.
415-433-2444

The Gold Spike
527 Columbus Ave.
415-421-4591

ice cream for dessert) at the Gold Spike, a North Beach staple since 1920, run by three generations of the Mechetti family. The small dining room is covered from floor to ceiling with tchotchkes and bric-a-brac, and the tables sport red-checked tablecloths. Go on Friday for the cacciucco feed, a robust Italian seafood stew made with prawns, clams, crab, and calamari.

Zachary's Pizza—Always packed, and always worth the wait (and the drive to Oakland). The deep-dish Chicago-style pies are simply the best—my favorite is the basil-tomato, but many people swear by the smoked chicken and mushroom.

Hard Rock Cafe—The granddaddy of theme restaurants, this bastion of rock-and-roll memorabilia packs in the  tourists like it's a roach motel, especially now that it's moved to Pier 39. The thing is, it's still fun. Sit under the front end of the Cadillac or beneath Huey Lewis's gold records and be prepared to shout your order over the blasting music.

Video Café—Cheap, solid fare (burgers, fries, malts, and so on) for kids of the TV age. This 24-hour restaurant and video store lets you rent movies to play while you eat, or you can just watch the house selection played on monster-size wall-mounted televisions all around the room (also a great spot for all-nighter extrovert types).

Weird Museums

In my family, no vacation came without a visit to at least one museum and one old church. Though later in life I was grateful for the cultural exposure, at the time I think I would rather have had my gums scraped. The key to making museums attractive to kids is to find a subject they can relate to, or a collection that's just weird enough that they'll think it's cool. Here are some favorite oddball museums:

Cartoon Art Museum—Past exhibits at this comic strip and animation cel collection have included art from "The Tick" and "The Flintstones," a survey of MAD magazine drawings, a Peanuts retrospective, and work by tons of cult and underground comix artists.

Musée Mécanique—This is technically not a museum but a collection of great vintage carnival arcade games, all restored and fully functional. Parents will wax nostalgic over the mechanical gypsy fortune teller (like that one in the movie *Big*), the baseball game with the painted wooden players and the spring-wound bat, the hand-crank nickelodeons, and the miniature mechanical carnival of trains, Ferris wheels and shooting galleries, which all spring to life with a coin deposit. Kids will get a glimpse of life before Nintendo. Don't forget to say hi to Laughing Sal, the cackling fat lady who used to grace the entrance to Playland-at-the-Beach, and visit the *USS Pampanito*, the World War II submarine that is parked out back.

Blackhawk Museum—For car freaks, this East Bay museum is worth the hour or so drive from the city. It features more than 100 classic and one-of-a-kind cars in several large showrooms, including a 1935 Mercedes-Benz, a 1936 MG Model PB, and a 1968 Bizzarrini Spyder.

Pez Museum—A whole museum devoted entirely to dispensers for those little rectangular candies—*way* cool. There are Tweety heads, Batman heads, and even Japanese characters—some 300 in all.

Santa Cruz Surfing Museum—Located in a lighthouse overlooking Steamer Lane, Santa Cruz's most gnarly surfing spot, this one-room museum displays old surfboards (including one bitten in two by a great white shark), surfing memorabilia, wet suits, photographs of famous surfers, and a brief rundown of the history of the sport. After you're done looking at the stuff inside, find a perch at the cliff's edge and watch 'em ride the waves live and in person. It's teenager nirvana.

San Quentin Prison Museum—Unlike Alcatraz, this is still an operating maximum security prison, which may make the museum here that much more appealing. It has old tools of incarceration, such as a ball-and-chain and an Oregon boot, a gun collection, and a re-created 1913 prison cell.

Zachary's Pizza
5801 College Ave.,
Oakland
510-655-6385

Hard Rock Cafe
Pier 39
415-956-2013

Video Café
21st Ave. and Geary
Blvd.
415-387-3999

Cartoon Art Museum
655 Mission St.
415-227-8666

Musée Mécanique
Embarcadero and
Taylor at Pier 45
415-386-1170

Blackhawk Museum
3700 Blackhawk
Plaza Circle,
Danville
925-736-2280

Pez Museum
214 California Dr.,
Burlingame
650-347-2301

Santa Cruz Surfing Museum
West Cliff Dr.,
Santa Cruz
831-420-6289

San Quentin Prison Museum
just before the
Richmond/San
Rafael Bridge
415-454-1460

Museum of Vision—Some of the things in this tiny museum—diseased eyeballs; glass eyes; strange, creepy surgical devices used in early eye surgery—might put you off your lunch, but the kids will probably think it's great. The museum, part of the American Academy of Ophthalmology, is located near Fisherman's Wharf and is open Monday through Friday 8 a.m. to 5 p.m. by appointment only.

Lou's Living Donut Museum—It's a bit further afield in San Jose, but it might just be worth the drive for anyone craving a truly old-fashioned glazed (with the hole still attached). The "museum" is actually a shrine to late owner Lou Ades, former amateur film star and World War II flying ace, who opened up this small donut factory in 1955. Mementos and memorabilia line the walls of the shop, but of course, the donuts are the real star. If you call ahead, you can tour the factory and see how donuts are made. Admission is free; donuts extra.

BAY MODEL

I take back part of what I said about Sausalito. The Bay Model (2100 Bridgeway, Sausalito, 332-3870) is a fascinating feat of engineering that's definitely captivating for older kids. Built by the Army Corps of Engineers, the two-acre hydraulic scale-model of the San Francisco Bay and Sacramento Delta shows the flow of the tides and currents at 100 times actual speed (an entire cycle takes 14 minutes). There's also a small museum, and a good self-guided audio tour explains about the bay environment. Call ahead; the tide test schedule is erratic.

The Usual Suspects

It would be impossible to write about kids' activities without mentioning some of the tried-and-true places that are givens on any tour of youthful San Francisco.

Academy of Sciences/Steinhart Aquarium—Currently in temporary digs until the new building opens in 2008, the Academy still has a plethora of must-sees (and touches and tries): the scale where you can see how much you weigh on different planets; the earthquake simulator; the giant pythons and glow-in-the-dark fish display; the gem and mineral hall; and (for grown-ups) the Far Side Gallery of Gary Larson cartoons.

Japanese Tea Garden—Certain rituals must be observed here. Climb the Moon Bridge and throw a penny into the wishing pond. Have tea and cookies at the tea house; pick out the almond and sesame cookies and save them for last. Play with the funny little Japanese dime-store toys and ogle the origami papers at the gift shop. Leave a rice-cracker offering at the giant Buddha.

Exploratorium—The giant spirograph, the tree that lights up when you clap, the device where you hear yourself on a split-second time delay, the giant bubble-blowing pool, holograms, and the two-way mirror where you can put your head on someone else's body—these are only a tiny sample of the hundreds of exhibits at this enormous hands-on science playpen. Sure it's for kids, but you'll have a hard time dragging adults out of here at the end of the day.

Monterey Bay Aquarium—If you have time, a trip south to this remarkable living aquarium is a must. From the neon-jellyfish tank to the outdoor sea otter habitat and the walk-through tour of the Monterey Bay that starts underwater and works its way up in elevation to a shorebird aviary—there's nothing quite like it anywhere else. The surrounding Cannery Row area is basically Fisherman's Wharf South, but fun for an afternoon of walkaway crab cocktails, factory outlet shopping, arcade games, and taking a portrait of yourselves dressed up like Old West gunslingers.

Paramount's Great America—At the Bay Area's version of Disneyland you get more rollercoasters and thrill rides for your buck, as well as the chance to bond with life-size stars of Nickelodeon. Worth the long waits are the Vortex stand-up rollercoaster, the Top Gun inverted coaster (your legs swing free), the giant-screen IMAX movies, and—for those can stomach it—the Xtreme Skyflyer, in which you free fall 17 stories in a simulated skydive.

WHERE TO STAY

If the lure of an outdoor swimming pool with hammocks and palm trees isn't enough, then the family suite at the Hotel Del Sol—complete with bunk beds, toys, and games, VCR, and clock radios that play rain and wave sounds—should do the trick. The hotel rises above motor-lodge status with its bright cabana décor, a great Marina district

Museum of Vision
655 Beach St.
415-561-8502

Lou's Living Donut Museum
387 Delmas Ave.,
San Jose
408-295-5887

Academy of Sciences/ Steinhart Aquarium
875 Howard St.
415-221-5100

Japanese Tea Garden
Golden Gate Park,
9th Ave. near
Lincoln St. entrance
415-752-1171

Exploratorium
Marina Blvd. and
Lyon St.
415-563-7337

Monterey Bay Aquarium
886 Cannery Row,
Monterey
831-648-4848

Paramount's Great America
Great America
Parkway, Santa Clara
408-988-1776

Hotel Del Sol
3100 Webster St.
415-921-5520

locale, and clever amenities such as a Pillow Library for picky sleepers and free kites, beach balls, and sunglasses for kids. All this and free parking, too!

The hip, high-tech decor and celebrity handprints in the cement in front of the entrance to **Hotel Diva**, plus its location directly across from the Geary and Curran theaters and down the street from David's Deli (a classic Jewish nosh palace), make this a good compromise for families. The Diva's sister property, **Hotel Metropolis**, may be an even better bet, offering the city's first kid suite (parents stay in an adjoining room), outfitted with bunks beds, a drawing chalk-board, kid-size desk and chairs, toys, Nintendo games, Cookie Monster soap dispenser, and a radio tuned to the Disney channel.

Hotel Diva
440 Geary St.
415-885-0200

**Hotel
Metropolis**
25 Mason St.
415-775-4600

tour 9 Romantically Inclined

Scenario #1: You were introduced to her through a friend of a co-worker of your ex-roomate's on Friendster.com. You spent hours "talking" online about deep philosophical matters—how you hate Starbucks and reality TV, that there's no good way to convey sarcasm in an e-mail, your stance on genetically modified foods. Finally, after exhausting your extensive repertoire of clever computer smileys and

acronyms, you decided it was time to meet face to face. She's flying out for a visit, and you're nervous. Very nervous. You're determined to impress her with your knowledge of San Francisco and show her that the sensitive romantic you revealed in that intimate discussion on Michael Stipe wasn't just a figment of her Macintosh.

Scenario #2: You met riding the 38 Geary each morning to work. He lives in the Richmond; you live in the Western Addition. You both know the city like

Desiree
in the San Francisco
Film Centre, 39
Mesa St. next to
Main Post, Presidio
415-561-2336

the back of your hands. You finally got up the nerve to ask him out, and now you're thinking, "If I take him to some place like Julius' Castle, he'll dump me faster than an old transfer." You want romance, but you don't want it wrapped up in a box of truffles, tied with giant corsage ribbon, and rammed with a drip-wax chianti bottle down your throat. What will you do? What *will* you do?

MORNING

Granted, most dates don't start out first thing in the morning (unless it's the morning-after, and then we're not exactly talking "date" anymore). Morning dates are usually spend-the-day-together-and-see-if-we-run-out-of-things-to-talk-about affairs. They're low-stress in the sense that there's not that "are we, or aren't we" pressure you get at the end of a nighttime date; but they're high stress in the sense that there are a lot more hours to fill with actual, nonnaked activities.

The Presidio, I've decided, has something for just about everyone, but this pristine, private, wooded glen is particularly suited to romantics, both on sunny days, when the views make you want to dance a jig, and on cool, misty ones, when you can pretend you're John and Yoko watching the play of light and fog as it sweeps through the Golden Gate.

Before you begin your amorous adventures, stop in for breakfast or even better, pick up a box breakfast or lunch, at **Desiree**. First, you will score points with your date for even knowing about this place, hidden as it is at the end of a narrow hallway, inside the SF Film Centre building, which is off an obscure side street behind the Main Post.

Once you've stepped inside the café and are greeted by the smell of fresh-baked tarts, warm goat cheese, and sugar cookies, and the sight of five tables (along with the staff) all tucked snug and cheery into a room the size of a postage stamp, your companion may even consider your marriage material.

Desiree is actually the low-key baby of high-profile chef Anne Gingrass, who once helmed the kitchens at big-deal restaurants Postrio and Hawthorne Lane. The small, delightful box-lunch menu feels like something your mom might pack for you—if your mom was a five-star chef and had time to make you things like grilled Saint George cheese and ham, or warm goat cheese, pine nut, zucchini and basil puree sandwiches, that is.

My advice is to stow your sandwiches, your pasta salad, and your bag of fresh, housebaked cookies in a knapsack and head down Lover's Lane before you enjoy this feast.

In answer to your next question, yes, there is in fact a footpath in the Presidio called **Lover's Lane**, a tiny byway

marked by a little street sign. It's nothing fancy or terribly official, but somehow it makes you want to hold hands and sing about moon and June and spoon nonetheless. Pick it up just past the Presidio Boulevard Gate at the southeast entrance and walk slowly (the whole trail only takes about 15 minutes), making sure to point out all the silly romantic stuff along the way—squirrels sharing their nuts, the brick footbridge built for two, the huge weeping willow at Tennessee Hollow that's the perfect place to hide love notes or have a clandestine tryst.

When you're ready to step up to the big leagues, there's also a spot in the Presidio called **Inspiration Point**. Located near the top of Arguello Boulevard, just past the Presidio Golf Course clubhouse, the spot looks out over the Palace of Fine Arts and the Golden Gate. The Ecology Trail takes you right to it, but if you're already heading for a spot known as Inspiration Point, why not do it properly: drive here and "park."

Alternate Route

Start by sharing a pains au chocolat and frothy bowl of au lait at a sidewalk table at **Boulange de Cole Valley**, one of the city's homiest and Frenchiest cafés. Then walk west up Parnassus Avenue to Willard Street, hang a left up the hill, and you'll find yourself on a cobbled lane that time forgot—and your date probably never knew existed. After admiring the Wurster-esque shingle-style houses along Willard and nearby Edgewood Avenue and Farnsworth Lane (a treasure of a secret, cottage-dotted stairway), turn around, head back to Willard Street, and follow it to the end, where you'll find the entrance to **Sutro Forest**. Walk hand-in-hand along the footpaths, through the shady woods, beneath the fragrant eucalyptus trees, until you emerge into the sunlight at a destination that's invariably surprising. One trail leads to the back of UCSF; one to the houses along Stanyan Street; another to tiny Belgrave Avenue, just below Tank Hill. Depending on which way you go, you might happen upon a lovely glade, a redwood grove, or a perfect vista point. Half the fun is in not knowing.

NOON

There are dozens of romantic spots in Golden Gate Park, none of them completely undiscovered, but the **Shakespeare Garden** is certainly one that often gets overlooked. Grab a bottle of wine, some grapes, and a volume of Shakespeare's sonnets, and sit on the grass under a canopy of flowers and plants, every one of which is mentioned somewhere in the Bard's works. If you forgot your Penguin compendium, you can read from the inscriptions on the stone wall at the south end, or hum a few bars of "How Do I Love Thee . . ." and fake the rest.

A dozen roses is always a sure-fire date-pleaser, but also a tad on the cliché side if you ask me. If you really want to impress, take a drive up to the **Berkeley Rose Gardens** and present him/her with a thousand roses—along with a spectacular view of the San Francisco Bay and skyline. The lovely stone-terraced amphitheater, a WPA project of the 1930s, is filled with every imaginable variety and color of rose, like some kind of English grandmother's fantasy run amok. If things are going well, slip your hand in his or hers and stand under the trellis at the bottom, where dozens of couples get married each year.

Drake's Beach

Sure, you could do the whole oysters-aphrodisiac routine at a restaurant somewhere and be one of six other couples

Lover's Lane
near southeast entrance to the Presidio, at Presidio Blvd. Gate

Inspiration Point
in the Presidio, off Arguello Blvd., next to golf course

Boulange de Cole Valley
1000 Cole St.
415-242-2442

Sutro Forest
end of Willard St., Parnassus Heights

Shakespeare Garden
Golden Gate Park, near 9th Ave. and Lincoln St. entrance

Berkeley Rose Gardens
at Euclid and Eunice streets, Berkeley

Drake's Beach
Point Reyes National Seashore, off Highway 1

DINNER DATES

These restaurants constantly come up on people's "most romantic" lists. Who am I to argue?

Acquerello, 1722 Sacramento Street, 415-567-5432

Fleur de Lys, 777 Sutter Street, 415-673-7779

Woodward's Garden, 1700 Mission Street at Duboce, 415-621-7122

Café Jacqueline, 1454 Grant Avenue, 415-981-5565

Café Mozart, 708 Bush Street, 415-391-8480

Café Kati, 1963 Sutter Street, 415-775-7313

doing exactly the same thing. Or you could take a leisurely drive up Highway 1 to Point Reyes in the middle of the afternoon, make your way to romantic Drake's Beach, grab a dozen barbecued Hog Islands, Johnsons, or Tomales Bay oysters from the beachside grill, curl up on a blanket, and feed them to each other while swapping swigs from an impertinent bottle of sparkling rosé. You make the call. The sheltered beach is surrounded by tall, dramatic, white cliffs—the kind you might imagine Catherine running out across with Heathcliff in close pursuit. In between slugs of wine, gaze out toward the horizon and weave a tale about the Golden Hinde sailing into the lagoon with Sir Francis Drake at her helm. The English adventurer purportedly landed here in that ship in 1579.

Saying "They Do"

In most towns, going down to **City Hall** to get hitched is about as romantic as getting your driver's license. But most towns don't have a City Hall as magnificent as ours. Each year, hundreds of couples say their vows in the stunning rotunda at the foot of the grand marble staircase, beneath the soaring copper dome of this 1915 French Renaissance masterpiece. Sometimes the ceremonies are conducted en masse, followed by a formal presentation of the newlyweds, who descend the stairs like they're walking on air. Even if you may be years away from marriage, you can't deny that a good, three-hanky wedding will put you in the mood. Bring flowers and give them to a bride who's bouquetless, be a witness for someone who doesn't have one, or just stand on the sidelines and beam.

NIGHT

Lots of people come down to the **Palace of Fine Arts** in the afternoon, but for romantics, nighttime is definitely the right time. In the still of the evening, with the dome lit up and casting its shimmering reflection onto the lagoon, the palace looks like something Zeus created for Hera to hold all her earthly treasures. Chances are, unless it's a warm night or there's an event at the theater, people will be few and far between. Take full advantage of this. Walk slowly around the pond and take in the pavilion from all sides. Make sure to ponder architect Bernard Maybeck's mysterious weeping maidens wreathing the top of the pavilion. Then stand under the dome at the very center (there's usually a small circle marking the spot) and yodel for a haunting echo. Frequently, you'll encounter a lone flutist or saxophone player using the ethereal acoustics to great effect. Don't squander this opportunity. Ask your date for a dance.

Screen Gems

Dinner and a movie is probably the oldest dating ritual in the book, but it needn't be (roll eyes) "the oldest dating ritual in the book"—if you know what I'm saying, and I think that you do.

For instance, as opposed to the East Coast's Cinema 'n' Drafthouse, where patrons watch action flicks while tossing back pitchers of Rolling Rock, San Francisco has **Foreign Cinema**, where you can pitch woo over Kurosawa, Bertolucci, Truffaut, and vintage Eastwood while running the oyster circuit from Fanny Bay to Phantom Creek (some 15 varieties of oysters in all). Follow those up with a King salmon "B.L.T" or a Moroccan duck breast salad, and that's what I call dinner and a movie. The films, screened on a wall in the restaurant's neo-industrial open-air courtyard, can work as main feature or background chatter, depending on how high you turn up the volume on your tableside speaker. Or sit inside, bask in the glow of the wood-fired oven and the beautiful people, and provide your own soundtrack to one of the seduction scenes from *Jules et Jim*.

Since the demise of the drive-in movie in San Francisco, old-fashioned romantics have found fewer and fewer opportunities to employ the old "yawn and stretch." Seize the moment at the **Film in the Fog** fest on the Main Post in the Presidio. Held each October, the free event

City Hall
between Polk St. and Van Ness Ave., Grove and McAllister
415-554-4000

Palace of Fine Arts
Bay and Lyon streets
415-567-6642
(theater line)

Foreign Cinema
2534 Mission St.
415-648-7600

Film in the Fog
San Francisco Film Society, 39 Mesa St., Suite 110, The Presidio
415-561-5000

provides a rare chance to curl up under a blanket, nibble on a picnic dinner, and watch a big-screen movie without being hampered by sticky-soda floor or Huge-Head Boy. The show kicks off with a misty twilight band concert, followed by a cartoon (remember when Looney Tunes before the main feature was a given, just like maltballs?), and the screening

of a creepy classic—usually a sci-fi monster movie like *The Blob* or *It Came From Beneath the Sea*. Squeeze his/her hand, fake a few gasps and involuntary twitches, and watch in abject horror (read: delight) as a gelatinous creature devours the earth.

During the summer, the best place to combine the drinking with the movie viewing is at **Pyramid Alehouse, Brewery & Restaurant** in Berkeley. The brewery/restaurant shows cult comedy favorites—*So I Married an Axe Murderer, Spinal Tap, Strange Brew*—on the wall of their parking lot, weekends from July through September. Best part: the adjacent beer garden and barbecue grill, which beats jujubes and soy-bean-oil-slathered popcorn hands down. Bonus: live music before the show, and your movie dollars go to support a good cause (c'mon—it's Berkeley, of course there's a cause).

Progressive Dinners

One of my all-time most romantic date memories involves sneaking Chinese food into a movie theater and filling the auditorium with the smell of garlic chicken as we giggled over *Gregory's Girl* and our neighbors salivated. There's nothing sneaky about the reciprocal arrangement between **Giorgio's Pizzeria** and the **Plough and Stars** on Clement, but it's somehow impressive (and therefore romantic) when you've got an insider's edge on local rituals. The routine goes like this: arrive at Giorgio's about the same time as the live Irish minstrel music starts up across the street at the pub (between 8 and 9 p.m.). Order a couple of the stellar calzones. Peruse the shop windows for a little while, and then scope out your table at the P&S (the long, wooden tables are designed for conviviality rather than intimacy, but you can usually find a good niche on one of the benches along the wall). After about twenty minutes you can pick up your steaming stuffed popover and bring it back to your table in the bar. Immediately order a perfect, room-temperature Guinness—with a bartending staff that is almost exclusively Irish, you may not find a more perfectly poured pint in town—then sit back and tap your toes as the fiddles and the flutes infect you with their mischievous spirit.

On a slightly more extravagant level, you can do what I like to think of as the date trifecta (if you don't get him/her out of the gate with the first course, you've got two more chances to win in the stretch). Begin with an overflowing stem glass and a bowl of caviar at the **Bubble Lounge** champagne bar. Set the mood for the evening by settling into an overstuffed love seat and gazing at each other through the effervescent golden lens of Dom Perignon or a champagne cocktail. Most certainly order the Petrossian caviar degustation—30 grams each of Beluga, Ossetra, and Sevruga—and toast to the world of possibilities (and extended credit).

After the preamble, walk over a couple of blocks to **Kokkari Estiatorio** for dinner. If your date isn't swayed by the tale of Orion, who fell in love with the daughter of the King of Chios, and scoured the island Kokkari seeking game and seafood so he could prepare elaborate banquets for her, she's bound to fall for the haute Hellenic menu—food fit for the gods, if you ask me. For insurance, reserve the table in front of the fireplace where the aroma of roasting meats and the sound of crackling logs combine for a guaranteed toe-curler.

If you're feeling ambitious and you managed to save your dessert square, follow dinner with a stroll up to North Beach and share a slice of tiramisu or a cannoli at **Mara's Italian Pastry**. The cozy little bakery is open 'til midnight on weekends and will win extra points if your date is from the Boston area—this is about as close to Mike's on the North End as SF gets.

Romance in the 'Hood

Certain concert venues are so exceptional, for one reason or another, that I'll go to a show there almost regardless of who's playing. The Greek Theatre is one of them (can't beat

Pyramid Alehouse, Brewery & Restaurant
901 Gilman St.,
Berkeley
510-528-9880

Giorgio's Pizzeria
151 Clement St.
415-668-1266

Plough and Stars
116 Clement St.
415-751-1122

Bubble Lounge
714 Montgomery St.
415-434-4204

Kokkari Estiatorio
200 Jackson St.
415-981-0983

Mara's Italian Pastry
503 Columbus Ave.
415-397-9435

the views of the stage and the bay). The **Noe Valley Ministry** is another. This little church auditorium provides an incredibly intimate concert experience, and you'd be amazed at the performers they slip in the back door—Gypsy Kings, Box Set, Tracy Chapman, Jonathan Richman, X. Begin the evening at **Elisa's Health Spa** with a dip in a cozy outdoor Jacuzzi (suits optional) and a sauna or steam. Tucked off the street, this neighborhood spa has been soothing sore muscles for more than 25 years. Next, walk up to **Bacco's Ristorante**, easily the most romantic Italian restaurant this side of Twin Peaks. Order the risotto or gnocchi—both out of this world—and a bottle of chianti, or ask for the chef's recommendation (sometimes they put together special romantic, prix fixe dinners). From here proceed to the ministry for your living room concert. Unlike the big arenas, if the seats are all taken, they'll often let you sit on the stage behind the performer—it's like having a backstage pass without knowing the bouncer.

IT'S RAINING MEN

The flesh may be willing but the selection can be weak: Some spots for snagging single men.

The Canvas Gallery/Café— Every time I've set foot in this cheery café-cum-artspace next to Golden Gate Park there have been a half-dozen cute, smart, single-looking (straight) guys hanging out with cups of coffee and their laptops or the *New Yorker* or making origami (no joke!). 1200 9th Avenue, 415-504-0060.

Thursday nights at MOMA— The Museum of Modern Art's monthly mixer (half-price from 6 to 9 p.m.) attracts well-dressed guys who like jazz and are interested in art. What's not to like? 151 Third Street, 415-357-4000.

Mad Dog in the Fog—Some days it's just another Irishly inclined Lower Haight bar, but during Women's World Cup, you can separate the beer-swilling boys from the equal-opportunity men. 530 Haight Street, 415-626-7279.

Star Wash—You can simultaneously play "find the missing sock" and talk classics of the silver screen at this campy Laundromat between the Mission and Castro, decorated to the nines with old movie posters and memorabilia. If it's a movie night, stick a couple of extra quarters in the dryer and get cozy with your sock-mate. 392 Dolores Street, 415-431-2443.

Cruise and Snooze

Note: this is more of an anniversary date than a first date, as the sleeping arrangements don't leave much room for ambiguity.

There's nothing like a moonlight cruise to put you in the mood—the ocean breeze in your hair, the lights of the Bay Bridge reflecting off the water, the foghorns calling forlornly to anyone who'll listen. Begin with a sunset ferry ride to Jack London Square (the **Alameda/Oakland Ferry** leaves from Pier 39 and the Ferry Building every two hours or so); ride topside if it's not too cold, so you can see the underside of the bridge as you pass beneath its vast span. From the

Oakland docks, it's a short stroll along the main drag, past shops, restaurants, and wharfy knickknack parlors to **Yoshi's** for an evening of top-notch jazz and Japanese food (make sure to order lots of sake). The club, which moved to the Oakland waterfront in 1997, features some of the biggest and best names in the business—from Ron Carter to John Pizzarelli. After the show, when your date is starting to wonder how you're going to get home, lead him or her to the Voyager, a 46-foot ketch-rigged sailboat docked in the marina looking out over the bay to the San Francisco skyline. The Voyager is one of six yachts that make up the East Bay arm of **Dockside Boat & Bed**, a sort of floating bed and breakfast inn (another seven are moored at Pier 39, but it's hard to imagine a romantic evening shouting over sea lions and dodging Instamatic cameras). For between $110 and $270 a night, you can sleep aboard a private luxury yacht equipped with TV/VCR, stereo, sundeck, wet bar, coffee maker, and continental breakfast. For an all-out mush fest, charter the boat (captain provided) for a cruise and a catered candlelight dinner. Dance in the moonlight with the ocean lapping against the hull and let the waves work their magic.

WHERE TO STAY

At the **Archbishop's Mansion**, a sumptuous, restored 1904 Victorian mansion, you get to have breakfast in bed, take baths by candlelight in a claw-foot tub, and sip brandy in front of the fireplace. It all adds up to the ultimate honeymoon (or popping the question) hotel.

Inconspicuous and inexpensive, **Petite Auberge** is a little pension on the slopes of Nob Hill that snuggles up to you like a warm cat on a rainy day. Besides a crackling fire, a bottomless cookie jar, and a homey kitchen that serves bountiful breakfasts, the hotel offers one of the most romantic suites in all the city. For a little over $200, you get a trellis-enclosed pied-à-terre, hidden from the prying eyes of neighbors and guests by overgrown climbing roses and vines, with a private deck, large deep tub, and complimentary champagne and chocolates. It's like you stepped off the mean streets into your own private Provence.

Noe Valley Ministry
1021 Sanchez St.
415-454-5238

Elisa's Health Spa
4028-A 24th St.
415-821-6727

Bacco's Ristorante
737 Diamond St.
415-282-4969

Alameda/ Oakland Ferry
from Ferry Building or Pier 39 on the Embarcadero
510-749-5837

Yoshi's
510 Embarcadero, Oakland
510-238-9200

Dockside Boat & Bed
67 Clay St., Oakland
510-444-5858

The Archbishop's Mansion
1000 Fulton St.
415-563-7872

Petite Auberge
863 Bush St.
415-928-6000

tour 10 Neo-Bohemians

They came, they saw, they snapped their fingers. For better or worse, the beatniks' mystique lingers on in cafés and dark alleyways, in bookstores and jazz clubs, along sleek, cool underground corridors, and of course, on the road.

Unlike many movements that have captured the imagination of San Franciscans for a time (tie dye, smart drinks, and chat rooms come to mind), the fascination with '50s Beat culture never really went away. Consider, for instance, the accouterments of modern-day Bohemia: cigarettes, experimental jazz, pouty lipstick, poetry, cult film, coffee, and a tendency toward unemployment. Yes, open the closet door of just about every Beck-listening, low-rise-jeans-wearing 20-something and you'll likely find a beret and a copy of *Naked Lunch*.

Granted, the neobeatnik's hipper-than-thou idio-syncrasies can occasionally get annoying, but this particular group may very well be the best kind of visitor. Why? Because for many of them, hanging out in cafés and coffeehouses (sometimes several during the course of a day) is considered an actual event. No doubt you see the inner beauty of this scenario: while indulging in one of your favorite activities, you get to feel like you're showing your friends the sights.

MORNING–NOONISH

The key is to pick coffeehouses with character (and charac-ters) that perhaps offer something beyond the standard indie filmmaker/philosophy major/bike messenger banter. In the old beatnik quarter of North Beach, there's an embar-rassment of café riches, but not too many have . . . how you say? . . . the right "vibe." On boho Grant Avenue, eschew the obvious lures—Caffè Trieste, Savoy Tivoli—in favor of the **Italian/French Baking Company**, a small storefront with a big bakery in back that offers a half-dozen kinds of biscotti and breadsticks as well as some heavenly specialty treats such as eccles cakes (don't ask, just try 'em). Grab an espresso and a hazelnut biscotti, perch on a stool, and gaze out with appropriate insouciance at the tantalizing North Beach street scene.

Another good stop is **Mario's Bohemian Cigar Store**, which, despite its touristy location (on the corner of Columbus and Union) and popularity, still feels authentic. A narrow corridor—about wide enough for a person to stand with one arm extended dangling a long cigarette holder—divides the tables from the bar. They have coffee, but you might want to opt for a pale ale instead. And don't leave before trying one of Mario's eggplant focaccia sandwiches. Afterward, head down the street to **Lyle Tuttle's Tattoo**

Italian/French Baking Company
1501 Grant Ave.
415-421-3796

Mario's Bohemian Cigar Store
56 Columbus Ave.
415-362-0536

Lyle Tuttle's Tattoo Parlor and Museum
841 Columbus Ave.
415-775-4991

Parlor and Museum, where the now-retired Lyle displays an interesting collection of early tattoo equipment and designs. Tuttle's a legend in the biz, having inked everyone from Janis Joplin to Cher. Hard to believe we've come so far in this peculiar realm that looking at old flash (popular tattoo images) of hula girls and sailors would make one nostalgic. But there you are.

If you're seriously thinking about adding a couple of chain-links to that permanently penned fence around your ankle, there's a bigger stable of skin artists working a few blocks away at **Tattoo City**. Owner Ed Hardy also specializes in tattoo makeovers for those, like Johnny Depp, who needed to transform "Winona Forever" into something more au courant.

Though it's a cliché by now, I would be remiss if I talked about North Beach and beatniks and didn't mention **City Lights Bookstore**, Vesuvio, or Specs'. City Lights, of course, is where Beat bard/publisher/artist Lawrence Ferlinghetti has kept the candle burning for 50 years, and where you can find nearly everything ever written by and about Kerouac, Corso, McClure, Rexroth, Ginsberg, et al. The poetry section is outstanding, as you might imagine—and not just filled with tributes to '50s counterculture. Ferlinghetti and his Little Publishing House That Could have continued to champion emerging voices in contemporary poetry, and the bookshop is a whirlwind education for anyone even remotely curious about San Francisco's predilection toward waywardness and unconventional thinking.

Once you've found the obscure literary journal of your fancy, take it into **Vesuvio**, the famous bar and literary hangout that was once the favorite watering hole of Jack Kerouac. (Even blasé Bohemians will enjoy the oft-told tale of the night Kerouac was supposed to head down to Big Sur for a historic meeting with writer Henry Miller, but instead ended up at Vesuvio on an all-night bender. The 'twain never did meet.) Vesuvio's interior looks like what might have happened if Queen Victoria had hired the Mad Hatter as her decorator. And though the crowd these days consists mostly of "squares," you can still feel the Beat in the bar stools. Kerouac fans might also want to make a side trip to

29 Russell Street on Russian Hill, where the Beat icon lived while writing *On the Road.*

Across the street on tiny Adler Place, the cast of characters at **Specs'** is a bit less predictable and therefore all the more tantalizing. Once a beatnik hangout managed by Henri Lenoir, the same guy who owned Vesuvio, the bar has maintained a healthy sense of irreverence over the years. Ponder the deeper meaning of the shrunken head collection, have your handwriting analyzed, or attempt to explain the ramifications of the hanging whale penis bone to a group of Spanish sailors on shore leave. If you hang out here long enough, there's a good chance you'll have a close encounter with an actual poet, novelist, or someone who knows someone who's working on a screenplay. Spend a few minutes with the baskets of postcards at the bar, written by tourists from around the world.

A few blocks and a million ideological light years away from Specs', on the border of Fisherman's Wharf, is **Cafe Francisco**, which, considering its precarious locale, is one of the last places you'd expect to find any self-respecting hipster. But somehow this quiet café manages to skirt the wharf scourge. Hardwood floors, old wood-back booths for two, and a collective of crusty salts who hang out at the sidewalk tables lend an air of ingenuousness to the place.

Lower Haight

Divisadero is the dividing line between the old Haight (or what's left of it) and the new Haight, which resides—philosophically—somewhere around the intersection of New Bohemia and Gen X/Y Slackerville. Middle ground can be found at the **Horseshoe Coffee House**—the kind of place where the beatniks might have met the hippies halfway. It's a great spot to scope out the next big thing: tattoos, piercing, mayoral candidates—but probably not ideal for resolving the problems of the world (hard to hear yourself think over the music). The coffee's strong and cheap, though, and there are a half-dozen computer terminals in the back—a few with great design applications on them— for latter-day poster artists (believe it or not, this was purportedly the country's first Internet café). The food is

Tattoo City
700 Lombard St.
415-345-9437

City Lights Bookstore
261 Columbus Ave.
415-362-8193

Vesuvio
255 Columbus Ave.
415-362-8193

Specs'
12 Adler Pl., at Columbus Ave.
415-421-4412

Cafe Francisco
2161 Powell St.
415-397-2602

Horseshoe Coffeehouse
566 Haight St.
415-626-8852

minimal café fare, and if you're hungry, you should be across the street at **Kate's Kitchen** anyway, chowing down on either Flannel Hash (a heaping plate of corned-beef chunks, potatoes, bell peppers, carrots, and red onion, topped with fried or poached eggs), or the cornmeal buttermilk pancakes (topped with fresh fruit and maple syrup).

SoMa

South of Market used to be more of a weekday café place, but with the last few frenzied years of loft/condo building, coffeehouses down here have started to get that good, lived-in feel. **South Park Café**, a small, sunny French boite located on the bucolic oval between 2nd and 3rd and Bryant and Brannan, is a great place to go with neo-Bohemians who 1) did the whole expatriate stint in Prague, or 2) want to get a whiff of where the dot was during the dotcom boom. South Park Café, with its picture windows that open out

onto the sidewalk, reading racks of international newspapers, and café au lait served in big bowls, was oozing Euro-hip long before **Caffè Centro** and the **Butler and the Chef** plopped themselves down for a ride on the Internet gravy train. (Nothing against either of these, they are très bien in their own right; but when given a choice, you gotta go with the original.)

Down Bryant Street on the South Embarcadero waterfront, **Red's Java House** is the place to take your grunge refugee friends so they can bond with the regular crowd of longshoremen and tugboat operators. The coffee stinks, but so what? This is 100-percent, genuine, no-pretense Atmosphere. For under $4 you get to sit in a shack on the edge of the bay eating a burger, drinking a Budweiser, and imagining San Francisco's old working waterfront—back before the peach-and-teal set moved in. Now that's sightseeing.

Cole Valley

The **Reverie Café**, a relatively new addition to the sleepy Cole Valley scene, offers what may be the ideal neo-

Bohemian blend: exquisitely marbled espresso drinks, existential reading material, chess/backgammon, and dim arty lighting—all set to the soundtrack of Chet Baker.

The Mission

In the Mission, where New Bohemia has settled in for the decade, you might need to do a progressive café crawl, beginning at **Cafe Que Tal** on Guerrero for a low-key, read-the-morning-paper, get-your-bearings experience. Later, for more serious café dwelling (as opposed to café squatting), you should progress to **Muddy Waters** or (my personal favorite) **Café La Bohème**, where habitués have elevated the act of lingering to an art form. Sure, it's about coffee, but it's also about speed chess, temping, left-wing politics, burning out, art, and life in the slow lane. This is the spot to hit if you want your friends to get a sense of how fringe (if not sometimes frayed) San Francisco lives.

From here, head directly to **826 Valencia**, perhaps the most prominent sign of literary Bohemia's resurgence. The community writing salon, outlaw publishing house, and ersatz pirate den was started by local luminary Dave Eggers, who proved that the phenomenal success of his memoir, *A Heartbreaking Work of Staggering Genius,* could have benefits far beyond his own pocketbook. During the day, school kids find their muse among the coterie of young, hip, extraordinarily talented and well-published tutors who make 826 their classroom. For the culturally curious, 826 is also a great place to pick up the latest in cutting-edge fiction and journalism: from Eggers' quarterly review, *McSweeney's,* to *The Believer,* a literary magazine for the younger set—and if there's a reading/lecture/happening going on, these guys will know exactly *where it's at.* Oddly enough, though, it's the pirate supply store that puts the final spanner in the bridge between old and new bohemia—the odd-mod assortment of jolly roger flags, eye patches, spyglasses, mops, and glass eyes make for a curio shop worthy of a Beat poet or his first mate.

Potrero Hill

Farley's is perhaps the city's ultimate café. Highlights include a magazine rack that offers a wealth of intriguingly

Kate's Kitchen
471 Haight St.
415-626-3984

South Park Café
108 South Park,
between 2nd and
3rd streets
415-495-7275

Caffè Centro
102 South Park Ave.
415-882-1500

**Butler and
the Chef**
155-A South Park
415-896-2075

**Red's Java
House**
Embarcadero at
Brannan, no phone

Reverie Café
848 Cole St.
415-242-0200

Cafe Que Tal
1005 Guerrero St.
415-282-8855

Muddy Waters
521 Valencia St.
415-863-8006

Café La Bohème
3318 24th St.
415-643-0481

826 Valencia
826 Valencia St.
415-642-5905

Farley's
1315 18th St.
415-648-1545

bizarre reading, including (at last peruse) *Morbid Curiosity* (a magazine containing articles of esoterica ranging from testicular injury to childbirth), *Mental_Floss*, and the always-popular *TooMuchCoffeeMan* comic books. I also love their "One Cup, One Milk" policy—the best anti-Starbucks statement for miles, and their assortment of quasi-famous T-shirts, including the aforementioned cup/milk and the classic "~~Sex, Drugs, Alcohol, Tobacco, Rock Music, Socialism~~, Caffeine." This should have been the place filmmaker Mike Moore referred to in *Roger and Me* when he said, "San Francisco is a city where everyone has a job, but no one seems to be working."

Richmond District

The **Blue Danube** is a traditional favorite, and it's close to lots of other places that could substitute for coffeehouses, such as the **Plough and Stars** pub. With its long, wooden tables, perfect-temperature Guinness (which looks a lot like coffee), and authentic Irish angst (accompanied by live Irish music), retro beatnik types should have no trouble making the transition. While you're down here, you must drag anyone who's ever thought about wearing a beret to **Green Apple Books** for a spin through the fiction annex, where you might pick up a dog-eared copy of *A Confederacy of Dunces*.

Sunset District

In the Inner Sunset, nothing's really been the same since the Owl and the Monkey closed, but **Java Beach**, out at Land's End, constitutes something of a landmark: a cool coffeehouse in a valley of culture death. The decidedly low-budget café attracts a groovy little mix of surfers, beachies, and cheap-rent hipsters who while away the hours playing board games, reading, and drinking French roast. On a clear day, you can sit and watch the breakers and bikers from sidewalk benches as you contemplate the minutiae of life. For a true

San Francisco beatnik experience, take your bad poetry to
the beach and burn it in a ritual bonfire. Then head back to
the café for a little existential banter about what it all
means. Java Beach is open every day until about 11 p.m.

Oh, and in case you're wondering—by definition,
Bohemian and Marina district are two mutually exclusive
terms. Nuff said.

See the Light

After you've had enough caffeine and you're feeling the need
to cleanse and purge, head down to the **Church of Saint
John Coltrane**, one of the best ways I've ever found to
spend a slacker Sunday. Services at this African Orthodox
Church begin around noon, but you needn't be African or
orthodox to get enlightened. All you need is a beat and a
fondness for the music of patron saint and jazz genius John
Coltrane (which, in Neo-Bohemia, is like asking if you like
strong coffee). While it's not quite as colorful a scene as it
was a few years ago (they were booted from their storefront
on Divisadero and now share quarters with another church
on Gough Street), this is still an earth-moving experience.
Step through the doors and you'll find yourself swept up in
a cacophony of saxophones and hallelujahs as Bishop
Franzo King, saxophone in hand, leads the congregation in
a service that is part gospel, part all-out jam session.
Accompanied by Ohnedaruth, the house band (usually a
drummer, bassist, keyboard player, and several saxophon-
ists), the weekly event unfolds like a half-scripted improv
session: the reverend, resplendent in fuchsia robes, alternates between congas and the soprano sax, more saxophones come crawling out of the woodwork, a full-throated
chorus of gospel singers joins in the fray, and pretty soon
everyone's stomping their feet and clapping their hands
until the room's rocking in a full-on jazz jam. Should you
feel inspired, the congregation is invited to join in the
band—you can bring your own instrument or you can
borrow a tambourine or sleigh bells. By the time you leave,
you may find yourself wondering if it's pure coincidence
that John Coltrane and Jesus Christ have the same initials.

Blue Danube
306 Clement St.
415-221-9041

**Plough and
Stars**
116 Clement St.
415-751-1122

**Green Apple
Books**
506 Clement St.
415-387-2272

Java Beach
1396 La Playa, at
Judah
415-665-5282

**Church of Saint
John Coltrane**
930 Gough St.
415-673-3572

NIGHT

As evening falls and the conversation shifts from intense coffee chatter to more languorous, squinty-eyed discussion, latter-day Bohemians head to **Cafe du Nord**—a place so hip that one visit is the equivalent of two or three just about everywhere else. Just like the Cellar in the beatnik days of yore, this bar/club lures the hepcats down, down, down to a subterranean former speakeasy where you'd expect some guy named Jocko to ask you for a password through an eye-level slot in the door. Du Nord is like a museum of cool: retro lounge lizards in Quiana shirts pose against a magnificent 40-foot mahogany bar (an original from the club's Roaring Twenties days); cigarettes dangle off the full lips of modern-day flappers, their long black fingernails tapping

out rhythms on high ball glasses; hep cats nod expectantly to the edgy groove of an acid jazz combo. Du Nord has been almost prescient in its ability to foresee the next hot thing, from bachelor pad music to swing dancing to storytelling by up-and-coming fiction writers. It's easy to see how coming here can turn into an all-night outing, especially if you decide to eat (the food's not half bad). Peak people-watching hours don't begin until after 9 p.m.

For a more low-key sit-down experience, slink down the alley behind Zuni Café on Market Street to the **Hotel Biron**, which does not in fact offer lodging but does provide a fantastic array of a wine and art in a champagne cave-style antechamber that bespeaks a brand of cultivated carelessness attained only by the truly avant-garde. Sip cabernet, nibble on cheese and caviar, and wallow in moody lighting and muted jazz as you ponder the sometimes obtuse work of local artists.

Rarely do you find a place where Bohemians can be fastidious and cool at the same time, which is why **Brainwash** is such an anomaly. A groovy café and bar that offers a fun mix of live music acts, beer, and Internet access, it is also a laundromat. Tucked in back are dozens of high-tech, computerized washers and dryers where you can air (or dampen) your dirty little secrets. A numbered light board in the café gives you the blink and nod when your load is done. If this set-up doesn't pose enough of a dilemma for your anti-establishment-type guests, try the bathrooms, which are segregated for "readers" and "writers." Sit midroom, so you can overhear some truly bizarre conversations, which veer wildly from German philosophy (a result of Brainwash's proximity to the Global Youth Hostel) to multimedia techno-talk.

You'd think any place that bills itself as a "bohemian café" would be precisely the opposite, but in fact, **Frankie's Bohemian Café** in Pacific Flats (the no-man's-land between Pacific Heights and the Western Addition) is pretty hep. High points include good beers on tap, a youngish and pleasantly unmotivated crowd, and a groovy menu of big, healthy dishes, including a yummy Czechoslovakian one called a brambory, a giant zucchini-and-potato pancake topped with everything from barbecued shrimp to guacamole, sour cream, and cheese.

Beat Crazy

The resurgence of spoken word events and performance art is one of the biggest tip-offs that the Beat goes on in San Francisco. This time around, however, you're more likely to encounter the young avant-bard engaging in full-scale word warfare—complete with vocal heckling, foot stomping, and judges who cut you off in mid-rhyme—than mild-mannered finger snapping. Poetry slams, where spoken-word artists battle each other in a fast-paced and raucous tournament of tongues, are introducing a whole new generation to the art form. Around town, you can usually catch one (or if you're feeling bold, participate in one) every fourth Sunday at Café du Nord, and every second Sunday at **Studio Z**, where poetry bouts are rounded out with hip hop and soul music acts, and DJ dancing.

For regular-old readings full of adjective-laden angst, poets still hold court in the coffeehouse. Prep yourself by watching Mike Meyers' hilarious tribute to beatnik coffee-house culture in the movie *So I Married an Axe Murderer*,

Cafe du Nord
Market St. at
Sanchez
415-979-6545

Hotel Biron
45 Rose St., behind
Market St.
415-703-0403

Brainwash
1122 Folsom St.
415-861-3663

**Frankie's
Bohemian Café**
1862 Divisadero St.
415-921-4725

Studio Z
314 11th St.
415-252-7100

A WORLD OF EATS ON VALENCIA STREET

Running on empty? Valencia restaurants offer some of the most diverse dining in the city.

You can join the tapas revolution (or as I like to call it, Spanish dim sum) at **Picaro** (3120 16th St., 415-431-4089), **Esperpento** (3295 22nd St., 415-282-8867), **Ramblas** (557 Valencia St., 415-565-0207), or **Timo's** (842 Valencia St., 415-547-0558). **Ti Couz** (3108 16th St., 415-252-7373) is the spot for savory and sweet crepes (for dessert, try the one with Nutella).

If your tastes swing east, there's **Amira** (590 Valencia St., 415-621-6213) for pan-Arabian cuisine, **Saigon Saigon** (1132 Valencia St., 415-206-9635) for Vietnamese food, **Firecracker** (1007 Valencia St., 415-642-3470) for Chinese, and **Rasoi** (1037 Valencia St., 415-695-0599) for Indian.

For good, cheap Mexican food, hit **La Cumbre** (515 Valencia St., 415-863-8205) or **Pancho Villa** (3071 16th St., 415-864-8840), where the burritos are the size of small babies. The Mexican food at **La Rondalla** (901 Valencia St., 415-647-7474) isn't stellar, but you go here more for the entertainment value anyway. Sip a cheap margarita and admire the year-round Christmas decor while mariachis serenade you with "Guantanamera."

then make your way to the **Yakkety Yak Coffeehouse** downtown (Friday nights) or **Dalva** in the Mission (second and fourth Thursdays).

Performance art crosses over into cult film at **The Werepad** on Potrero Hill, a place that could very well have been swept up in a Wizard of Oz tornado circa 1961 and plunked down 50 years later in this Dogpatch locale, and no one would have been the wiser. Part beatnik lounge, part underground cinema venue, part B-movie poster gallery, and one giant homage to kitsch—the Werepad is the unofficial gathering spot of the neo-Boho "it" crowd. Featuring a cozy padded bar, rigged with Tiki imagery and lava lamps, a modern DJ booth, and hosts dressed in period costume, the Werepad hosts regular film nights, when hipsters, mods, cineastes, and self-described hicks gather in the private screening room and unveil one of the delights from their huge collection of exploitation and B-Movie fare from the '60s and '70s. Whether you're watching *Death Race 2000* or *Teenage Jailbait*, there's no escaping the allure of trash cinema projected onto the big screen from the gaudy and wonderfully low-tech 16mm prints.

Good, traditional theater is fine and well, but experimental, occasionally bad theater is what Bohemians live for. Performances at the **Exit Theatre** are rarely bad, but occasionally you do hit something that's just completely out there, especially during the annual Fringe Festival held here in September. How could any nonconformist not be thrilled with plays boasting such titles as *The Almost True Adventures of an Ex-Mormon Stripper and the Cursed Generations That Came Before* and *The Disco Prophecies*, which is described as "a true story (mainly) of how Disco brought the world to Australia."

Valencia Street

If you're short on time, you might want to do the "add water and stir" tour of Beat San Francisco along Valencia Street—a one-stop boulevard for all your nightly boho needs. Park (carefully) around Fifteenth Street and work your way down the promenade, beginning with a drink at **Liquid** (so hip it's almost square), **Elixir** (more tap beers than you can think of), **Doctor Bombay's** (less-crowded, more surreal), Dalva (poetry, sangria, and a secret back room), or **Zeitgeist** (an odd convergence of biker bar and literati den, sort of *The Wild One* meets *Bucket of Blood* in a sea of tattoos, beer, Gauloise, and tamales).

Then catch a noir flick at the fabulous **Roxie Cinema** (showings at recent fests have included *The Life of Allen Ginsberg, Burroughs: The Movie,* and the aforementioned *Bucket of Blood*). Next, peruse the bookshelves for a copy of *Howl* or *On Civil Disobedience* at **Dog-Eared Books** or **Modern Times**. Then head over to **Aquarius Records** or **Zen City Records** to bring yourself up to date on the alternative/hip hop/retro lounge music scene.

Local acid jazz favorites the Broun Fellinis and Mingus Amungus play regularly down the street at the **Elbo Room**, a formerly undergroundish bar/club that's toppled over into mainstream status (at last check, the bridge-and-tunnel crowds hadn't discovered it yet).

WHERE TO STAY

Hotel Bohème is the perfect hotel for latent Bohemians, emerging artists, or movie stars like Frances (*Fargo*) McDormand, whom you almost recognize. Step inside, walk up the narrow staircase, and know what it's like to be listening to Allen Ginsberg read *Howl* from the room above the club (Ginsberg, in fact, was a guest here, as were McDormand and husband/director Joel Coen). Some rooms look straight out over Columbus Avenue, others look

Yakkety Yak Coffeehouse
679 Sutter St.
415-351-2090

Dalva
3121 16th St.
415-252-7740

The Werepad
2430 3rd St.,
between 20th and
22nd streets
415-824-7334

Exit Theatre
156 Eddy St.
415-931-1094

Liquid
2925 16th St.
415-431-8889

Elixir
3200 16th St.
415-552-1633

Doctor Bombay's
3192 16th St.
415-431-5255

Zeitgeist
199 Valencia St.
415-255-7505

Roxie Cinema
3117 16th St.
415-863-1087

Dog-Eared Books
900 Valencia St.
415-282-9246

Modern Times
888 Valencia St.
415-282-9246

Aquarius Records
1055 Valencia St.
415-647-2272

Zen City Records
105 Valencia St.
415-437-1578

Elbo Room
647 Valencia St.
415-552-7788

Hotel Bohème
444 Columbus Ave.
415-433-9111

through an Old World maze of laundry lines and fire escapes. Press your face to the glass of one room and you even get a great view of Coit Tower. The rooms are small and creatively appointed with charming touches like mosquito-netting canopies. The hallways are decorated with marvelous Beat-era photographs by Jerry Stoll, who captured late-1950s North Beach in all its smoky, full-lipped, jazz cat, back-alley glory. To keep guests abreast of the nightlife on the street below, the staff maintains a culture chalkboard, which posts offerings such as Irish music at O'Reilly's pub and hours for opera singing at Caffè Trieste. Like, *crazy*, daddy-o.

Hotel Rex comes from the stable of Chip Conley, whose Joie de Vivre chain has taken the town by storm with theme-oriented, budget-minded, funky-chic hotels. The Rex has a Bohemian slant, geared toward artists, filmmakers, and writers (many of whom regularly stay here). Walls are covered with original, local art and books, some of them dating from the 1920s and '30s. Antique phones and typewriters are on display in the lobby bar, giving it the feel of a noir Sam Spade mystery. Scenesters make their way to the back salon, which hosts regular literary soirees, readings, and book signings, before retiring for a drink at adjacent Café Andrée, a chic little bistro named for Andrée Dutcher, wife of Beat poet Kenneth Rexroth.

BOHO IN BIG SUR

If you can rouse the café rats from their chairs (maybe bribe them with buzz beans), hop in the old Karmann Ghia and head down to Big Sur and the **Henry Miller Library and Museum** (Highway 1, 3 hours south of SF, 831-667-2574). Any hipster worth his or her salt had a *Tropic of Cancer* period in college, and will probably jump at the chance to make a pilgrimage to Miller's home turf, tucked in a redwood grove just off a wild, untamed stretch of coastline. The library/museum offers handwritten letters, books for sale, and artifacts such as Miller's typewriter. Pick up a copy of *Henry Miller On Writing*, sit in one of his hand-carved chairs in the whimsical sculpture garden, and reflect.

Hotel Rex
562 Sutter St.
415-433-4434

tour 11 Shopaholics

Shopaholics come in all shapes and sizes, and they feed their addiction for all kinds of reasons. For some, it's the bargain mentality. They've plowed

through every thrift store and outlet within a forty-mile radius of their home, and now they've come here looking for fresh meat. For others, it's the prospect of bringing back something that is uniquely San Francisco, something they can't find where they live. And for still others, shopping is simply their favorite form of entertainment, with a vacation in San Francisco merely being a conduit for pursuing their preferred pastime at their leisure, rather than on their lunch hour. Whatever their motives, it's your job as host to indulge their cravings—that is, as long as they're paying with their own credit card.

THE OUTLETS

For a while in the '80s, factory outlets were cropping up South of Market faster than trendy restaurants. And some of them were actually good deals. The Gunne Sax outlet alone provided me and thousands of other girls with the prom dresses of their dreams at prices that made moms sigh with relief. But along with the Gunne Saxes, the CP Shades, and the Esprits came shoddily made fake designer clothes, manufacturers that no one's ever heard of, and discount stores that offered very little in the way of real bargains. Then riding the wave of outlet mania came the gargantuan off-price outlet malls, many of which claimed to give deep discounts on designer merchandise but really just sold lower-end lines by the same label at very average prices.

All this whining is my way of saying that just because there's a slash through the $700 price tag on that Donna Karan dress, it doesn't automatically mean that you're getting a deal. Here are some places worth noting:

Jeremy's—While it's no longer just a locals' secret, the shoppers at Jeremy's still shoot furtive glances across the racks, hoping no one else has spotted the Prada skirt or Jimmy Choo sandals selling for a song. The store carries designer duds—end-of-season leftovers, samples, returns, and display merchandise (sometimes slightly damaged)—which they discount at between 40 and 70 percent off retail. Located on the corner of 2nd and South Park, it's the perfect place to while away an afternoon before settling into a house-brewed ale at the **21st Amendment** or a not-too-foamy cappuccino at **Caffè Centro**.

Isda and Company—This chic little boutique, kitty-corner to Jeremy's on South Park and a few doors down from her full-price retail store, is the wholesale outlet for local designer Isda Funari's classy, modern career and casual wear. The inventory includes samples, overruns, seconds, and returns from department stores—and everything is sold at wholesale prices (no markup). Search the sale racks for even bigger bargains: clearance items can go for as much as 50 percent off.

Red Dot Outlet—The younger, less monied set will find looks and prices more suited to their lifestyle at Red Dot, which sells a nicely edited selection of sports apparel from Athleta, Puma, Nike, Prana, and others, as well as casual wear and accessories from the likes of Lance and Laurie B. Discounts range from 40 to 80 percent.

Jeremy's
2 South Park
415-882-4929

21st Amendment
563 2nd St.
415-369-0900

Caffè Centro
102 South Park
415-882-1500

Isda and Company
29 South Park
415-512-0313

Red Dot Outlet
508 4th St.
415-979-1597

Christine Foley—Foley's hand-loomed, multi-colored and patterned sweaters (hearts, sailboats, hummingbirds) are not for everyone, but if you (or your mother-in-law) coveted them on the racks at Nordstrom when they were selling for $300, you'll no doubt be thrilled to find them at this outlet shop for under $200. The collection ranges from older styles to samples and discontinued patterns.

Nordstrom Rack—The clothing here seems almost unrelated to the stuff you find in the actual department store, but if you dig deep enough, there are bargain-priced popular brands to be found. It's mostly women's wear, with a smattering of men's stuff, lingerie, home décor, and of course, shoes. The shoes, in fact, may be the overriding reason to stop in here. With reductions as deep as 75 percent, the payoff for scouring the racks may be an Italian leather loafer that costs less than a good pair of pantyhose.

Napa Premium Outlets—If you're taking your shopa-holic friend to the wine country, you absolutely can't pass up this outlet center. Unlike the ones in Vacaville, this is not your typical London Fog/Bass/Levi's strip mall. In Napa, you'll find off-price outlets for labels you really like, including Barney's New York, J. Crew, BCBG, Ellen Tracy, Ann Taylor, Timberland, Liz Claiborne, Calvin Klein, Jones New York, and Kenneth Cole. Discounts average 25 to 65 percent; look for irregulars and overruns, and additional

reductions on clearance racks. I once walked away from the J. Crew outlet with three new outfits for under $100. Score!

St. Helena Premier Outlets—You'll find this petite, swank outlet center farther north on Highway 29, just past the Beringer Winery. It offers only a few stores, but if you like Brooks Brothers, Escada, Jones New York, Coach, Tumi, Movado or Donna Karan, you'll want to make a detour through here. To my mind, the Donna Karan outlet is a rip-off. Most of the inventory looks like it comes from a knockoff line that's inferior to her lower-priced DKNY collection, and it's still incredibly expen-sive. The Coach outlet offers some good deals on end-of-season handbags. And if you are a fan of the button-down

Brooks Brothers look, it may be worth a trip to snag a camel-hair sportcoat or herringbone jacket at $200 below retail.

Wine Club—While it's not technically an outlet store, the Wine Club is the place to shop in SoMa for wine bargains and a must-stop if you didn't have time to get up to the Napa Valley, but your friends would still like to sample a little fruit of the vine. Don't let the windowless warehouse exterior or the word "club" scare you away. You don't need to be a member, and the insides are quite hospitable and inviting. Belly up to the tasting bar and try some of the wines recommended by the staff of friendly experts (official tastings are usually held once a month, but if you ask, they will always oblige). It's really almost better than being at a winery, because here you get to taste a variety of labels and vintages. Plus, the prices are half what you'd pay at a winery.

SECOND-HAND CLOTHES AND OTHER WORLDLY GOODS

There are people who live for the pre-owned. My friend Paul is one of them. He is also the nattiest dresser I know, with closets full of '50s bowling shirts and burnt-orange golf cardigans, '60s leather blazers, zoot suits, and tons of '70s Quiana and psychedelic Austin Powers polyester shirts. He is the only person I know who could wear an authentic, circa 1977 rhinestone necklace that says "Foxy," and have people stopping him in the streets to tell him how cool he is. Why I'm telling you this, I don't know. But I do know that if your visiting friends are serious vintage and thrift store hounds, sending them to American Rag probably isn't gonna cut it.

For serious bargains on high-end stuff, peruse the chi-chi secondhand stores on Upper Fillmore, where the well-heeled residents of Pacific Heights toss the designer suits and dresses they've grown tired of. Profits from the **Next-to-New** shop go to benefit the Junior League, so you know what social strata the donations are coming from (though some of the items may be a bit too bridge-club stuffy for younger tastes). **Crossroads Trading Company** has a large inventory of stylish and trendy women's name-brand clothes, plus a lot of quality vintage stuff from the '30s

Christine Foley
430 9th St.
415-621-8126

Nordstrom Rack
555 9th St.
415-934-1211

Napa Premium Outlets
629 Factory Stores St., Napa
707-226-9876

St. Helena Premier Outlets
Highway 29, St. Helena
707-226-9876

Wine Club
953 Harrison St.
415-512-9086

Next-to-New
226 Fillmore St.
415-567-1267

Crossroads Trading Company
1901 Fillmore St.
415-775-8885

and '40s. **Victorian House** is the place to pick up Brioni suits, double-breasted cashmere trench coats from Barney's, and the other stuff the sartorially splendid ex-Mayor Brown has discarded, for pennies on the dollar. **Departures—From the Past** specializes in theatrical vintage looks and costumes, with an emphasis on hats. This is the store to find a felt fedora or a '40s-era leather driving cap.

Nearby on Sacramento Street, **Good Byes** sells men's and women's new and pre-owned top-quality clothing and shoes. I once saw a practically brand-new women's Armani tuxedo for $200. In the women's shoe section are brands such as Ferragamo and Bally; good deals can also be found on men's sportcoats and ties.

Like the Salvation Army, Goodwill stores are generally only for the dedicated bargain hunter who doesn't mind rifling through racks of junk to find an overlooked gem.

Make an exception for the **Goodwill Boutique** tucked away on West Portal Avenue midway between Stonestown and the Sunset district. This is one of the clearinghouses for upscale clothing items culled from all the local Goodwill stores. I've found nice, if slightly outdated, designer dresses, blazers, and suits, plus lots of tops, skirts, and pants from places like the Gap, the Limited, and Banana Republic. And prices are dirt cheap (like a Jones New York dress for $15).

So maybe they didn't come here looking for a set of 1920s cookie cutters, or a classic, stainless-steel blender, but once inside **Cookin'**, it's amazing what your guests will find they absolutely can't live without. The small store sells vintage and refurbished gourmet cookware and kitchen gear—everything from hand-crank meat grinders to cake molds and crockery.

Anyone into vintage tableware should head from Cookin' directly to **Dishes Delmar**, where Burt Tessler has amassed a fabulous collection of dish sets from Fiesta, Harlequin, Starburst, Lu-Ray and other luminaries of '50s dining-room Americana. The 'store' is really Tessler's house in the Haight, and you have to shop by appointment, but he's usually able to accommodate last-minute drop-ins—it'll be worth the extra effort if you finally find that avocado green fruit bowl you need to complete your set.

ONLY IN SAN FRANCISCO

Souvenir hunting is an essential part of the whole tourist ritual and really shouldn't be overlooked if you want to create a positive shopping experience for your purchase-happy friends (even if they clearly suffer from some kind of obsessive-compulsive disorder). A few suggestions:

Mark Reuben Galleries—This gallery, with locations in Ghirardelli Square and Sausalito, has a huge inventory of old San Francisco photos, including classic images like the half-built Golden Gate Bridge, Sutro Baths, Joe DiMaggio when he played for the San Francisco Seals in the Pacific Coast League, and the aftermath of the 1906 earthquake.

Golden Gate Bridge Shop—Most of the stuff at this toll plaza shop is ticky-tacky crap. But the one thing they do sell that's worth making a shopping stop for are authentic pieces of cable and rivets from the Golden Gate Bridge. If your pals are looking for something even more substantial, perhaps an original Lombard Street brick from the City Store (at City Hall and Pier 45) would do (see the Green Fiends tour for more info).

Paxton Gate—Just weird enough to make your friends shake their heads, Paxton Gate is part taxidermist, part Amazonian flea market, part garden shop—and always entertaining. Delight your friend's teenager with the collection of glass eyes, a mouse skull, or a box of chocolate-covered insects. The wall of dried and mounted exotic beetles and butterflies is reason alone to make a pit stop.

826 Valencia—Literary groupies make a pilgrimage here to catch sight of writer Dave Eggers and his clan, who publish the marvelous *McSweeney's* journal upstairs and tutor local high-school students below decks. But the faux-pirate's den offers something wholly unique for errant shoppers as well: a treasure chest of oddball gifts and curiosities—eye patches, jolly roger flags, maps, music box mechanisms, song lyrics, and back-issues of Eggers' growing empire of brainy lit publications. Buccaneer booty aside,

Victorian House
2033 Fillmore St.
415-567-3478

Departures—From the Past
2028 Fillmore St.
415-885-3377

Good Byes
3464 Sacramento St.
415-346-6388, and
3483 Sacramento St.
415-674-0151

Goodwill Boutique
61 West Portal Ave.
415-665-7291

Cookin'
339 Divisadero St.
415-861-1854

Dishes Delmar
by appointment
415-558-8882,
www.dishesdelmar.com

Mark Reuben Gallery
Ghirardelli Square,
900 North Point St.
415-346-1120, and
34 Princess St.,
Sausalito
877-444-3767

Golden Gate Bridge Shop
at the bridge toll plaza on the San Francisco side
415-923-2331

Paxton Gate
824 Valencia St.
415-824-1872

826 Valencia
826 Valencia St.
415-642-5905

where else can you go shopping and run a better than 50-percent chance of brushing elbows with the likes of David Byrne or Michael Chabon?

Gump's—Since 1861, Gump's has been the arbiter of San Francisco tastes: the East/West imports emporium that guided an uncouth city of newly minted roughnecks into the new century with style. Call it what you will—stuffy, the city's most expensive bridal registry, baubles for people with too much disposable income—Gump's sense for design is unerring. It's worth stopping in just to see the pearl collection, the art glass, and the enormous 18th-century Ch'ing Dynasty Buddha that has been a fixture in the store since the days of Solomon Gump.

Marshall's—Weirdly enough, this national discount clothing store out in Metro Center in Colma has a small housewares department. And believe it or not, in that housewares department you can often find good, hand-painted

Italian ceramics—plates, vases, bowls, salt-and-pepper shakers, mugs, and more. But instead of paying $100 a plate, you pay $19.99. Va bene! Unfortunately, the stock varies wildly from month to month, and there are times when you may come up dry. But it's worth trying your luck. Just make sure to look on the back for the "Made in Italy" stamp.

Biordi—Unlike Marshall's, you won't find many bargains here, but you are guaranteed a full selection of beautiful, handmade Italian pottery. All the famous artisans and designs are represented, in pieces as small as card-holder trays and as a large as outdoor planters.

Exploratorium Store—The science geek in you will go into sensory overload at this great museum shop, which carries everything from kaleidoscopes and kinetic energy balls to glow-in-the-dark maps of the night sky, science experiment kits, and M.C. Escher clocks.

La Tienda—This is the retail shop for the Mexican Museum (which moves into grand new Yerba Buena digs in 2005) and a great place to go Christmas shopping. The place is filled with handmade Mexican crafts, folk art, tin ornaments, tree of life dioramas, Day of the Dead shrines, coconut masks, and other delights.

Panetti's—There have been years where I did all my holiday gift shopping at this store. My best friend got the earrings shaped like tiny chairs and the refrigerator magnet poetry; my sister-in-law got the enormous silver spoon mug rack; my other sister-in-law got the hand-enameled cat pin; my mom got the frog garden torch; and my mother-in-law got the handcrafted ceramic teapot.

Flax—It bills itself as an art supply store, but it's so much more. I've spent hours looking at the handpainted clocks, boxes, and Russian eggs, the art chairs, the rubber briefcases shaped like cats and Scottie dogs, the handmade paper, and the 3-D jigsaw puzzles.

Gamescape—Located in the Western Addition, this little shop sells every kind of game imaginable, but their specialty is nonstandard games—the kind you won't find at places like Toys R Us. Look particularly for imported items, party games, strategy and role-playing games (including five varieties of Go), unique chess sets, darts, and unusual word games.

SAN FRANCISCO DESIGNERS

When you absolutely, positively must have that "Made in Frisco" label, may I suggest…

Laku—This tiny jewel-box shop in the Mission is a labor of love for owner Yaeko Yamashita, who creates adorable cloche hats, baby dresses, hair accessories, and (the main attraction) tiny Japanese silk-and-velvet slippers with pointy toes, adorned with her signature velvet roses.

Dema—Dema Grim's Valencia boutique is the place to shake (and decorate) your groove thing. A selection of her bright creations for 21st century mods (youthful enough for a mature teenager, but not so silly that her mom couldn't find something as well), is augmented by pieces from Petit Bateau, Custo, Michael Star, and other cool customers.

Metier—This chic downtown shop carries a large selection of local and international designers, including Anna Molinari, Katayone Adeli, and Rozae Nichols, and a fabulous original jewelry selection (don't miss local artist Jeanine Payer's message rings and bracelets—big with Hollywood types).

Gump's
135 Post St.
415-982-1616

Marshall's
65 Colma Blvd.,
Metro Center,
Colma
650-992-5350

Biordi
412 Columbus Ave.
415-392-8096

Exploratorium Store
Marina Blvd. and
Lyon St.
415-561-0390

La Tienda
in the Mexican
Museum, Mission
St., between 3rd and
4th streets
415-202-9700

Panetti's
3927 24th St.
415-648-2414

Flax
1699 Market St.
415-552-2355

Gamescape
333 Divisadero St.
415-621-4263

Laku
1069 Valencia St.
415-695-1462

Dema
1038 Valencia St.
415-206-0500.

Metier
355 Sutter St.
415-989-5395

Cicada—Cicada is the modern reincarnation of the late Sandra Sakata's famed Obiko gallery/boutique (one of Robin Williams's favorite pre-awards-show haunts), featuring handcrafted, highly textural clothing that doubles as wearable art. Owner Monique Zhang spotlights 80 to 100 fashion artists, most of them local and many using Asian-inspired, custom-printed fabrics, crafted into everything from hand-dyed silk mandarin coats and intricately beaded evening wear to ethereal scarves and wraps. Upstairs, the one-of-a-

kind bridal gowns are worth ogling, even if you don't have any wedding plans.

Knitz & Leather—Designer Julia Relinghaus has amassed a fanatical, almost cultlike following for her limited-edition leather jackets. Why? Simple, unadorned designs (button and zip) made from buttery-soft leather that never look like they were all the rage . . . last year. Partner Katarina Ernst's "knitz" (hand-knitted sweaters, dresses, and wraps in microfiber and mohair) are the perfect complement to all that calfskin.

Lily Samii—Lily Samii began her dress designing business across the Bay in Marin County. A few years ago, she opened a salon above Union Square so her regular clientele of society divas wouldn't have to drive so far. She also enlisted the masterful hands of designer Jacques Pantazès to create her couture confections: lemon-yellow silk cocktail dresses, beaded opera gowns, ice-blue bridesmaids' attire, lavender chiffon shifts with matching jackets. It's a look that manages to be contemporary and retro at the same time.

Diana Slavin—Located on tiny Claude Lane, this boutique features the designs of its namesake, who creates smart, slimming, but not-too-flashy skirts, menswear-inspired jackets, pants, and dresses that you can wear to work or out on the town. Lots of black.

Margaret O'Leary—Also on Claude Lane is a retail outlet for the Irish-born O'Leary, who comes from a long line of knitters and weavers. O'Leary is one of San Francisco's secret designer treasures, though her exquisite hand-loomed sweaters, dresses, tunics, and twin sets are very familiar to buyers at places like Neiman Marcus and Saks. Both this shop and the one on Fillmore feature a full line of seasonal knits: lightweight rayon crepe, ultra-soft cashmere, merino wool, and mohair that you could get lost in.

WHERE TO STAY

Although just about every hotel located in the vicinity of Union Square could be considered a shoppers' hotel, only one really positions itself as such: the **Maxwell**. Part of the Chip Conley/Joie de Vivre chain of quirky boutique hotels, the Maxwell has unique services designed specifically for shoppers: high-tech foot spas for post-pavement-pounding pampering; a unique, personal guide to Union Square retailers; gift-wrapping and department store coupons; shopping bags in your room; and a shopping newsletter that highlights best buys and interesting items. They also frequently offer great shop/stay packages (as do a number of Union Square hotels), which include a room, continental breakfast, parking, and shopping guides.

Cicada
547 Sutter St.
415-398-4000

Knitz & Leather
1429 Grant Ave.
415-391-3480

Lily Samii
260 Stockton St.,
4th floor
415-445-9505

Diana Slavin
3 Claude Lane
415-677-9939

Margaret O'Leary
1 Claude Lane
415-391-1010

The Maxwell
386 Geary St.
415-986-2000

tour 12   *Gender Blenders*

This tour is by no means the final word on gay and lesbian hangouts and activities in the Bay Area. There are other books and periodicals that collec-

tively cover the scene in full—among them: *Betty and Pansy's Severe Queer Review, The Gay Guide, Odyssey Magazine,* and *San Francisco Bay Times.* But, as a straight person with gay friends, living in a gay mecca, I have often been faced with the problem of trying to come up with places that are fun for both persuasions—places that are gay- or lesbian-oriented, where straight people won't feel out of place, or places that are fairly mainstream, but simultaneously gay-friendly. After all, your friends presumably came here to see you, not just to galavant off by themselves every night to the clubs.

MORNING

Call it what you will, but **Café Flore**—aka Café Hairdo,
Café Whore, Café Bore—is still the place to be on weekend
mornings. You'll have to get there at opening time to get a
seat on the outdoor patio, especially in warm weather. This
Castro institution is usually 90 percent homo at any given
time of day, but heteros won't feel uncomfortable. There's too
much activity, chatter, coffee banter, breakfast, people-
watching, and eye contact going on for it to be an issue. The
main thing for foreigners is that Café Flore is fun, the food
and the coffee are good (though a tad overpriced), and you
really get a feel for the pulse of the gay scene—at least this
side of Twin Peaks.

For women, **Mabel's Just for You Café** in Dogpatch is a
nice introduction to the San Francisco lesbian scene—a low-
key dyke-run diner that in its new expanded digs attracts its
fair share of all persuasions: slackers, Muni drivers,
politicos, you name it. The frighteningly long list of breakfast offerings includes eggs made every which way but loose
(Luis, Blackstone, Bennie, and other names I'm hankering to
get familiar with), served with homestyle potatoes or grits;
buckwheat, cornmeal, or buttermilk pancakes; and three
different kinds of huevos rancheros.

One of the most fascinating, social, and educational
gay-oriented outings (no pun intended) I've come across is
Trevor Hailey's **Cruisin' the Castro Tour**, which meets most
mornings June through December at the corner of Castro
and Market at 10 a.m. The irrepressible Trevor is a retired
army nurse who came to San Francisco and the Castro
district in 1972, just as the gay revolution was coming to
full flower. On her tour you'll learn all about gay history in
the district and the city; about the Lavender Cowboys, an
all-male square-dance group of the Gold Rush era; about the
rise and violent death of Supervisor Harvey Milk, including
a visit to the site of his old camera shop; about the pre-
Castro gay ghettos such as North Beach and Polk Street;
about the Castro Cathedral (a.k.a. the Castro Theatre); and
about the Sisters of Perpetual Indulgence. Midway through

Café Flore
2298 Market St.
415-621-8579

**Mabel's Just for
You Café**
732 22nd St.
415-647-3033

**Cruisin' the
Castro Tour**
Tuesday through
Saturday, June
through December
415-550-8110

the tour there's a stop for lunch at **Firewood Café**, a warm, homey spot for wood-fired roast chicken, pizza, and pastas.

For real dishy brunch drama, the kind where the waiters snap at and flirt with the customers who all mysteriously know each other and seem to be avoiding eye contact as a result, nothing really has come close to approximating The Patio. But if we're all a bit older, wiser, and more mature these days, so are the Castro's brunch cafés. **Luna** (formerly Caffè Luna Piena) and **Home** still manage to capture that community diner ambience—though (a little sadly) without the side of bitchiness.

The lush garden patio at gay-owned and -operated Luna is definitely the place to park on a warm day for omelets, poached Dutch eggs with smoked salmon, or a midday burger. For something a little more lively, Home's high-decibel crowd and Bloody Mary bar (see Extroverts) provide a sturdy celery-stalk bridge between Castro regulars and their het friends.

Afterward, stroll up the street and pick up a copy of Betty and Pansy's or Diane Middlebrook's *Suits Me: The Double Life of Billy Tipton* at **A Different Light**, one of the few bookshops in the country that dedicates the majority of its space to gay and lesbian authors and subjects.

NOON

Marina Green is one of those odd confluences—a mecca for straight yuppies and gay men alike, both of whom compete for volleyball space and the best washboard stomachs on the grass just west of the yacht harbor. The recreation field, with its fabulous Golden Gate views, affords one the opportunity of cruising (lots of brief briefs and shirtless sunbathers) and sightseeing at the same time.

Of course, if you really want to see some skin, you should head over to **Baker Beach**, famous the town over for its nude status (see the Extroverts tour). Send your gay friends to the far north end; naked heteros should veer slightly south.

If they like the lounge-in-the-sun lifestyle and prefer the company of women, take them to **Osento** for a little hot tub/cold pool R&R. This women-only (mostly lesbian) spa and massage facility, located in an old Victorian on Valencia Street, has a great relaxed attitude that will make straight women feel instantly at ease. (For more details, see Artsy Aunties.)

In the Market

You've gotta buy groceries anyway, so why not have a little fun? The **Diamond Heights Safeway**, located in what is referred to as the "Swish Alps," is to clean-cut gay men what the Marina Safeway was to straight swingles in the early '80s. Direct your shopping cart to the produce aisles and see what's ripe.

On Market Street just below Castro, the **Harvest Ranch Market**, a great gourmet deli and natural foods café, features a huge assortment of ready-to-go items including an extensive salad bar with all kinds of fancy offerings as well as sushi, fresh focaccia and sandwiches, homemade soups, and veggie burritos. It's a great place to stock up for a picnic with the help of a handsome grocer; or you could plunk yourself down on one of the benches out front and let the Castro scene unfold.

Remembrance Sites

The **AIDS Memorial Grove** is without a doubt the most serene and special spot in Golden Gate Park. And it's not just a place to take your gay friends. It is a place to take your straight friends, parents, grandparents, and teenage nephews. Centered around a small grove of redwoods, volunteers and city park workers have fashioned a quiet, reflective, peaceful glen filled with singing birds and hundreds of forget-me-nots. A small creek lined with round stones runs through it, and all around are small stone benches where you can sit and contemplate. A circular platform at the head of the grove has the names of the major donors carved into it Vietnam Memorial-style. In the center, people have placed flowers,

Firewood Café
4248 18th St.
415-252-0999

Luna
558 Castro St.
415-621-2566

Home
2100 Market St.
415-503-0333

A Different Light
489 Castro St.
415-431-0891

Marina Green
along Marina Blvd.,
from Fillmore to
Lyon streets

Baker Beach
follow signs on
Lincoln Blvd., before
Golden Gate Bridge

Osento
955 Valencia St.
415-282-6333

Diamond Heights Safeway
5290 Diamond
Heights Blvd.
415-824-7744

Harvest Ranch Market
2285 Market St.
415-626-0805

AIDS Memorial Grove
Golden Gate Park,
off Middle Drive
east

tokens, and remembrances. Surprisingly, the grove is not a sad place, but a place of healing.

In Grace Cathedral, just to the right of the entrance, is the **AIDS Memorial Chapel** with its Keith Haring altarpiece, a beautiful triptych in gold, alive with the playful dancing figures that were Haring's hallmark. This stunning work of modern art, Haring's last work before he died of AIDS, offers a wonderful message of hope, as well as a quiet place to reflect, for those whose lives have been touched by the disease.

A small gallery in Yerba Buena is the temporary home of the **Gay, Lesbian, Bisexual, Transgender Historical Society** and headquarters for the yet-to-be-built Museum of Gay and Lesbian History. The society launched its inaugural exhibition in 2003 with "Saint Harvey: The Life and Afterlife of a Modern Gay Martyr," and plans to host other shows in this small space until the museum is built (target date 2012). A visit to the gallery or reading room (which houses the society's extensive archives, including more than 400 oral histories of gay, lesbian, bisexual, and transgender Americans) is a nice way to kick off a cultural tour of the district, which blossoms every year with marvelous new offerings (2005 alone will see the opening of the Mexican and Jewish museums and the Museum of the African Diaspora).

Celebrate Good Times

Since its opening in 2002, the new LGBT Community Center (known as **The Center**) has had to fill the wide and disparate gaps left by both Josie's Cabaret and the Names Project headquarters. It has managed to do so ably, offering a colorful, comfortable visitor center and café where people of all stripes can get information on events, queer history, and general happenings about town, as well as providing a hang out for a day or an evening's entertainment. The upstairs Rainbow Room hosts regular events, lectures, and readings; dances are held on the roof deck; and on Monday nights, the Q comedy showcase features an array of gay stand-up comics and performers.

The **Gay, Lesbian, and Transgender Pride Parade** every June is not just a party for gays, lesbians, and transgenders. It's a celebration of diversity. It's street theater. It's Fluorescent Wig Day. It's What-the-Hey Day. It's a day when life is indeed a cabaret, and anyone who shares this spirit should feel right at home. The parade is traditionally led off by the notorious Dykes on Bikes, San Francisco's very own gender-bending Wild Bunch; they're followed by everything from contingents of drag queens and gay cops to the ever-popular Lesbian/Gay Freedom Day Marching Band. From the sidelines, the crowds cheer in rainbows of support and good humor. Best strategy is to grab a beer, find a pair of shoulders to sit on, and let it all hang out.

The **Castro Street Fair** in October is like a small version of the parade, except that you get to shop for nifty arts and crafts, snack on gourmet goodies, and stay in one place. And of course there's always Halloween (see the Extroverts tour), which has gotten so big they've sent the rubberneckers to Civic Center. The best and most elaborate costumes are still in the Castro on Halloween Eve proper (not the weekend preceding or following).

For something a little more on the dark side, the **Folsom Street Fair** in October may be more to your liking. This festival of leather, chains, piercing, bare buns and breasts, and general S&M kinkiness is definitely *not* for everyone. But if you and your friends are feeling open-minded (or curious), it's certainly an interesting and unusual way to see an edgy slice of gay life in San Francisco.

NIGHT

Bernal Heights and Hayes Valley are San Francisco's less visible lesbian/gay-oriented neighborhoods, though neither are predominantly same sex, making them a nice compromise for mixed-group socializing. Hot spots in Bernal Heights include the dyke bar **Wild Side West**, at 35, the oldest women's bar in the city. When I lived in Bernal Heights I used to come here to play pool, and it took me several visits before I realized it was a lesbian hangout, though all the signs were certainly there (the naked women artwork on the walls

AIDS Memorial Chapel
Grace Cathedral,
1100 California St.
415-749-6300

Gay, Lesbian, Bisexual, Transgender Historical Society
657 Mission St.,
Suite 300
415-777-5455

The Center
1800 Market St.
415-865-5555

Gay, Lesbian, and Transgender Pride Parade
last weekend in June, Market St. from Embarcardero to Castro
415-864-3733,
www.sfpride.org

Castro Street Fair
mid-October,
Castro St. between 18th and Noe
415-841-1824,
www.castrostreet fair.org

Folsom Street Fair
late September/ early October,
Folsom St. between 5th and 11th streets
415-861-3247,
www.folsomstreet fair.com

Wild Side West
424 Cortland Ave.
415-647-3099

and the toilets that double as chairs and planters—one painted with hungry-looking teeth—should have been a dead giveaway). That's because above all this is a homey, friendly, neighborhood bar where you can have a beer, chit chat with strangers, and play pinball or pool.

Just up the street from Wild Side West, the **Liberty Café** is one of the best New American restaurants in town, catering to a mix of neighborhood regulars and cross-town

foodies (don't miss the chicken pot pie or the Caesar salad). Across the street, the lesbian-owned **Red Hill Books** offers a great selection of literature for and about women.

Hayes Valley is inhabited by a fairly well-heeled and culturally astute crowd of hip straights and gays. The see-and-be-seen, ripped-and-cut guys like to work out at **Muscle Systems** on Hayes Street, a men-only gym which features a Jacuzzi and sauna along with the requisite exercise equipment. Afterward, they fortify themselves with glasses of cabernet at the **Hayes and Vine** wine bar, a pleasantly androgynous (and cozy) establishment that offers a great selection of small and unusual vintages from near and far.

Over on Gough Street, underneath the Albion House Inn, is **Miu Miu Bistro and Bar**, a warm, friendly gathering place for middle-aged tourists and gay couples that serves good French bistro fare, and offers a lively inexpensive happy hour (4:30 to 6:30 p.m. weekdays, $4 for 2 tap beers and a small appetizer).

If you had something a little more haute and haughty (and I mean that in a good way) in mind, head over to **Paul K**, where gay gourmets sup on scallops and duck with pomegranate sauce and sip martinis. The Mediterranean small-plate menu is perfect for those who like to pick off of others' plates.

Stepping Out

The **Metronome Ballroom** on Potrero Hill is a mainstream dance hall where most nights you can take lessons in swing, fox trot, tango, salsa, or two-step, and later practice what you learned at a dance party. It's primarily hetero, but everyone is made to feel welcome. If you swing the other way, try hitting this hot spot on same-sex night, usually scheduled for two evenings each month.

If your friends are here around Christmas and they want to shake their groove thing and get in the holiday spirit at the same time, take them to the **Dance-Along Nutcracker**, which is rapidly becoming one of the city's most beloved holiday traditions. Performed by the Lesbian/ Gay Freedom Band and the San Francisco Cheer, this wacky version of the ballet classic involves a bunch of guys dressed in tutus performing various parts of the Nutcracker and getting the audience to dance along with them in the aisles. Lots of audience members, children and adults, dress up in tutus, too (there are tutus for rent, if you forget yours). It's wonderful silliness for kids of all ages.

If that's not sweaty enough for you, head directly to **The Stud**—once a strictly gay dance club, now a place where leather and lace, straights and gays mix it up to hip hop and techno-funk.

More serious gay performance art can be found at **Theatre Rhinoceros** in the Mission, where you might encounter anything from Cuban performance artist Carmelita Tropicana to serious dramas to light-hearted romps (a recent offering on the main stage promised a comedy about "sex, drugs, and drag queen denial"). If your friends are visiting in late November or early December, definitely take them to the Rhino's annual reading of Truman Capote's *Christmas Story*.

If the theater is your destination, make a night of it by starting off with dinner at **Mecca**, a smart, chic restaurant/club on upper Market Street that attracts a cool, gender-bending crowd and sports an excellent menu of Southern specialties masterminded by foodie darling, chef Stephen Barber. Entertainment in the form of both DJs and live bands keeps the room swinging most nights, but the event of the month is Edie, an elegant drag crooner from New York, whose monthly shows attract a lively crowd of the queer and the curious.

Liberty Café
410 Cortland Ave.
415-695-8777
415-255-1355

Red Hill Books
178 Andover St.
415-648-5331

Muscle Systems
364 Hayes St.
415-863-4701

Hayes and Vine
377 Hayes St.
415-626-5301

Miu Miu Bistro and Bar
131 Gough St.
415-252-1369

Paul K
199 Gough St.
415-552-7132

The Metronome Ballroom
1830 17th St.
415-252-9000

Dance-Along Nutcracker
held at Center for the Arts in December; for information call the Lesbian Gay Freedom Band
415-255-1355

The Stud
399 9th St.
415-252-7883

Theatre Rhinoceros
2926 16th St.
415-861-5079

Mecca
2029 Market St.
415-621-7000

If you didn't have time for supper, there's always **Sparky's**, the late-night wonder diner on Church Street. This is one of the few places in town where you can actually get decent food at three in the morning—that is, if you stick to the burgers, omelets, and pizzas. I can't vouch for the fancy food items.

Club Compromise

It's taken a long time, but San Francisco has finally arrived at a place where parents and their outgoing gay children can bond in an atmosphere of mutual fun and show tune appreciation. **Martuni's** is also the kind of place to take visiting New Yorkers who have aspirations of playing the Algonquin Room. An upscale, mainstream gay bar of the smoky-mirrors-and-marble-column variety, Martuni's features open-mic cabaret singing. As you sit and sip cocktails, "amateur" singers (some of these guys and gals seem like they're warming up their chops for professional careers) get up and

perform standards and show tunes to piano accompaniment. There's something for everyone: aspiring lounge acts can work on their audience appeal; the folks can sing along to Gershwin, Rodgers and Hammerstein, and Sinatra; and you can suck down a few martinis while you secretly admire the chanteuse in the corner.

If you want to see drag the way it was done in the old days, back when female impersonators were popular with the middle-aged and middle America crowd, then you may be out of luck— the legendary Finocchio's closed a couple of years ago. But if you want to see drag the way it's done nowadays, head to **AsiaSF**, where stunning "gender illusionists" lip-sync and dance on the runway/bar for a crowd that's usually more straight than gay (it's not unusual to see a bachelor party camping it up here). Creating a menu that can stand-up (ahem) to the entertainment is no easy task, but the "baby got back" ribs and sake-steamed mussels in red curry are good enough to make diners look down at their plates once in awhile. All in all, this is a great place for an evening of not-quite-whole-some fun.

There are no drag queens at **Bimbo's 365**, unless you have suspicions about Dolphina, the busty "optical illusion" mermaid in the fish bowl, who occasionally appears behind the bar, but it's still one of the most fabulously plush night-clubs in town. The lounge hasn't changed much since it opened in the 1940s, and there's something about all that red velvet and vinyl, the Final Net and curlers in the bath-room, and the cocktail cabinets filled with miniature liquor bottles, that gives the place a decidedly campy edge. At any moment you might expect to see Ricky Ricardo or Louis Prima bursting through the curtain leading a conga line. Come here for a Copacabana-style dance party.

The Lexington Club off Valencia Street, has been the first all-grrl bar to surface since the demise of Maud's and Amelia's all those years ago. Rife with lipstick lesbians and plain-ole good-time gals, the bar sits in one of the current groovy spots in the Mission—reason enough to drop by for a cocktail, no matter what your persuasion.

El Rio (see Cheapskates to find out about Friday night happy hour) is a down-home bar and performance venue that welcomes a happily integrated crowd most nights. The trop-ical Caribbean/tiki garden out back is a great hangout on salsa-dancing Sunday afternoons—particularly if you're a girl who likes girls. If you aren't, there's always shuffleboard.

WHERE TO STAY

Of course, all the hotels in this town are gay-friendly. So if your friends are here to hang with you, and not to prowl the corridors in the wee hours, then the hotel choice should be based mostly on convenience of location. If they want to get specific, there are also a number of good gay and lesbian lodging options in the city.

The **Parker Guest House** is a magnificent restored Victorian with a garden that will leave you and your friends with a bad case of green-thumb and statuary envy. Catering to a primarily gay clientele, the 21 rooms feature luxe poster beds, terry robes, dataports, and voicemail. Extended continental breakfast served in a lovely sunroom is included in the price, as well as afternoon wine social and access to the steam room.

Five rooms are available at **24 Henry Guesthouse**, which is a beautiful, 122-year-old Victorian home that promotes itself as a gay inn. The house also features communal sitting rooms, a library, and a full buffet-style breakfast.

The inexpensive and pedestrian-looking **Beck's Motor Lodge** is an updated Travelodge–style motel conveniently located in the heart of the Castro. From the outside, it's the kind of place you'd think of putting up your relatives from Kansas, but frankly the balcony cruising (especially during Pride Month) and after-hours activity make this a better bet for people with a more seasoned world view.

Located on 14th Street and Church, the country-style, twelve-room **Willows Inn** caters mostly to men, and features furnishings made out of bent willow branches. Other nice touches include continental breakfast served in your room, kimonos, and decanted port on your bedstand. One drawback: shared bathrooms (though there are washbasins in each room).

Bock's Bed and Breakfast is a comfortable spot for women here for long-term stays (30-day minimum). Located in a safe and sane part of town (on Willard Street right near UC Med Center), it offers three spacious suites, one with a private deck and view. From here, you can walk to Cole Valley, the Haight, or up the hill to Mount Sutro.

24 Henry Guesthouse
24 Henry St.
415-864-5686

Beck's Motor Lodge
2222 Market St.
415-621-8212

The Willows Inn
710 14th St.
415-431-4770

Bock's Bed and Breakfast
1448 Willard St.
415-664-6842

tour 13 Foodies

In San Francisco, sooner or later, it always comes down to food. Where are we going to eat? What kind of food do you want? Have you tried that new restaurant? Have you tried to get into that new

restaurant? How the *hell* did you get into that new restaurant?

Indeed, in this town, eating is hardly ever just a bite before the main event. Eating *is* the main event. And when company comes to town, the value of the food factor grows by exponential leaps and bounds. Because aside from the bridges, the hills, and the cable cars, almost everyone who comes here has heard about the restaurants.

It's hard enough choosing the right dining spot when you live here and you've got time to try them all, but when your days are limited and your eating companions are from out of town, picking just the right restaurant can become a paralyzing decision.

So you turn to the guidebooks, which present you with 100 more choices that you hadn't even thought of, and pretty soon you just want to give up and order take-out. What you really need is someone to make the decision for you. Someone to tell you where to go and what to order when you get there. Then if they hate it, you can just blame it on me.

BREAKFAST

There are three kinds of breakfast people: nibblers, diner and coffee shop types, and serious brunchers. As you can tell by the number of divey countertops I've described in this book, I'm a diner kinda gal. (If you're looking for a dissertation on breakfast's constant companion, coffee, see Neo-Bohemians and Politically Correct.)

For nibblers of the bagel variety, **House of Bagels** on Geary is where the cream cheese meets the onion stick. There will be many who will disagree vehemently with this assessment. They'll say Noah's makes softer, cushier bagels (in my inner circle, these are called "sponge muffins"); they'll argue that you can't get blueberry or chocolate chip bagels here; they'll say that they don't have date-walnut or tofu-dill schmears. Tough toenails. It's not your book. No one can touch House of Bagels' traditional onion bagels, sticks, or bialys. They're chewy without being mushy, they're not enriched in any way, they're kosher, they're not completely coated with onions or salt or poppy seeds to the point that that's all you taste, and they're so incredibly flavorful (especially right out of the oven), you won't even need any of those fancy spreads. The bakery also makes fabulous pumpernickel, egg twist, and New York corn rye bread. Everything's baked fresh daily, and for cheapskates, whatever's left over is sold for half price the next day.

I'm not a donut fanatic, but many people I know belong to the Church of the Old-Fashioned Glazed, and they tell me there's one word in donuts in this town: Bob's. If you don't believe them, the morning traffic jam on Polk Street in front of this no-frills bakery should convince you. **Bob's Donuts and Pastry Shop** makes donut from scratch every day. They're baked in small batches that are sold immediately so they don't sit around and get stale. Nothing is over-fried or over-sugared, and they don't use any artificial flavors or colors. When five out of six buttermilk bar addicts agree, who am I to argue?

Italian pastries really fall more into the realm of afternoon coffee break, but if your friends like them with breakfast, the **Italian/French Baking Company** (see Neo-Bohemians), **Danilo**, and **Stella**, on Columbus Avenue, are the places to go. Get your biscotti, your semisweet hard cookies, and your panettone at one of the first two; get your sacripantina (a Marsala-soaked sponge-layer cake topped with zabaglione) and your cannoli at Stella.

On to bigger and butter things. Diner rats can read in these pages about It's Tops for atmosphere; Art's for big piles

of good cheap eggs and hash browns; Herb's for celebrity sightings and parental bonding; and Manor Coffee Shop for a '50s time-warp experience. To these I must add **Tyger's Coffee Shop** in Glen Park for the quintessential, neighborhood eggs-over-the-fence encounter. This corner coffee shop is one of the few diners in town that's full every day—and not just with retirees. People actually spend their days off reading the newspaper and lingering over scrambles and toast here. On par with Tyger's for conviviality and hometown hospitality are **Al's** "Good Food" diner on Mission and **Hungry Joe's** in outer Noe Valley. Any one of these should satisfy your friends' counter culture itch.

Kate's Kitchen bridges that delicate gap between a diner and a full-fledged brunch restaurant. In the grand diner tradition, the small room is filled with regulars who know the kitchen staff and each other. But the food is no greasy truckstop fare. Come here for the Red Flannel Hash, a huge combo of eggs, potatoes, corned beef, onions, peppers, and carrots, or the much-acclaimed buttermilk cornmeal pancakes, served with real maple syrup and a hunk of butter. This is also one of the few places around where you'll find biscuits and gravy made with genuine sausage gravy.

For unusually flavored, delicate, fluffy flapjacks, my vote goes to **Miss Millie's** for their lemon-ricotta pancakes. In the French toast category, not too many can argue with the **Liberty Café's**, made with challah and topped with fresh fruit or pralines and real maple syrup. A recent foray into the banana bread French toast with banana-rum sauce at **Beach Chalet**, however, has made a believer out of me, especially when combined with the showstopping views.

Foodies staying downtown should go directly to **Dottie's True Blue Café** for the housemade cornbread with jalapeno jelly or the cinnamon-streusel coffeecake. And when breakfast's gotta carry you all the way to dinner, you'll want to head to **Squat & Gobble** in the Lower Haight, where you can fill up on omelets and crepes the size of carry-on bags.

LUNCH

You can't please all of the people all of the time. And when it comes to foodies, you're lucky if you hit it right once or twice. For the gourmand on your roster, consider some of my favorite dishes and the locales where they're served:

Ferry Plaza Farmer's Market—The new market is a revelation, both for your palate and your pocketbook. But even among the $10-an-ounce mushrooms and $20 artisanal cheeses there are finds. One of them is the pumpkin/green chile or zucchini/white corn tamales at the Cocina Primavera kiosk, which is usually out back near the ferry docks. The other is Bruce Aidells' yummy bier sausage with whole mustard seed, which is available on a roll only at his Ferry Plaza market stand.

So—This New Wave Chinese restaurant is like a breath of fresh chili for folks who are tired of trotting out to the Richmond and ordering the tried-and-true staples by number. The broccoli beef is so full of flavor (garlic, ginger, chili), you'll wonder if you ever really had this dish properly made before. The chicken noodle soup with mustard greens is a hangover cure for two-and-a-half.

Bob's Donuts and Pastry Shop
1621 Polk St.
415-776-3141

Italian/French Baking Company
1501 Grant Ave.
415-421-3796

Danilo
516 Green St.
415-989-1806

Stella
446 Columbus Ave.
415-986-2914

Tyger's Coffee Shop
2798 Diamond St.
415-239-4060

Al's
3286 Mission St.
415-641-8445

Hungry Joe's
1748 Church St.
415-282-7333

Kate's Kitchen
471 Haight St.
415-626-3984

Miss Millie's
4123 24th St.
415-285-5598

Liberty Café
410 Cortland Ave.
415-695-8777

Beach Chalet
1000 Great Hwy
415-386-8439

Dottie's True Blue Café
522 Jones St.
415-885-2767

Squat & Gobble
237 Fillmore St.
415-487-0551

Ferry Plaza Farmer's Market
Market and Embarcadero
415-291-3276

So
2240 Irving St.
415-731-3143

Café Bastille—Down on Belden Place, that tiny Financial District alley with all the Frenchies and the sidewalk tables, you could make a progressive meal going from mussels at **Plouf** to escalivada (warm roasted vegetables with manchego cheese in sherry vinaigrette) at **B44**, to hachis parmentier at Café Bastille (a true Parisian bistro, complete with surly French waiters, art nouveau posters, and a menu of butter-, ham-, and cheese-heavy dishes). Sure, you could stick to the lowfat ahi tuna salad, but the hachis parmentier, a traditional baked casserole of ground beef, cheese, and potatoes, puts the *ooooh* in ooh la la.

And while we're speaking French, no one does the classic steak pommes frites like nearby **Le Central**.

Mayflower—So much dim sum, so little time. This Outer Richmond Hong Kong-style restaurant gets overrun on weekends by Asian families hankering for tender steamed dumplings and roast duck—and with good reason. There is not a bad dish on a menu of 80+ offerings; the potstickers will make you wish you hadn't filled up on all that har gao and siu mai beforehand. If you're doing the tourist circuit downtown, steer over to **Harbor Village** in the Embarcadero Center. While its not big on authentic Chinatown atmos-

phere or prompt service, it has my vote for the largest, freshest, and tastiest assortment of dim sum this side of Twin Peaks.

Sai's Restaurant—My favorite alternative to a double latte is Vietnamese iced coffee at this popular Financial District lunch spot. The coffee is made in individual brewers that sit atop your glass. Inside is a dollop of sweetened, condensed milk. When it's done dripping, you stir it up and pour it over ice—better than a milkshake and with a caffeine jolt that will have you running a marathon while writing the great American novel. They also make some of the best pho ga (Vietnamese chicken noodle soup) in town.

ABC Bakery Café—The Hainan chicken over rice at this hole-in-the-wall Chinatown eatery is guaranteed to put a "wait 'til I tell them about this at home" kind of smile on any adventurous foodie's face. The yellow–feathered, free-range bird is sweeter, plumper, and more chickeny and tender than your average hen. At ABC, it's simply known as "chicken on rice," and it comes with bok choy soup and a ginger/scallion dipping sauce.

Arizmendi Bakery—After an afternoon paddling around Stow Lake, nothing revives the spirits like moist, tangy asiago cheese rolls from this worker-owned cooperative bakery (note to PC-types: it's named for and inspired by Basque priest and labor organizer José Maria Arizmendi-arrieta). Afterward, satisfy your sweet tooth with Auntie Mabel's Kookie Brittle, a crunchy slab of chocolate chips, nuts, and home-baked heaven.

Tartine—There are not enough m's in "mmmmmm" to describe Tartine's croque monsieur. The pedestrian toasted ham-and-cheese sandwich gets elevated to a higher plain in the hands of chef/owner Liz Prueitt, who combines fromage blanc, gruyere, applewood-smoked ham and béchamel atop partner Chad Robertson's transcendent crusty French bread. Tartine is also the perfect spot to rub latte bowls with hipster foodies who have their finger on the pulse of the next big (edible) thing.

Acme Bread—We could argue the merits of Grace and SemiFreddi and Metropol until we're blue in the face. Good bread is in the taste buds of the beholder. Acme is the one you should use as an example of what sourdough is all about. If you're in Berkeley, get it straight from the source, or on Saturday head down to the Ferry Plaza farmer's market, where Acme has a satellite bakery.

Bullshead—If you're still on the beef bandwagon, this neighborhood hole-in-the-wall has been serving "great meats, no bull" since 1979—the kind of juicy, chin-dripping burgers vegetarians dream about. Granted, the location (in West Portal) isn't exactly a tourist mecca—for that you need to go to **Mo's** in North Beach, where the burgers are thick and juicy and the skin-on fries are shoestring.

La Taqueria—Burritos come and burritos go, but guacamole is forever. La Cumbre, Pancho Villa, and La Corneta all make stellar contributions to the burrito vernacular, but La Taqueria makes a guacamole that surpasses all—fresh avocado, no creamy additives, seasoned with a little cilantro, lemon, and spices.

Café Bastille
22 Belden Pl.
415-986-5673

Plouf
40 Belden Pl.
415-986-6491

B44
44 Belden Pl.
415-986-6287

Le Central
453 Bush St.
415-391-2233

Mayflower
6255 Geary Blvd.
415-387-8338

Harbor Village
4 Embarcadero Center
at California St.
415-781-8833

Sai's Restaurant
505 Washington St.
415-362-3689

ABC Bakery Café
650 Jackson St.
415-981-0685

Arizmendi Bakery
1331 9th Ave.
415-566-3117

Tartine
600 Guerrero St.
415-487-2600

Acme Bread
1601 San Pablo Ave., Berkeley
510-524-1327,
and Ferry Plaza farmer's market,
415-288-2978

Bullshead
840 Ulloa St.
415-665-4350

Mo's
1322 Grant Ave.
415-788-3779

La Taqueria
2889 Mission St.
415-285-7117

Chava's—I am fairly convinced that Chava's caldo de res could cure cancer. Luckily, I've never had to put it to the test. At the very least, a bowl of their beef vegetable soup after a day traipsing through the Mission has power to soothe the savage tourist.

DINNER

Many of these entrees are offered for lunch as well, but somehow they seem to taste better after the sun goes down.

Crustacean Restaurant and **Thanh Long**—You can search the wharf over for Dungeness crab, but to my mind you'll find the most succulent and savory examples at these Euro/Vietnamese seafood restaurants on Russian Hill and

the outer Sunset. Owned and run by the respected An Family, their whole roasted crab will have you licking your fingers long after they take away your plate.

Andalu—I suspect the onslaught of tapas and small-plate restaurants has peaked, and soon the weak will die off and the strong will prevail. Trendy Andalu could survive on its polenta fries alone. Crispy, golden, and delicate on the outside, simultaneously airy and lava-like on the inside, they come zestily seasoned and served with a spicy tomato vinaigrette dipping sauce.

Duarte's Tavern—Folks come from near and far to Pescadero (below San Gregorio on Highway 1) to sample the creamy, delicious, secret-recipe artichoke and green chile soups at this venerable bar and restaurant. If you can't decide between the two, get the half and half. It's dinner in a bowl.

LuLu—A revolving door of chefs hasn't bumped the iron-griddle roasted mussels off its pedestal: they remain tender, smoky, and delicious—one of the reasons this hot, hip restaurant has survived boom and bust.

Home—It's a tough choice between the macaroni and cheese here and the one at **Chenery Park**. Home gets the edge for a slightly more piquant balance of cheeses and better prices, but the panko breadcrumb topping gives

Chenery's version that indescribably satisfying crunch. (*Note:* If you've got children in tow, or people who have the patience of children, family-friendly Chenery Park is definitely your best bet.)

Ton Kiang—After a day of sightseeing in the gale-force fog, nothing warms the bones like a steaming clay pot stew with mustard greens or won ton soup from this Richmond District institution. Oh, also the Singapore-style noodles (you have to ask for them; they're not on the menu).

Tommy's Joynt—I feel about Tommy's Joynt the way I feel about the nachos at the ballpark—I've always harbored the fact that I love them like a guilty secret. In a town lousy with high-brow cuisine, it somehow seems crass to hanker after hofbrau food. But then I found out that Tom Petty had Tommy's delivered nightly to his hotel room when he was here for the concert series in 1997, so now I don't feel so bad. I'm partial to the open-face turkey sandwich with mashed potatoes and gravy, but nothing preps the stomach better for a night at the Great American Music Hall down the street than Tommy's spicy buffalo chili. Yes, it's real buffalo—farm-raised just like cattle, only leaner, and without the mad cow disease.

Thep Phanom—I can't go to a Thai restaurant without sampling the tom kar gai, spicy-sour chicken soup with lemongrass and sometimes coconut milk. This one is sublime.

Khan Toke—The warm mushroom "farmer's" salad (infused with lime, cilantro, and chilies) at this atmospheric Thai restaurant brings me close to tears. No shoes; you sit on cushions at floor-level tables; traditional dancers entertain during dinner.

Hunan—The spicy-smoked ham and chicken (Marty's Special) is Hunan's pièces de résistance, but the cold noodle salad with chicken and cucumbers in spicy peanut sauce eclipses it in my book.

Fringale—I've never been disappointed with anything I've ordered at this wonderful little SoMa restaurant, but the traditional French cassoulet has my mouth watering just thinking about it.

Biscuits and Blues—This down-under downtown club is a big tourist mecca, but there are several reasons why it

Chava's
2839 Mission St.
415-282-0283

Crustacean Restaurant
1475 Polk St.
415-776-2722

Thanh Long
4101 Judah St.
415-665-1146

Andalu
3198 16th St.
415-621-2211

Duarte's Tavern
202 Stage Road,
Pescadero
650-879-0464

Lulu
816 Folsom St.
415-495-5775

Home
2100 Market St.
415-503-0333

Chenery Park
683 Chenery St.
415-337-8537

Ton Kiang
5128 Geary Blvd.
415-752-4440

Tommy's Joynt
1101 Geary St.
415-775-4216

Thep Phanom
400 Waller St.
415-431-2526

Khan Toke
5937 Geary Blvd.
415-668-6654

Hunan
924 Sansome St.
415-956-7727

Fringale
570 4th St.
415-543-0573

Biscuits and Blues
401 Mason St.
415-292-2583

transcends the tourist trap label. One is the weekly schedule of solid, talented blues and R&B bands; the other is the biscuits—flaky, tender, substantial, and totally addictive. Of course, they come as an accompaniment to the cajun/southern menu, which is also usually darn good, though inconsistent.

Zuni Café—For more than twenty years, chef Judy Rogers has kept foodies, tourists, and other chefs coming back to her hip Hayes Valley restaurant for wood-oven-roasted dishes—especially the roast chicken for two.

Ebisu—If you're gonna do sushi, you may as well impress them with a sushi bar that makes hand rolls artistic as well as tasty. Godzila does an exceptional job of this, but the caterpillar roll at Ebisu is truly something to behold. Small segments of sushi stuffed with avocado and spicy tuna (and hidden pockets of wasabi) snake down the plate—the seafood creature even has antennas and fish-roe eyes. The sight of it has been known to cause spontaneous applause.

Roosevelt Tamale Parlor—There are better places in the Mission to get tamales, but a lot of them aren't sit-down restaurants with a great homey Mexican kitchen kind of atmosphere. The portions at Roosevelt's are big, the price is right, and the tamales and chile colorado have been made from scratch daily since 1922.

Tommaso's—If you like your pizzas thick and deep and soupy with toppings, go to Zachary's in Oakland. But if you like them made the Italian way—thin and crispy, with an emphasis on perfect tomato sauce and uncluttered by a pile of toppings—then you should come to this North Beach institution. Tommaso's brick oven has been cranking out perfect pizzas for more than 65 years, and with any luck, they'll be around for another 65.

FARM FRESH

Many of the farms that put the regional in regional cuisine are small producers up in Sonoma and Napa counties. A sampling of a few that are open to the public for sales and/or touring:

Vella Cheese (dry Jack)—315 East Second Street, Sonoma, 707-938-4307

Kozlowski Farms (jellies, jams, mustards, sauces)—5566 Gravenstein Highway 116, Forestville, 707-887-1587

Cowgirl Creamery (cheeses include the house brand, Redwood Hill Farms, Cypress Grove, and Point Reyes blue cheese; they also sell organic produce, have a Niman Ranch charcuterie, and a lovely grassy picnic area out back)—80 4th Street, Point Reyes Station, 415-663-9335

B.R. Cohn (olive oil, vinegar, winery)—15000 Sonoma Highway, Glen Ellen, 707-938-4064

Marin French Cheese Company (Rouge et Noir camembert, schloss, and brie)—7500 Red Hill Rd., Petaluma, 800-292-6001

DESSERT

This could be a whole chapter in and of itself, but I'd probably have a heart attack doing the research. So here are just a few very worthy places:

Mitchell's Ice Cream—You can have your gelato, your frozen yogurt, your tofutti—none of it comes close to the ice cream at Mitchell's, an old-fashioned mom-and-pop shop (since 1953), located on the outskirts of the Mission. Along with all the traditional varieties, Mitchell's makes a whole series of unusual, tropical flavors—mango, langka (a tart melon), halo halo (sweet bean), and the incredible macapuno (meaty coconut) and buko (sweet baby coconut), which should be ordered on a cone with chocolate dip. Other standouts are their fresh fruit ices and sorbets made with big chunks of fruit. The best part is, they're open until 11:30 p.m. on weekends.

Polly Ann Ice Cream—The texture isn't nearly as creamy or satisfying as Mitchell's, but Polly Ann has more flavors than you could taste in a lifetime, all handmade. If you can't decide what you want, spin the wheel and let it decide for you (just hope durian isn't one of the choices; the tropical island fruit smells like gasoline). Another bonus—doggies (accompanied by owners) get free cones.

Dianda's—This Mission district Italian bakery is known the city over for its chocolate rum cakes, amaretto cookies, and layer cream cakes. The cannolis aren't too shabby, either.

Delancey Street—There many reasons to come here—fabulous waterfront locale, supporting a good cause—but the ultimate motivation is the sweet potato pie or chocolate-fudge Snickers Pie.

Something to Wash That Down With

Martinis   Believe it or don't: the martini was supposedly invented in a San Francisco bar by "Professor" Jerry Thomas back in the 1860s. The tale goes that the professor was asked to make something strong for a passenger embarking on the cold ferry ride across the bay to Martinez. The drink consisted of gin, bitters, vermouth, and maraschino. Later,

Zuni Café
1658 Market St.
415-552-2522

Ebisu
1283 9th Ave.
415-566-1770

Roosevelt Tamale Parlor
2817 24th St.
415-550-9213

Tommaso's
1042 Kearny St.
415-398-9696

Mitchell's Ice Cream
688 San Jose Ave.
415-648-2300

Polly Ann Ice Cream
2063 31st Ave.
415-566-9869

Dianda's
2883 Mission St.
415-647-5469

Delancey Street
600 Embarcadero
415-512-5179

HOT RESTAURANTS...

...That Are Worth the Wait

Fifth Floor (12 4th St., 415-348-1555)

Slanted Door (Ferry Building, Embarcadero and Market St., 415-861-8032)

Kokkari (200 Jackson St., 415-981-0983)

Baraka (288 Connecticut St., 415-255-0370)

Delfina (3621 18th St., 415-552-4055)

...Where There's No Wait

One Market (1 Market St., 415-777-5577)

Universal Café (2814 19th St., 415-821-4608)

Citizen Cake (393 Grove St., 415-861-2228)

Ana Mandara (865 Beach St., 415-771-6800)

Acquerello (1722 Sacramento St., 415-567-5432)

the formula and the name of the cocktail were abbreviated to the concoction we know today.

Whether or not it's true, San Francisco does have its fair share of stellar martini bars. Among my favorites:

The Red Room—What it lacks in authenticity it makes up for in volume and atmosphere. The oversized martini glasses look like they came from Pee Wee's Playhouse, and they're served by bartenders who are so cool you might feel the need for a warm coat. In deference to the bar's theme color (absolutely everything, down to the lighting and a wall of mysterious bottled elixirs, is red), you might consider ordering the martini's crimson cousin, the Cosmopolitan.

Top of the Mark—The 100 Martini Menu lives up to its name, as does the view.

Blondie's Bar and No Grill—If you can abide the Marina diaspora that frequents this swingles bar, you will find some of the tastiest and heftiest martinis in town. And for a few extra bucks they give you the shaker.

Maxfield's/Pied Piper Bar—The historic bar in the Palace Hotel seems like it was built for sipping martinis and

wearing cloche hats and kid gloves. Sit at the bar and gaze at Maxfield Parrish's *Pied Piper* mural while you daydream about Oscar Wilde cavorting in an upstairs parlor.

Margaritas No one can have just one margarita at **Tommy's**, because they're so damn good. A staple in the Outer Richmond since 1965, this platter-style Mexican restaurant is famous the town over for its margaritas, made with 100-percent pure agave. Tommy's stocks an enormous array of imported tequilas, which you can sample if you join the tequila club. Needless to say, the party atmosphere prevails here, as patrons order pitcher after pitcher and proceed to get completely snockered.

Beer　From a local brewpub angle, your best bets for beer are **Gordon Biersch**, **Magnolia Pub and Brewery**, **San Francisco Brewing Company**, and **Thirsty Bear Brewing Company**. Gordon Biersch's märzen is a consistent winner in most ale-lovers' books, and 30-somethings will find the atmosphere at the bar more than conducive to alliances of a romantic or professional kind. Magnolia's locale in the heart of the Haight makes it a magnet for once and future hippies, and they craft a large variety of interesting ales and stouts. The SF Brewing Company offers a few good ales too, but the place feels distinctly like a tourist attraction (which it is). Thirsty Bear's beers can be hit or miss, but their food—tapas, paella, and other Spanish specialties—is top notch.

For authentic, hearty German beers served in appropriate two-liter glasses and boots, make a detour to **SuppenKüche** in Hayes Valley, where the young and Euro-restless say "danke" and "bitte" as they pass the Spaten.

Wine　If you don't have time to hit the wine country, do some vertical tastings locally at **Hayes and Vine**, a cozy, chic wine bar in Hayes Valley that has none of the rarefied air you find in Silverado Trail tasting rooms. Snuggle up to the bar, where they offer 35 to 40 wines by the glass on any given day. The total inventory features more than 500 wines including a number of small, hard-to-find vintages which the knowledgeable (and occasionally pierced and tattooed) staff will be only too happy to tell you about.

Downtown, the bar at **First Crush** is the perfect overture to a night at the theater. The gargantuan wine list, served in tasting flights and by the glass and bottle, offers a well-rounded selection from both heavy hitters and up-and-comers. And if you have too many, you can just skip the show and stay for dinner.

The Red Room
827 Sutter St.
415-346-7666

Top of the Mark
Mark Hopkins
Hotel, 999
California St.
415-616-6916

**Blondie's Bar
and No Grill**
540 Valencia St.
415-864-2419

**Maxfield's/Pied
Piper Bar**
Palace Hotel, 2 New
Montgomery St.
415-546-5020

Tommy's
5929 Geary Blvd.
415-387-4747

Gordon Biersch
2 Harrison St.
415-243-8246

**Magnolia Pub
and Brewery**
1398 Haight St.
415-864-7468

**San Francisco
Brewing
Company**
155 Columbus Ave.
415-434-3344

**Thirsty Bear
Brewing
Company**
661 Howard St.
415-974-0905

SuppenKüche
525 Laguna St.
415-252-9289

Hayes and Vine
377 Hayes St.
415-626-5301

First Crush
101 Cyril Magnin St.
415-982-7874

tour 14   Ivy Leaguers

Back in the days when your college roommate wore IZod shirts and your sorority sister wouldn't be caught dead without a hairband and an oxford button-down, we referred to them as Preppies.

In some circles, Preppies morphed into the free-spending, expensive-gadget-obsessed subgroup

known as yuppies. But in the country clubs, aboard the yachts, and on the Cape, the Ivy Leaguers continued to engage in those pursuits—stock market dabbling, Hampton house-hopping, Gavin Newsom-worshipping—that befitted their social stature and their bank books.

Your debutante days may be behind you, and your rugby shoes may have been replaced by a pair of Uggs, but that doesn't mean you can't regress for a week or a weekend when your ex-Bachelor/Spinster pals roll into town. So throw on a pair of Docksiders,

hop in your SUV, and party like it's rush week at
Princeton all over again.

MORNING

If you are a genuine, card-carrying prep-school dropout, there
are three areas of town where you can comfortably brunch
and take your morning constitutional (which might consist
of rollerblading, sailing, golfing, or taking a brisk walk to the
newsstand to pick up the *Wall Street Journal*). Those areas are
Cow Hollow, the Marina, and Pacific Heights.

In Pacific Heights, the day begins at either **Pauli's Café**
or **Ella's**. If you live in the neighborhood, I'm not telling you
anything you don't already know. If you don't live here, but
aspire to, this is a great way to make your introductions.
Pauli's on upper Fillmore is the place for piles of potatoes,
eggs Benedict and Florentine, and Grand Marnier French
toast. The lines can get long in the late morning, so stop
first at **The Grove** down the street for a double cap and the
odd celebrity sighting (recent spottings include former
"Felicity" star Keri Russell and Robin and Marsha
Williams), and amuse yourself by window-shopping at
superchic boutiques like **Jim-Elle** and **Gimme Shoes**.

Ella's is technically in Presidio Heights, where the
serious Old Money resides, but that never stopped the
young and ambitious from overstepping their bounds.
Besides, this is the ultimate in gourmet brunches, worth the
invariable Sunday morning lines. Everything here is made
from scratch, even the bread for the French toast. Not only
is the orange juice fresh-squeezed, it's squeezed from blood
oranges. The coffeecake and sticky buns are to die for, and
my friend Rob swears there are no better buttermilk
pancakes in town.

On Union Street, the youthful denizens of Cow Hollow
and the Nut (as in Chestnut Street) crave the housemade
scones, turkey-bacon and avocado omelets, and fresh fruit
pancakes at **Home Plate** on Lombard. If you have a young
lawyer/realtor/stockbroker friend looking to meet someone
of his or her ilk, this is the breakfast spot for you. Sign up

Pauli's Café
2500 Washington St.
415-921-5159

Ella's
500 Presidio Ave.
415-441-5669

The Grove
2016 Fillmore St.
415-474-1419

Jim-Elle
2237 Fillmore St.
415-567-9500

Gimme Shoes
2358 Fillmore St.
415-864-0691

Home Plate
2274 Lombard St.
415-922-4663

on the outside chalkboard and don't let the parade pass you by. Afterward, work off the calories by joining the conga line of bra-tops and IPods as they blade down the boardwalk in front of **Marina Green**, leaving phone numbers in their wake.

FOR THE BOYS

Retail-wise, no lawyer working his way up to partnerhood will want to bypass **Thomas Pink** (255 Post St., 415-421-2022), with its stacks of tailored shirts; **Burberry's** (225 Post St., 415-392-2200), where a plaid trenchcoat is all the introduction you'll ever need; or **Brooks Brothers** (150 Post St., 415-397-4500), home of the classic three-button suit. From here, a requisite trip to the Italian designer boutiques **Giorgio Armani** (278 Post St., 415-434-2500), which carries the exclusive Black Label line, and **Salvatore Ferragamo** (233 Geary St., 415-391-6565) for Italian leather foot fashions (nothing this fabulous could just be called "shoes"). Then perhaps a button-down shirt, something in paisley, or a saddle blanket from **Polo/Ralph Lauren** (90 Post St., 415-788-7656); the accompanying saddle and harness can be found at **Hermès** (125 Grant Ave., 415-391-7200). Men looking to get sponsored at the club, or trying to get in good with the old man, will also need to drop a couple of hundred on Dominican cigars, clips, and humidor boxes at **Alfred Dunhill** (250 Post St., 415-781-3368).

The Yachting Set

Sure, you could take a ferry or a Hornblower tour around the bay with the commoners, or you could charter a yacht and brunch in style like Ari Onassis on holiday. **Signature Yachts** features a small fleet of luxury vessels just for the occasion, equipped with salons, bars, galleys, and dance floors—one even has a private state room with a Jacuzzi. **Adventure Cat Sailing Charters** offers bay sails and sunset cruises on catamarans that look like sailboats but feel like luxury liners. Unfortunately, you might have to share the boat with others, but you can keep up appearances for the people watching from the shore by gesturing demonstratively and pretending to give orders to the crew. Then, when you're far enough away, prop up your feet and let the hired hands do all the work.

NOON

No former Junior Leaguer leaves home without a platinum card (her own or her dad's), which makes the inevitable shopping tour of Union Square fairly painless. All you need to do is steer her to the stores with a pedigree.

Begin at the bottom of Sacramento Street at **Sue Fisher King**, who's outfitted high society tabletops and bedrooms for some 25 years. King's taste is impeccable: her shop boasts an array of imported linens, china, flatware, Venetian mirrors, cashmere throws, writing implements, silk pillows, soaps, and objets d'art that will leave you wishing you'd inherited the Italian villa to house it all.

From here, make your way up the street, dipping into **Forrest Jones** for a fondue set; **Sarah Shaw** for the latest cocktail party outfit from up-and-coming American designers such as Juicy Couture, Seven Jeans, and Trina Turk; the **Urban Pet** for a hand-drawn portrait of your pug by artist Rive Nestor; and **Bettina** for a silky French under-thing from La Perla.

Then duck down the secret cobbled alley to **True Body Wraps** for an amino-collagen wrap to tone up your thigh flab before settling into a courtyard table at **Sociale**, where the country-club crowd nibbles on poached shrimp salads and pappardelle with braised duck before their afternoon manicures.

Downtown, make a beeline for **Wilkes Bashford**, haber-dasher to socialites and their lineage for nearly 40 years. The always-dapper Wilkes, accompanied by his beloved dachshund, offers six floors of couture for tastes that run the gamut from modern to matronly, with ample collections from names like Pucci and Bogner to remind you of where you came from.

Next, hit the Brunello Cucinelli collection at **Saks Fifth Avenue** for a perfect pink cashmere sweater (guys can get their Dolce & Gabbana fix further down the street at the **Saks Men's Store**); **Chanel** for a pair of sunglasses with signature interlocking C's; **Prada** for, well . . . does it matter?; and designer darling **Marc Jacobs** for something hot, colorful, and fresh off the runway.

Then, even if your guests arrived with enough luggage to fill a small moving van, stop in at **Louis Vuitton**, because there isn't a Ivy Leaguer born who couldn't use a little some-thing extra emblazoned with a trademark "LV." Finish off the outfit with a rubber tote from **Kate Spade** (that black burlap is *so* last season).

After all that power shopping, join the Ladies Who Lunch (and by ladies, we mean men, too) at **Armani Café**.

Marina Green
Marina Blvd., west
of Buchanan

Signature Yachts
Pier 9
415-788-9100

Adventure Cat
Pier 39, J Dock
415-777-1630

Sue Fisher King
3067 Sacramento St.
415-922-7276

Forrest Jones
3275 Sacramento St.
415-567-2483

Sarah Shaw
3095 Sacramento St.
888-554-4300

The Urban Pet
3429 Sacramento St.
415-673-7708

Bettina
3654 Sacramento St.
415-563-8002

True Body Wraps
3665 Sacramento St.
415-292-9727

Sociale
3665 Sacramento St.
415-921-3200

Wilkes Bashford
375 Sutter St.
415-986-4380

Saks Fifth Ave.
384 Post St.
415-986-4300

Saks Men's Store
220 Post St.
415-986-4300

Chanel
156 Geary St.
415-981-1550

Prada
140 Geary St.
415-391-8844

Marc Jacobs
125 Maiden Lane
415-362-6500

Louis Vuitton
233 Geary St.
415-391-6200

Kate Spade
227 Grant Ave.
415-216-0880

Armani Café
One Grant Ave.
415-677-9010

The chic little lunch spot and espresso bar housed among the white-marble pillars of the high-fashion store is the perfect place for the diet-conscious shopper to graze on panini, pasta, and salads (eat too much and you won't fit into that gorgeous little black suit). Where else can you dine and be waited on by a staff wearing Armani-designed uniforms, who will put that little cocktail number aside for you in a dressing room until after your espresso? If the weather's not cooperating, skip the outdoor tables and grab a seat in the upstairs balcony—a better vantage point to eavesdrop on all the comings, goings, and air-kissing below.

The Sporting Life

For serious members of the horsey set, a trip to **Tal-Y-Tara Tea & Polo Shoppe** is a must. The tiny outer-Richmond District boutique and tea shop will outfit you head-to-stirrup in English equestrian gear and accouterments (all that smooth leather and riding crops may also make this a good

stop for your college roommate-turned-dominatrix). Afterward, scoot to the back for proper English Tea served on love seats or a sunny garden patio. The signature Motor Loaf—a hollowed out molasses bread filled with finger sandwiches—and the sherry trifle will satisfy bluebloods and commoners alike.

Missed a dues payment at the Olympic Club? Not to fret, while the **Presidio Golf Course** doesn't quite cultivate the same air of exclusivity, its former incarnation as a course for the military elite gives it a certain historical stature: Teddy Roosevelt and Dwight Eisenhower have played here, and it's located right next to Presidio Terrace, perhaps the city's most prestigious residential enclave, home to mayors, senators, and reclusive philanthropists. Plus, it's run by Arnold Palmer Golf Management, and you get to sip your 19th-hole gin and tonic in the comfort of a swanky clubhouse restaurant with floor-to-ceiling windows that overlook the first tee.

NIGHT

For fully credentialed Ivy Leaguers, getting into the St. Francis Yacht Club, the Pacific Union Club, or the Bohemian Club is usually just a matter of knocking on the door. If your pedigree isn't quite so polished, try happy hour at the **San Francisco Bay Club**, where the cream of Marina society mingles and sweats. The posh health club hosts a regular series of wine-and-cheese mixers for young movers and shakers who congregate to flirt and discuss upcoming alumni association fund raisers.

If your chums happen to be in town in April, May, or October, there's a gaggle of galas they can attend which give them an opportunity not only to wear the wardrobe they've just purchased, but also to hobnob with the hoi polloi at some of the city's most exclusive addresses.

In April, the **Junior League Home Tour** takes groups on walk-throughs of six Pacific Heights palaces, each more elaborate than the last; in May, you can dine, drink, and dance the night away at the bi-annual **Black & White Ball**, a fund raiser for the Symphony, and then plan your remodel at the **San Francisco Decorator Showcase**, when a couple dozen high-end designers are let loose in one of the city's historic mansions.

In September, if you have enough clout (and more importantly, cash) don your tuxedo or your best ball gown for **Opening Night at the Opera**, when everyone who's anyone in this town steps out for an evening of label-ogling and cleavage appreciation.

Cocktail Hour

In San Francisco, where so many young people with newly minted college degrees find themselves aloft on the executive payroll of the family business, there is no shortage of places in which they can congregate with like-minded folk. And when their wallets spilleth over, these are the bars that sop up the mess.

Balboa Café—The isosceles configuration of bars on Filbert and Pierce streets known as The Triangle (after the

Tal-Y-Tara Tea & Polo Shoppe
6439 California St.
415-751-9275

Presidio Golf Course
in the Presidio at the end of Arguello Blvd.
415-561-4653

San Francisco Bay Club
150 Greenwich St.
415-433-2200

Junior League of San Francisco
415-775-4100

Black & White Ball
San Francisco Symphony
415-552-8000

San Francisco Decorator Showcase
415-447-5830

San Francisco Opera
301 Van Ness Ave.
415-861-4008

Balboa Café
3199 Fillmore St.
415-921-3944

Bermuda Triangle—yuppies check in, but they don't check out) is not the meat market it was when the Dartmouth Social Club occupied the northeast corner, but it's still pretty darn beefy. If you've been looking to hobnob with the bridge-and-tunnel, tasseled-loafers-with-no-socks crowd, look no further: they're here, along with mayoral cronies and promising young D.A.s. Part of the Billy Getty/Gavin Newsom empire, the Bal's biggest asset is its menu, which goes far beyond the requisite cocktail nibbles. It's all good, but regulars usually rely on the thick, juicy burger on a long French roll.

City Tavern—Another anchor on The Triangle, this slightly more casual bar is a popular post-collegiate hangout where you can slam shots and play "quarters" and no one looks at you sideways. This is the place to go if you're not prone to claustrophobia or averse to rubbing up against slightly inebriated young advertising execs.

Bar None—This below-the-street sports bar is pretty much an ex-fraternity/sorority mecca—keep your eye out (and your head down) for chugging contests. It's a one-stop shop for all your private East Coast-college name-dropping needs.

Bix—Sidle up to the bar with the big boys at this elegant back-alley supper club, located in what was once a gold assayer's office. The place exudes just the right amount of two-olive ambience, from the handsome gent at the grand piano to the glittering crowd of double-breasted suits and three-strand pearls.

Royal Oak—This swank fern bar, a fixture on the pick-up scene for more than a decade, still packs in a posh Russian Hill/Pac Heights crowd, who cozy up on red-velvet sofas beneath Tiffany lamps and sip Cosmos.

Matrix—The former bar/music stage owned by a member of Jefferson Airplane is now is a styley elbow-rubbing joint for label-conscious financiers. But then, maybe that's exactly what you had in mind.

Blue Light Café—Oddly enough, this bar was started two decades ago by musician Boz Scaggs, who envisioned it more as a funky, low-key New Orleans addition to button-down Union Street. But it was adopted early on by the young, single, and monied crowd, and these days it feels like a throwback to the meat-market bars of the '70s—an end-of-the-night spot where highly lubricated Marina bachelorettes and Ivy League boys in alma mater sweatshirts go to hook up when the other spots have cleared out.

Le Colonial—With its palm trees, plantation shutters, rattan furniture and outdoor veranda, the upstairs lounge off this elegant southeast Asian restaurant feels like a scene out of *Casablanca*, if Casablanca were in French-colonial Vietnam. For Old Money, the back-alley location on the site of the famed Trader Vic's is enough reason to drop in for a tropical cocktail.

Redwood Room—The lines down the street attest to the fact that hotelier Ian Schrager didn't alienate too many people for too long when he transformed this legendary art deco piano lounge into a paean to post-modernism. Amidst the luminous redwood-paneled walls (it was built, after all, long before the days of Earth First), starlets poured into the latest runway fashions and gents wearing $400 lavender-tinted sunglasses drink Grey Goose martinis and sway under the weight of their lengthy last names.

Harry Denton's Starlight Room—Harry's penthouse suite is the kind of place where swank gents slip greenbacks to the door guy and glamorous gals get away with wearing dresses so revealing you'd think they were auditioning for Playmate "Fear Factor." Sip grown-up cocktails and do the white-man's overbite as you dance to Motown favorites and watch the twinkling light show of the city below.

Beauty Bar—Slumming among the unwashed masses is a time-honored tradition among Ivy Leaguers. And the most popular place to "get real" is the Mission, where genuine down-low spots bump up against ones that are just dressed that way, with drinking as the common denominator. The Beauty Bar is actually the sister of the hot New York original, which gives it an extra boost of Paris Hilton cred. Dolled up

City Tavern
3200 Fillmore St.
415-567-0918

Bar None
1980 Union St.
415-409-4469

Bix
56 Gold St.
415-433-6300

Royal Oak
2201 Polk St.
415-928-2303

Matrix
3138 Fillmore St.
415-563-4180

Blue Light Café
1979 Union St.
415-922-5510

Le Colonial
20 Cosmo Pl.
415-931-3600

Redwood Room
Clift Hotel, 495 Geary St.
415-775-4700

Harry Denton's Starlight Room
450 Powell St.
415-395-8595

Beauty Bar
2299 Mission St.
415-285-0323

like a Long Island hair salon, the gimmick here is that you can sip a Singapore Sling while you get your nails done (free manicure with a $10 drink).

WHERE TO STAY

Where does the Fortune 500 young exec sleep? Anywhere he or she wants. But probably the **Ritz-Carlton** will be acceptable. From the plush terry robes embroidered with that all-important insignia, to the feather beds, marble bathrooms, private town car, and full-time staff employed just to note guests' preferences—the Ritz will keep your friends in the style to which they are (or would like to be) accustomed.

Across town, the **Chateau Tivoli**, built in 1892, is one of San Francisco's most magnificent Victorians—a colorful, turreted mansion that was once the home of the Tivoli Opera House and hosted the likes of Mark Twain and Lily Langtry. If your to-the-manor-born friends aren't impressed by the hand-carved woodwork and crystal chandeliers, or they balk at the Alamo Square location, make sure to tell them that several of the furniture pieces came from the estates of the Vanderbilts, Charles DeGaulle and J. Paul Getty.

Ritz-Carlton
600 Stockton St.
415-296-7465

Chateau Tivoli
1057 Steiner St.
415-776-5462

Flower Children (and Their Parents)

I freely admit to having a bad case of '60s envy. I grew up in the Inner Sunset, not 15 minutes from the Haight-Ashbury, and yet as far as my consciousness was concerned, the psychedelic revolution could have taken place in Poughkeepsie.

I have two memories of the '60s. One is of a costume party my parents went to dressed up as beatniks. My mom wore a plastic miniskirt and a long cigarette holder; my dad a beret and goatee. I thought they were hippies. I bragged to all my friends. I was laughed out of second grade. The other is of our next-door-neighbor's daughter, who grew her hair wild, got pregnant before she was married, and refused to wear her dental bridge to fill the gaps where she had had teeth pulled. I was terribly impressed.

To this day, I have clung to the tragically romantic notion that because of some cosmically bad timing, I missed out on the greatest party the civilized world has ever known. I've held to this belief despite the testimony of actual hippies that the '60s were not nearly as much fun as they were cracked up to be.

It is clear that I'm not alone in my nostalgia. A couple of years ago, I was walking past a restaurant that was hosting a group of Japanese businessmen when, in what appeared to be a very formal exchange of gifts, the American hosts presented the Japanese visitors with an array of tie-dyed T-shirts, to which the Japanese responded with squeals of unmitigated delight, putting them on directly over their suits.

Even though the patchouli cloud of love, drugs, free sex, Beatle boots, and the Grateful Dead has long since dissipated, there are still a number of places you and your once and future hippie friends can go to recapture the spirit of '67.

MORNING-NOON

All trips back to the '60s eventually lead to San Francisco's former free love foyer, the Haight-Ashbury district, which long ago buried its ashes in a formal Death of the Hippie ceremony in Buena Vista Park. Still, the neighborhood holds symbolic appeal for those wishing to visit the sacred sites, so grab your favorite throwback and follow your inner flower child to the crossroads of Haight and Ashbury streets. As you stand at the famous intersection, reminisce about a time when LSD and smoking in public places were legal. Next, walk up two blocks to **710 Ashbury Street**, the stately Victorian that once housed the standard-bearers of the San

Francisco Sound, the Grateful Dead. Since the death of ring-leader Jerry Garcia, the house has taken on even more of a temple-like aura. Fresh flowers commonly appear on the steps; wandering waifs stare up at the windows with mournful, worshipful eyes, muttering bits and pieces of Grateful Dead song lyrics. But as corny as it sounds, the house is a piece of hippie history and worth a stop.

For breakfast, there are any number of granola-head hotspots, but the best food can be found at **Squat and Gobble** (huge omelets, scrambles, crepes, and home fries), the **Pork Store Café** (at 25 years, one of the stalwarts of the neighborhood, serving enormous piles of pancakes, hash-browns, and eggs over-easy), and **All You Knead** (muffins, scones, and other baked goods). Sandwiches, salads, and a spirit of tolerance and acceptance are on the menu at the aptly named **People's Café**, a harmonic convergence of a place where hippies and punks and Eurotrash happily shout over each other and the music, and gaze out the picture windows to the carnival that continues to provide diners with endless hours of far-out fun.

Next, take a stroll through the Panhandle, site of many of the Summer of Love concerts starring bands such as the 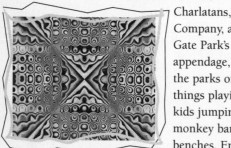 Charlatans, Big Brother and the Holding Company, and even Jimi Hendrix. Golden Gate Park's urban, slightly more gritty appendage, the Panhandle is SF's homage to the parks of New York City—twentysome-things playing pick-up basketball, inner-city kids jumping rope and swinging from the monkey bars, a few bums sleeping on benches. En route, make sure to pay your respects at 112 Lyon Street, the one-time residence of Country Joe McDonald and the late, legendary Janis Joplin.

At the west end of the Panhandle, in **Sharon Meadow**, is infamous Hippie Hill, a grassy knoll (located, appropri-ately, right next to the children's playground) that proves the old adage that the more things change, the more they stay the same. Once the hippies' central gathering spot, the place still resonates with groovy vibes. Grab a veggie burrito (with black beans) from **Zona Rosa** on Haight and Cole or a scoop of Cherry Garcia ice cream from **Ben and Jerry's**, sit on top of the hill, and watch the happening unfold—conga drummers doing their tribal thing, modern-day flower children twirling and dancing to the rhythm, little kids doing barrel rolls, dogs chasing Frisbees. It's a perpetual Human Be-In.

If that gets you in the mood, make sure to stop by the **Polo Fields**, site of the real Human Be-In, when San Francisco hippies and Berkeley radicals—Allen Ginsberg to Timothy Leary—united for a mass consciousness-sharing in January 1967. The pilgrimage to the field began at dawn, and by midafternoon tens of thousands of people had gathered to listen to music, poetry readings, invocations, chants, and prayers. Much to the police department's surprise, by nightfall the field had been left exactly as it was found—without a speck of trash.

There's really been nothing as all-encompassing since the Be-In (though I suspect Jerry Garcia's and Bill Graham's memorials came pretty close), but concerts at the Polo Fields and Sharon Meadow are still a great way to spend a free-to-be Saturday afternoon. Usually on the circuit are **Footstock** (the Bay to Breakers race post-mortem) at the Polo Fields in May, various blues and alt-rock jamborees at Sharon Meadow, including the **Now and Zen Festival** in the late-summer/early fall, **Reggae in the Park**, and the free **Strictly Bluegrass Festival**, both in October.

The biggest acid flashback of the year happens the first weekend in June at the **Haight Street Fair**. If you squint real hard and ignore the Gap store and some of other latter-day trappings of commercialism that have sprung up in the neighborhood, it might as well be 1967. The streets are awash in a kaleidoscope of tie-dye. Street musicians sing protest songs. Long-haired girls wear daisies behind their ears. There's dancing in the streets, tofu burgers on the grill, and a general feeling that people are once again making love, not war. This is a good time to pick up a set of love beads and other accessories of the aura. If your born-again Baby Boomers aren't here during the fair, send them to the following shops:

Positively Haight Street—For tie-dye anything, Guatemalan pullovers, granny dresses, psychedelic posters,

Squat and Gobble
1428 Haight St.
415-864-8484

Pork Store Café
1451 Haight St.
415-864-6981

All You Knead
1466 Haight St.
415-552-4550

People's Café
1419 Haight St.
415-553-8842

Sharon Meadow
Lincoln and JFK Dr.,
Golden Gate Park

Zona Rosa
1797 Haight St.
415-668-7717

Ben and Jerry's
corner of Haight
and Ashbury
415-626-4143

Polo Fields
Golden Gate Park
between 30th and
36th avenues

Footstock
Golden Gate Park,
Polo Fields
415-359-2800

Now and Zen Fest
Alice Radio
415-765-4097

Reggae in the Park
Golden Gate Park,
Sharon Meadow
415-458-1988

Strictly Bluegrass Festival
Golden Gate Park,
Speedway Meadow,
www.strictlyblue grass.com

Positively Haight Street
1400 Haight St.
415-252-8747

beads, and a very bright, upbeat attitude. The place still embodies the best intentions of that summer long ago.

Golden Triangle, Pipe Dreams, and **Psychedelic Sun—** These genuine, card-carrying head shops have gone right on providing the paraphernalia for the pot generation, completely unfazed by the whole medicinal marijuana brouhaha (Pipe Dreams, open since 1969, is the oldest head shop on Haight Street if not in the entire city). At these shops you'll find every kind of smoking accessory ever

made, from handmade ceramic bongs and rolling papers to hookahs and carved wooden pipes, as well as necessary adjuncts such as posters, hemp clothing, and incense.

Haight Ashbury T-Shirts—The selection is enormous and includes my favorite T-shirt slogan: "Haight-Ashbury: When the Going Gets Weird, the Weird Turn Pro."

Distractions—For starters, they've got candle votives, patchouli oil, incense, and lava lamps. Head to the back of the store and you hit the throwback pièce de résistance—black-light posters (and black lights) just like the ones you used to have on your ceiling.

ArtRock—One minute in this gallery and you'll kick yourself for throwing away those old '60s concert posters, 'cause now they're worth some serious bucks. The good news is that these days you have a legitimate job and can buy back your wild youth. The Folsom Street gallery carries an enormous collection of original and reissued '60s rock posters and handbills, including classics by Stanley Mouse, Victor Moscoso, and Rick Griffin. They also carry original Jerry Garcia lithographs, album cover art, and an extensive selection of new poster art. If your friends don't see the poster they're looking for, or can't make up their minds, ArtRock does a huge mail-order business with fully illustrated catalogs of their complete inventory.

Where the Spirit Is Still Willing . . .

Ironically, the coffeehouse that most exemplifies the lost ideals of the Love Generation is not even in the Haight.

Sacred Grounds on Hayes and Cole is a 1960s ersatz community center for genuine hippies and earthies. The coffeehouse features impromptu jam sessions, poetry readings, literature to aid your spiritual awakening, homemade soups and salads, and really good strong coffee. Coincidentally, it's also located a block from the site where the Blue Unicorn—the first official hippie hangout—once stood.

Born-again hippies may perhaps feel more at home in the digital Haight—that no-man's land between the Mission District and Potrero Hill. Here the spawn of the dotcom generation have established a fiber-optic network of likeminded souls who hold to many of the same ideals as the Love Generation, only with wireless DSL. A prime example is the **Atlas Café**, a place for anyone who laments the loss of "those" kind of San Francisco places . . . you know, where weirdos and gypsies and kids and tattooed guys and technogeeks and middle-aged guitar pickers and pierced-tongue lesbian moms all hang out together in an atmosphere of convivial eating, drinking, music-appreciating frivolity. Atlas Café is the keeper of the torch. It's the kind of place where employees past and present are enshrined on a website hall of fame, and where every Thursday and Sunday you can hear free live music—bluegrass to Tin Pan Alley vaudeville— alongside your sea of humanity. It's a gathering hall for 21st century children of the counterculture: cool enough for eight year olds, homey enough for hip baby boomers, and there's soup for everyone.

NIGHT

The **Red Vic** movie house is one of the few places left in the Haight that still seems to uphold the one-for-all, all-for-one spirit of the community. An independent cooperative that shows art, foreign, cult, and downright unusual films, the movie choices seem to be based more on the quirky tastes of the owners than held together by any sort of cinematic theme-glue (in a typical week you might encounter a surf movie fest, *Pumping Iron,* or *Last Tango in Paris*). The theater itself is really more of a glorified living room furnished with hand-me-down sofas and love seats, which you share with a

Golden Triangle
1340 Haight St.
415-431-6764

Pipe Dreams
1376 Haight St.
415-431-3553

Psychedelic Sun
1736 Haight St.
415-750-1368

Haight Ashbury T-shirts
1500 Haight St.
415-252-8751

Distractions
1552 Haight St.
415-252-8751

ArtRock
893 Folsom St.
415-255-7390

Sacred Grounds
2095 Hayes St.
415-387-3859

Atlas Café
3049 20th St.
415-648-1047

The Red Vic
1727 Haight St.
415-668-3994

friendly assortment of neighborhood types. Be sure to sample some of the atypical movie snacks, including fresh juices, raisin-carrot muffins, and popcorn served with an optional topping of brewer's yeast (kinda like butter, but well, yeastier).

Sharing the spotlight with the Red Vic is **Magnolia Pub & Brewery**, which has only been around since the late '90s but feels somehow like it's always been here, taking up the reigns as unofficial neighborhood social hall where two of the Haight's most infamous residents—the Drogstore Café and Magnolia Thunderpussy's—left off. While the name is more likely an homage to Ms. Thunderpussy (a former exotic dancer who ran an ice-cream and dessert business from this address) and not a tribute to "Sugar Magnolia," the Dead vibe is everywhere, from the soundtrack to the

groovy murals on the walls. On most nights, throngs of modern-day Hashburians happily quaff pints of house-brewed cask ales and chow down on burgers, sandwiches, salads, and soups (almost everything organically and locally grown) while they gaze through the enormous windows at the scene that's continuously unfolding outside.

Down the street at **Kan Zaman**, a crunchy Middle Eastern restaurant, you can pretend you're George Harrison visiting the maharishi as you sit on large floor pillows smoking honey-apple tobacco through an enormous hookah, while belly dancers hypnotize you with their hips. Assume the lotus position, nosh on hummus, kebabs, tabbouleh, and other tasty fare, and give peace a chance.

The Music Never Stopped

At the core of the hippie experience was the music, and even though Janis, Jerry, and Jimi are all gone, San Francisco hasn't entirely let the music—or that freewheeling feeling—fade away.

To relive the altered-state experience, with or without the help of illegal substances, go to a show at the reincarnated **Avalon Ballroom**, salvaged from the cobwebs by

**Magnolia Pub
& Brewery**
1398 Haight St.
415-864-7468

Kan Zaman
1793 Haight St.
415-751-9656

**Avalon
Ballroom**
1268 Sutter St.
415-847-4043

**Fillmore
Auditorium**
1805 Geary Blvd.
415-346-6000

**John Lee
Hooker's Boom
Boom Room**
Fillmore at Geary
415-673-8053

latter-day hippie Steve Shirley, aka Morning Spring Rain, who grew up under the rainbow tent of Wavy Gravy and friends on the Hog Farm Commune. Amazingly, Shirley was able to resurrect much of the Avalon's original charms, including psychedelic light shows projected on sheets along the wall, balcony seating, and even some of the original bands. Regulars include Big Brother and the Holding Company (21st century edition) and the house band, the Avalon All-Stars, whose roster reads like a Who's Who of the San Francisco Sound, with former members of the Jerry Garcia Band, and Frank Zappa and the Mothers of Invention. The concert line-up also features modern-day spiritual soulmates such as Reggae sensation Beenie Man and the Steve Kimock Band. It's an opportunity for multigenerational bonding that hasn't been seen since the closing of Laserium.

For erstwhile flower children, a trip to (or at) the **Fillmore Auditorium** is a must. Get there early, head upstairs to the café, and spend an hour perusing the phenomenal psychedelic poster collection culled from the archives of Bill Graham. Here, perfectly preserved in all their letter-squashing, neon-drenched splendor, are the most famous artworks of the era—all advertisements for concerts at the Fillmore. Among the gems are the original Grateful Dead skull-and-roses poster, the white dove/peace sign Jefferson Airplane poster, and colorful bills announcing shows for performers ranging from Otis Redding to Pink Floyd and Led Zeppelin. While the opening band plays, prowl the hallways and corridors looking at the photos of the musical greats who have graced this stage over the years. It's like being in the rock and roll hall of fame. After the show, grab a free apple from the box at the top of the stairs (a tradition started by Bill Graham back in 1965), and on your way out, pick up a free poster commemorating the performance—it'll probably be worth something someday.

If you haven't quite had your fill of jam sessions for one night, cross the street and have a nightcap at **John Lee Hooker's Boom Boom Room**, a hard-working blues bar with live music almost every night of the week. Before the Boom Boom, there was Jack's, and before that, other blues clubs dating all the way back to 1932. The room is loud—often so loud you have to use sign language with your tablemate—but the bands can knock your socks off.

Still jonesing for Jerry? Join the throng of 20-something Deadheads who manage to "have a great show" every Monday night at **Nickie's BBQ** on funky-dodgy lower Haight, where tapehead Dan plays the best of his live recordings of the Dead. It's a hand-twirling, head-bobbing, tie-dye-saturated jam session worthy of a parking lot outside the Oakland Coliseum.

For a great granola-and-guitar night, head over to Berkeley's **Freight and Salvage**, a concert venue for old folkies and new singer-songwriters. Offerings on the mostly acoustic music menu include bluegrass, klezmer music, and artists such as Mare Winningham, Peter Rowan, and the Modern Mandolin Quartet.

WHERE TO STAY

The **Red Victorian Bed and Breakfast** is a great place for those who remember the Summer of Love and those who wish they could. A delirious conglomeration of inn, peace center, gallery of meditative arts, and flowerchild dream-house, the Red Vic B&B was in fact a hippie crashpad in its 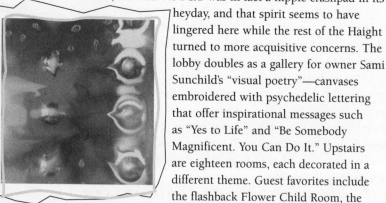 heyday, and that spirit seems to have lingered here while the rest of the Haight turned to more acquisitive concerns. The lobby doubles as a gallery for owner Sami Sunchild's "visual poetry"—canvases embroidered with psychedelic lettering that offer inspirational messages such as "Yes to Life" and "Be Somebody Magnificent. You Can Do It." Upstairs are eighteen rooms, each decorated in a different theme. Guest favorites include the flashback Flower Child Room, the Peacock Suite (which verily overflows with peacock feathers and patterns), and the room boasting an aquarium in the bathroom.

Pam Brennan lives in and runs the very respectable, but definitely funky/hippie B&B known as **Herb'n Inn**. Pam's husband Bruce leads Flower Power tours of the Haight on Tuesdays and Saturdays. Inside the small inn/ residence is a modest but steadily growing psychedelic history museum with photos, personal memorabilia, and posters. And if you ask, Bruce will probably show you his Woodstock ticket stubs.

For flower children who grew up, moved off the commune, and became successful despite their best intentions, there's **Inn 1890**, a restored 1890 Victorian on a quiet corner just a stone's throw from the heart of the Haight. The house may indeed at one time have been a crash pad, but it's cleaned up real nice. Antiques and oriental rugs adorn the bright rooms, many of which boast bay windows, fireplaces, and kitchenettes (if you can't picture it, check out the inn's website, www.inn1890.com, which offers one of the most complete room-by-room virtual tours I've ever seen). Other creature comforts include bathrobes and slippers, TVs, daily continental breakfast, a sunny private patio, and health club privileges.

Nickie's BBQ
460 Haight St.
415-621-6508

Freight and Salvage
111 Addison St.,
Berkeley
510-548-1761

The Red Victorian Bed and Breakfast
1665 Haight St.
415-864-1978

Herb'n Inn
525 Ashbury St.
415-553-8542

Inn 1890
1890 Page St.
415-386-0486

Fitness Freaks

Anyone who lives here knows that just going from your office to your car can be more exercise than most people get in a week. We live in a giant, natural gymnasium, where getting from Point A to Point B inevitably involves navigating up and down steep hills. Most people, rather than replace their clutch every few months, opt to hoof it, bike it, skate it, or public transport it (which can entail a bizarre sort of standing, balancing, stretching yoga exercise of its own). So with all these inadvertent workouts, a lot of us feel like we don't really need to do a whole lot more—that is, until Mr. or Ms. Gym Rat shows up at our door with weights in hand, sweating and panting from having just jogged in from the airport. And there we are at 11 a.m., still in robe and slippers, pint of Ben and Jerry's in hand, and the queasy look of the unmotivated on our faces. Best

Mount Davidson
off Portola Drive via
Teresita and Myra
Way

**Glen Park
Canyon**
just off
O'Shaughnessy at
Bosworth

strategy: suck in the gut, strap on the old Nikes, and show them what those 43 hills are really made of.

MORNING–NOON

There are more places to hike in San Francisco than you can shake one of those fancy walking sticks at—and they're not all in Golden Gate Park. After your breakfast of champions (heavy sweaters don't do fattening, lethargy-inducing brunchy-brunchy, remember?), pack up a couple of Clif Bars and go climb the city.

If you can set aside your religious beliefs (or, perhaps, embrace them), the hike up **Mount Davidson** is truly inspirational and a good aerobic workout. The trail to the summit is best reached off of Portola Drive (take Teresita to the intersection of Myra Way and Sherwood Court). From here, a wide path leads up the mountain. At 938 feet, this is the highest peak in San Francisco, and though others offer more flashy bay and ocean views, when you get to the top of Mount Davidson you really feel like you've climbed right through the marine layer to the top of the world. Though you may have mixed feelings about the 100-foot concrete cross that pierces this wooded mountaintop, walk to the base of it and look straight up. The sheer bulk and size of the thing is quite awesome and humbling—it's easy to see why putting crosses on mountaintops has been common practice for conversion-happy padres over the centuries.

I have to admit I'm a bit partial to **Glen Park Canyon**, since I live nearby, but honestly this is one of those rare places where you feel like you're in the country, in the middle of the city. Glen Canyon was the spark that set off the local environmental movement back in the '70s, when developers threatened to pave over the green hills, free-flowing creek, and craggy buttes. The fight goes on: as recently as 1997, park preservationists won a battle to keep cars out of the canyon.

Start off your trek with a leisurely stroll across the grassy fields, past the softball diamonds, to the clubhouse. Just behind the rec center, you can pick up the path that leads through the canyon. Follow the bouncing-ball-chasing dogs down the dirt trail until you reach the bridge, under which a rare natural creek trickles during the winter, spring, and sometimes even through the summer months. It's a picturesque little habitat that residents have lovingly restored with native plants. From here you can hike your way up the sides of the canyon, scaling the various rock formations for different overviews of the terrain. Any one of these vista points makes a great sun-and-snack stop.

For serious weekend warriors or aspiring decathletes, **Lake Merced** has it all. Start by jogging, rollerblading, or biking around the lake (approximately five miles). Next, rent a rowboat for a strenuous sculling exercise amid the shorebirds (watch out for stray tee shots and fly fishermen). Afterward, maybe take in nine holes of golf at the newly revamped Harding Park links or a little windsurfing on the lake (all-equipment-included beginners lessons are offered).

No law says sightseeing can't be part of a training regimen. So rather than run the bleachers at Kezar, do a thigh-burner up and down the city's secret stairways, where hidden San Francisco reveals itself in hillside cottages clambering with rambling roses and ivy, magical keyhole views, and neoclassical sculpture. The granddaddy of stairway walks is of course the **Filbert Street Steps** (see the Virgins tour) which, with fitness fiends, should be done from the bottom of Sansome Street, up.

In the Upper Market area there are the wonderful **Vulcan Stairs**, located at the end of Ord Street, off 17th Street. This tiny byway invariably produces a chronic case of address envy among both residents and tourists. Tucked along the steps are sweet little cottages with flower gardens and cobblestone terraces that should, by all rights, be up in Sonoma or along some sleepy country lane. The serenity of this spot may even cause your endorphin-loving friend to take a breather. Not a problem; he can finish his set on the staircase located just a few blocks higher, on the equally pretty Upper Terrace Street.

Just a stone's throw away, the steep **Pemberton Steps** probably offers the best balance of calorie burn to scenic rewards. They begin at the curve of Clayton Street right before Corbett and climb 20 feet up a brick stairway, at which point car noise and urban angst fade into the leafy overgrowth. By the time you reach the first cross street (Villa Terrace) you'll find yourself wondering if this hilly perch has always been here or if it magically appears like Brigadoon whenever the planets align just right. On the next flight, the steps become mossy and cobbled, and the gardens better tended and more elaborate. You can turn around now for a show-stopping vista or save it for the top (Corona Terrace), where geranium pots spill over the sides of balconies that seem straight out of *Under the Tuscan Sun*. (If you or your friends are feeling particularly ambitious, wend your way south and climb all the way to the Twin Peaks parking lot.)

The **Pacheco Street Stairs**, which begin at the bottom of Pacheco Street or the top of Mendosa (depending on which end you start at), win the award for longest set and are a guaranteed thigh burner. They're also a great sight-seeing jaunt, located in the district of Forest Hill, one of the least-known ritzy neighborhoods in the city. Forest Hill is almost like a separate village (up until about 15 years ago, the residents paved their own streets). The stairs are actually divided into three sets: from the top, the first one starts at Mendosa and goes down to Santa Rita; from here you jog around the bend and catch the next set at Ninth Avenue and Castenada; and the third tier goes from Castenada to Magellan on Pacheco. On your descent, you'll get a residen-tial-architectural eyeful—modern Tudors next to Maybeckian shingle-styles, next to modern neoclassical mansions, abutting Mother Goose houses. From the bottom, if your knees are still intact, head down to West Portal Avenue for some nonfat frozen yogurt at **Double Rainbow** or **Shaw's** (now there's a blast from the past), or a shot of liquid energy at **Peet's Coffee**.

The majestic **Lyon Street Steps**, located at the western end of Broadway, rival Filbert Street for spectacular panoramic vistas. From the top you gaze down upon the Palace of Fine Arts, the Marina, and the bay all the way to Alcatraz. For maximum ooh and aah effect, start at the bottom, run to the top, and don't turn around till you get there. The pretty flower boxes, statuary, and cameo celebrity appearances along the way should keep you distracted.

Out of the city, my favorite coastal places to hike with tourists are the Palomarin Trail to the waterfall on the beach at **Point Reyes National Seashore**, a singularly spectacular combination of surf and turf with a freshwater swimming lake thrown in for good measure (about five-and-a-half

miles); the ever-popular **Tennessee Valley Trail** to the beach, a short jaunt (if you don't take any strenuous detours) that leads to a sweet little beach/cove with panoramic views of the Pacific; and the **Point Bonita Lighthouse** trail, a stunning (if brief) path that takes you along steep ocean cliffs to a working lighthouse, which sits on a point on the edge of the earth. The park service regularly schedules evening and full-moon walks out to the lighthouse (a photographer's dream come true), but reservations are required; call 415-331-1540.

Beer lovers and woodsy types should not miss the trail at the top of Muir Woods that begins at the **Tourist Club**, a hidden gem of Old World hospitality in the form of a Bavarian chalet that offers overnight accommodation, German wurst and beers on tap, and outdoor tables that look out over the redwood groves and the horizon (for a real *oom pa pa* experience, come during one of the festivals in June, around Labor Day, or in October, when the lederhosen and polka dancers are out in full force). A great medium-level loop hike goes from here down to Muir Woods, up the Dipsea Steps, and along the Sun Trail back to the club, where you can soothe your sore limbs with a cold lager (or three).

Pedal Power

So, okay, motorists and politicos aren't so crazy about this event, but how better to give your out-of-town exercise hound a Tour d'EssEff than by riding in **Critical Mass**, held the last Friday of every month beginning at 5:30 p.m. at the Embarcadero BART station at the foot of Market Street. The organizers' motto—"promoting pedaling, not petroleum"—is really just the tip of the iceberg. Critical Mass is about free-spiritedness and grassroots activism, two of the fundamental principles that San Francisco was founded on. From stockbrokers to bike messengers to the guy whose dog stands behind him on his bike seat with its paws on his shoulders, there's no better way to experience the diversity of this wacky town. It's also a great way to see the city and get a little exercise while you're at it. Routes are made known on the day of the ride, so just go with the flow and see where you end up.

As far as recreational biking in the city goes—why mess with tradition? I'm not a huge biker, but I have tried to steer my two-wheeler down Valencia Street in traffic, and frankly, it ain't no fun. Anyway, out-of-towners want to see something besides asphalt and cars while they sweat up those hills. To my mind, the two best routes for your money are still Golden Gate Park to Ocean Beach and along the Great Highway bike path 'til it ends. If you want to extend that trek, stay on the Great Highway past Fort Funston until it curves around and drops you off at Lake Merced, where you can continue for another five miles before heading home.

The most scenic trip is, of course, the ride across the Golden Gate Bridge, which you can begin in the Presidio, on the Golden Gate Promenade in the Marina, in Fisherman's Wharf, or in the bridge's south parking lot if you're feeling wimpy. My choice is usually Fisherman's Wharf, because it allows you the option of taking the ferry back. After you make your way carefully across the bridge's west side (make sure to warn novices about scary speeding bikers; a shove in the wrong direction can launch you into oncoming traffic), head down the road past Fort Baker into Sausalito. Toodle along Bridgeway to the end of town (stopping for snapshots and souvenirs along the way), and hook up with the jogging/bicycling path that skirts the Mill Valley waterfront. Follow the trail to the Tiburon/East Blithedale overpass and take the bike path all the way to Tiburon. Park your bike and enjoy a well-earned seafood salad and cold beverage at **Sam's**. After you've knocked back a few, you'll be glad that all you have to do is walk your bike onto the ferry and let the sag wagon take you home. (If your friends are renting bikes and attempting to explore on their own,

Point Reyes National Seashore
Hwy. 1 to Olema-Bolinas Road
415-464-5100

Tennessee Valley Trail
Take Highway 101 to the Highway 1/Stinson Beach exit; turn left at fruit stand

Point Bonita Lighthouse
take the Alexander Ave. exit off Highway 101, go through the tunnel toward Rodeo Beach, then turn left at the Marin Headlands Center.

Tourist Club
30 Ridge Ave., Mill Valley
415-388-9987, look for the hand-carved sign on Panoramic Hwy, a couple miles past the Muir Beach turnoff.

Critical Mass
last Friday each month, 5:30 p.m., Justin Herman Plaza, Embarcadero at Market St.

Sam's
27 Main St., Tiburon
415-435-4527

steer them to **Blazing Saddles**, which rents bikes equipped with a map holder and a computer navigation system that tells you your mileage, what the best routes are, and what to see along the way).

Mountain Biking on Mount Tamalpais

Marin County is generally acknowledged as the cradle of mountain biking civilization, and most serious mountain bikers already know about the most popular trails, and probably the obscure ones, too. But if you're only spurred to occasional action by a visit from your fanatical two-wheeling friends, you might want to have the following route up your arsenal.

Bike trails crisscross **Mount Tamalpais State Park** (often to the chagrin of hikers), and many of them lead to Old Railroad Grade. You can pick up the grade at any number of spots, depending on how far you want to go. If you're feeling ambitious, start in Mill Valley off West

Blithedale Avenue. If not, drive up Summit Avenue and park at the end (about halfway up the mountain). The steady, not-too-steep climb follows the old Mount Tam railway tracks. About a mile-and-a-half from the summit of the East Peak is **West Point Inn**, a rustic log cabin built in 1904 that's accessible only to hikers and bikers. Take a break here for a pancake breakfast (available weekend mornings throughout the summer) or a PowerBar and a fresh lemonade before making your way to the top and a rewarding view of the Marin coastline all the way to the Pacific. Once you've reached the peak, there's a snack bar with more substantial items such as hot dogs and bagels with cream cheese. If you're lucky they'll have frozen fruit bars (ask for them; they're not on the menu).

Option two is to make a weekend out of it and stay the night at the West Point Inn. If fitness-dude/dudette happens to be here in June, get up in the morning and hike down the Bootjack Trail to the **Mountain Theater**, where they present old Broadway musicals such as *South Pacific* and *Guys and Dolls* on weekends. Finish off the day with a cold one on the deck overlooking the world at the **Mountain Home Inn**.

Points North and South

South of the city, you can't beat **Crystal Springs Reservoir** for a pleasant, picturesque little jaunt on foot or on two wheels. The biking/jogging path starts at the gate just off the Highway 92 West exit (going toward Half Moon Bay). Though you might have to dodge joggers, the nice, flat path takes you along the reservoir through a lovely wooded area and up to the dam where you can hook up with the trail that goes over Skyline Boulevard.

The granddaddy of all-inclusive combo recreational/ sightseeing areas near town is probably **Angel Island State Park**, where you can mountain bike, hike, or kayak while soaking up some truly amazing views of the city from the sheltered beachhead. The best part for out-of-towners is that you don't have to bring anything with you except your stamina. There's a bicycle and sea kayak rental shop on the island (kayakers can paddle on their own or take a guided tour with Sea Trek) and a snack bar. Catch the Angel Island Ferry from Tiburon, and don't miss the last boat back to the mainland, or you'll be camping out for the night (if it's any compensation, the campsites are pretty nice).

Wine Country

Touring wineries on bicycles is a guilt-free way to indulge, because whatever calories you gain drinking and noshing, you lose biking to the next stop. My suggestion is to steer clear of Highway 29 and the Silverado Trail—basically avoid the Napa Valley entirely. There's nothing that'll kill your buzz quicker than the sight of a Lincoln Town Car weaving its way at full tilt down the road you're pedaling on. Instead, head to the less-trafficked, more pastoral confines of Sonoma County, specifically the nice, flat, wide Dry Creek Valley. Park the car in Healdsburg, so later you can come back and hang out in the park, explore the shops, or eat

Blazing Saddles
1095 Columbus Ave.
415-202-8888

Mount Tamalpais State Park
take Highway 101 to Stinson Beach exit, follow the signs to Muir Woods
415-388-2070

West Point Inn
1000 Panoramic Hwy., Mt. Tamalpais
415-388-9955

Mountain Theater
Mount Tamalpais State Park
415-383-1100

Mountain Home Inn
810 Panoramic Hwy., Mill Valley
415-381-9000

Crystal Springs Reservoir
off Hwy. 280 at Hwy. 92 West

Angel Island State Park
415-435-1915, ferry info: 415-435-2131

dinner at one of the charming restaurants around the old town square. Dry Creek Road starts at Healdsburg Avenue, and you can pretty much stay on it until you get tired or too drunk. Turn off at Lambert Bridge Road to West Dry Creek Road to make a loop of approximately fourteen miles. On the way, you'll run into about six wineries, including the outstanding **Pezzi King** and **Kendall-Jackson**.

Another nice, easy course is through the Sonoma town center, a pretty self-explanatory route—just follow the signs to the nearby wineries (Gundlach-Bundschu, Ravenswood, Sebastiani, and Buena Vista are all nearby). Of course, if you're up here already and you're a health nut, you can't really stay anywhere but the **Fairmont Sonoma Mission Inn**, where you can massage, Jacuzzi, aromatherapy, and lounge your aching muscles by a natural hot spring pool while dining on lowfat spa cuisine (see Big Spenders).

More Recreating

Sure, you can stand on the shore and gaze out at the bay like a normal person, or you can jump in and see the surf up close and personal with the weathered veterans of the **Dolphin Club**. It may not be the cleanest water around, but

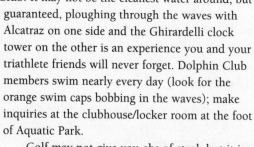

guaranteed, ploughing through the waves with Alcatraz on one side and the Ghirardelli clock tower on the other is an experience you and your triathlete friends will never forget. Dolphin Club members swim nearly every day (look for the orange swim caps bobbing in the waves); make inquiries at the clubhouse/locker room at the foot of Aquatic Park.

Golf may not give you abs of steel, but it is a nice way to spend a sunny afternoon. And at least here in the Bay Area, walking the course can double as a sightseeing excursion, particularly at the **Lincoln Park Golf Course**. Tell your friends to bring their cameras for the photo ops at the thirteenth and seventeenth holes.

Rollerblading became the mountain biking of the '90s, and while its popularity has waned in other places, it's still going strong here. My rollerblading friends recommend the

Marina Green and Promenade and Golden Gate Park as best blading terrain (advanced skaters will want to try the obstacle course located next to the Conservatory of Flowers off JFK Drive in the park on Sundays). You can rent blades at **Skates on Haight**. If you feel like combining exercise with a little socializing, join the party thrown every Friday night by the **Midnight Rollers**, a large, impromptu group headed up for the last 25 years by Golden Gate Park skate godfather, David "D" Miles. The group meets around 8 p.m. at the plaza across from the Ferry Building and skates 12.5 miles through the city—from Fisherman's Wharf and Cow Hollow, through the Broadway Tunnel and Chinatown, down to Union Square and back to the Embarcadero.

There are hundreds of places where people do this for real, but if you don't have time for Class 5 training on actual rocks and yet you have a hankering to rappel down a steep wall, **Mission Cliffs** is a great way to spend a strenuous afternoon. This indoor rock-climbing gym looks like some kind of set for Cirque du Soleil: dozens of people hang on ropes at various levels, clinging to the sides of a fifty-foot wall which is covered with colorful loops, toeholds, and niches. Some are practicing for an ascent on El Capitan; others are just doing it for grins. Drop-in beginner classes are offered daily; they provide instruction and all the equipment. The gym's location, at 19th and Harrison, is not exactly common tourist stomping grounds, but you're not far from **La Cumbre** and **La Taqueria**, two of the Mission district's best burrito joints (hey—athletes need to carbo load).

NIGHT

News flash: Dancing counts as exercise (the accompanying twelve-ounce curls are pushing it). For the maximum sweatfest, the 11th Street corridor still holds court with stalwarts **DNA** and **Paradise Lounge** both offering nightly DJ dancing. Paradise, revamped since its days as a live-music and spoken-word venue, features a 600-person dance floor down below and two smaller lounges upstairs, where you can sip a bubbly water and survey the scene. DNA, a club that came of age in

Pezzi King
3805 Lambert
Bridge Road,
Healdsburg
707-431-9388

Kendall-Jackson
337 Healdsburg
Ave., Healdsburg
707-433-7102

**Fairmont
Sonoma
Mission Inn**
100 Boyes Blvd.,
Sonoma
707-938-9000

Dolphin Club
at the foot of
Hyde St.
415-441-9329

**Lincoln Park
Golf Course**
300 34th Ave.
415-221-9911

Marina Green
Marina Blvd.,
between Fillmore
and Lyon streets

**Skates on
Haight**
1818 Haight St.
415-752-8375

Midnight Rollers
415-752-1967

Mission Cliffs
2295 Harrison St.
415-550-0515

La Cumbre
515 Valencia St.
415-863-8205

La Taqueria
2889 Mission St.
415-285-7117

DNA Lounge
375 11th St.
415-626-1409

Paradise Lounge
1501 Folsom St.
415-621-1912

the '80s and closed briefly in the late '90s, has come back with a vengeance in the 21st century, as popular with the young het set as it ever was. Video screens and internet kiosks augment the dance floor, which varies between live and DJ acts. Upstairs, there's a slightly lower-decibel lounge scene for taking a breather.

One of the silliest, yet strangely alluring, phenomena to come along in the last few years is the video dance pad. For a few coins, contestants (you can compete with others or "play" against yourself) stand on a pad lit with arrows and try to match moves with a video screen, while keeping the beat. It's not easy, and from an observer's standpoint it looks a bit like Devo in an aerobic step class without the haz-mat suits, but if you've got enough change, you will definitely get a major workout (and probably have some Japanese tech-pop song running through your head for the next few months). Try the one in **Metreon** (it's upstairs in Portal One, the center's game room); that way if you get bored or embarrassed, you can say you were just waiting for a Hyperbowl alley to open up.

GYM JUNKIES

Despite all the refreshing, outdoor ways to get your endorphin highs, some freaks, er folks, need that sweaty locker room smell to make them feel legit. Most decent hotels have fitness rooms these days, and if they don't, they have an arrangement with a local health club (day-use fees average $10-$20). But if you want to combine their workout with an only-in-SF experience, head to **Gorilla Sports**, inside the old Alhambra art deco movie palace on Russian Hill (2330 Polk, 415-292-5444). In lesser towns the theater would have been scrapped for more elliptical-trainer space, but here in culturally enlightened San Francisco, they not only left the silver screen intact, they built the gym around it and now present feature films to distraction-starved fitness buffs on the main floor. There are different themes each week; bring a headset if you want the soundtrack.

Combining healthy living with a Mission hipster bar scene seems like a contradiction in terms, but at the **22 02 Oxygen Bar**, you can inhale and imbibe all you want and not worry about hangovers or weight gain. Pure oxygen is the only thing on-tap at this bar, and for $10 to $25 (depending on the length of your session) you can sit and enjoy aromatically endowed hyper-oxygenated air through a nasal tube while sipping an herbal elixir pumped up with natural stimulants such as ginseng, St. John's Wort, and white peony. Admittedly, the set-up sounds like a place that would attract its fair share of Star Wars geeks, but surprisingly, the scene is pure Mission—nose rings, tattoos, henna hands, and all.

WHERE TO STAY

Perhaps the best reciprocal hotel/gym deal in town is through the **Harbor Court Hotel** and the **Hotel Griffon**, both adorable little boutique properties located on the Embarcadero waterfront that offer complimentary guest use of the next-door **Embarcadero YMCA**, a plush facility with all the latest machines and equipment, plus a regulation swimming pool, racquetball courts, Jacuzzi, steam, and sauna. After working out their issues on the Stairmaster (issues like, why they have to stay in a hotel when you have a perfectly good sofa), your friends can sip a well-deserved glass of chardonnay or a sake cocktail and nibble on sushi and salmon tartare with seaweed salad at the Franco-Japanese **Chaya Brasserie**.

    Nob Hill Lambourne is the place to put up your fitness-obsessed executive type. Each room comes equipped with a "balancing basket" of dumbbells, bottled water, energy bars, beta-carotene tabs, and a yoga mat, and if he/she is feeling really reclusive (or is recovering from a face-lift), the accompanying yoga lesson, along with the follow-up massage, can be performed within the privacy of their room (more social types might want to opt for the nearby Club One inside the Fairmont Hotel).

Metreon
101 4th St.
800-METREON

22 O2 Oxygen Bar
795 Valencia St.
415-255-2102

Harbor Court Hotel
165 Steuart St.
415-882-1300

Hotel Griffon
155 Steuart St.
415-495-2100

Embarcadero YMCA
169 Steuart St.
415-957-9622

Chaya Brasserie
132 The Embarcadero
415-777-8688

Nob Hill Lambourne
725 Pine St.
415-433-2287

tour 17 Big Spenders

San Francisco is no stranger to the nouveau riche, or to the plain old filthy rich for that matter. Ever since the Gold Rush made mansion owners out of former tent dwellers, we've had places that cater to folks who want to indulge in—and can afford—the finer things.

But even if your pocketbook isn't heavily padded, the moment may come when you find your-

self staring at the business end of a menu at Masa's, or lingering over a 'for sale' sign in front of a Victorian pied-à-terre and you're suddenly overwhelmed by the urge to splurge. (Hey, we weren't voted "most likely to live beyond our means" for nothing!)

It's a common malady: Yuppies, tight-fisted yummies (young urban millionaires), guppies (gay upwardly mobile professionals), even Sics with

Above the West Ballooning
800-627-2759

San Francisco Seaplane Tours
Stinson Beach/Mill Valley exit off Highway 101, or Pier 39
415-332-4843

Tweenies (single income with children ages 5-12) all eventually come to the realization that there are pleasures to be had in Baghdad by the Bay that are worth maxing out the credit card for, extravagances that make blowing the college fund seem like a reasonable trade-off, and luxuries that cause you to hesitate for a split-second before shouting, "What the hell!"

These places are for those moments.

MORNING

You've seen it on the Travel Channel, you've read about it in guidebooks, and be honest—you've always wanted to try it, so why not use your Big Dealio friends as an excuse to hop in a hot-air balloon and float over Napa Valley? The only downside is that you'll have to get up and hightail it to **Above the West Ballooning** in Yountville by the crack of dawn. (If your friends are staying in a downtown or Wharf hotel, shuttle service may be available.) Once you're there, however, it's smooth sailing—from the pre-flight refreshments to the post-flight champagne brunch in a private vineyard. As you soar over hill, dale, and endless rows of golden grapevines, you can pretend you're Phileas Fogg—or even better, Steve Fossett, the non-fictional character who keeps trying to fly a balloon solo around the world.

Closer to home, for about $170, you can fly over the Golden Gate Bridge and the Pacific coastline while sipping champagne in a private seaplane. **San Francisco Seaplane Tours** take off from the Bay at Pier 39 or the Sausalito/Tiburon harbor. Then, depending on which tour you've chosen, you'll either fly over both bridges, Muir Woods, and Crissy Field, landing near Treasure Island, or head down the Headlands coastline along the Financial District, over Angel and Alcatraz Islands, and back to Tiburon. If you balk at the price, keep in mind that unlike the jumbo jet you flew in on, a seaplane allows you to stay (relatively) low to the ground, affording a genuine bird's-eye-view of land and sea.

There are bay cruises, and then there are Bay Cruises. If you've got the cash to spare, forget the ferries and the party boats, head to **Rendezvous Charters** on Pier 40 and reserve a day on the *Yukon Jack*, the yacht that won the San Francisco to Tahiti race in 1995. Handmade by famous boatbuilder Bill Lee, the sailboat's interior is crafted from hand-rubbed teak and contains a below-deck dining area with sea-level views. There's also a full navigation station, but you'll probably want to leave the driving to the crew; it's hard enough work keeping up appearances for envious shore-dwellers.

Okay, it's not exactly sightseeing, but you will get a new perspective on yourself and the city when the Big Flaming

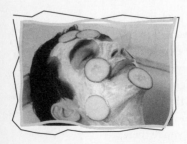

Entourage from **Guerilla Makeovers** gives you a top-to-bottom Mega Overhaul. Similar in concept to "Queer Eye for the Straight Guy" (only without the cameras or the budget), the sassy crew behind Guerilla will take you from fashion boutique to hair salon, leaving one-liners and the frumpy old you in their wake. A five-hour overhaul with a cast of three experts, which includes hair cut and style, new eyewear, grooming/cosmetic products, and a new outfit with shoes, runs around $349 (plus the price of all the products, services, and clothing). A tad steep, *fer sher*, but then, what price beauty?

NOON

What else are vacations for if not to treat yourself to the kind of indulgence you would never consider at home? When money's really no object....

Take Me Out to the Ballgame

I'm the first one to admit going to a Giants' game is no bargain anymore. Between the $15 parking spots, $12 bleacher seats, and $7 beers, you could easily drop a C-note before the first inning. But if you can just accept that SBC Park is not the Candlestick days of yore (thank goodness), then going the extra mile and spending another $110 with **Giants Scoreboard Messages** to put, "Bonnie: Happy 29th birthday . . . again" on the big electronic scoreboard won't seem painful at all. And heck, if you're going that far, why not throw a few thousand more into the pile and rent a field-level luxury suite behind home plate, with leather couches, a wet bar, TVs, and room service? (And if you've gone completely off the deep end, you can even rent out the whole stadium for around $100,000).

In-spa-ration

Day spas offer everything from quickie lunch-hour de-stress sessions to full days of pampering that leave you feeling like a well-coiffed wet noodle. For the latter treatment (c'mon, what's the point in skimping?) head to Nob Hill Spa or 77 Maiden Lane.

The view from **Nob Hill Spa**, located next to the Huntington Hotel, is probably worth the price of admission alone, but imagine gazing out over the downtown skyline to the Bay while soaking in a whirlpool after a hot-stone massage and plant-extract exfoliation. If money is no object, go for the all-day Longevity package ($550), which begins with a ritual involving tea tree cleanser and a detoxifying clay body mask, followed by massage, body therapy, facial, hand and foot treatments, and lunch.

The clientele at **77 Maiden Lane** are the sort who keep a private masseur on retainer, but come here when they want the full treatment—hair to toenails. Sherlee Rhine's salon and spa is a popular pre-wedding and pre-Oscars stop, but even if you're not practicing an acceptance speech, you can get done up in style with the Deluxe Day Package ($474), which begins with an hour massage and a loofah salt glow, followed by a deep-cleansing facial, manicure with a hand treatment, aromatic pedicure, lunch, scalp treatment, shampoo, blow dry, and makeup application.

Up in Wine Country, the official spa capital of Northern California, there are few places old or new that can compete with the **Fairmont Sonoma Mission Inn**. For one thing, the century-old resort, completely renovated a few years ago

Rendezvous Charters
Pier 40
415-543-7333

Guerilla Makeovers
866-293-7895,
guerillamakeovers.com

Giants Scoreboard Messages
SBC Park,
King St. at 3rd
415-972-2000, suite rentals: 415-972-2252

Nob Hill Spa
1075 California St.
415-474-5400

77 Maiden Lane
77 Maiden Lane
415-391-7777

Fairmont Sonoma Mission Inn
Highway 12 at
Boyes Blvd., Sonoma
707-938-4250

and now part of the Fairmont chain, comes with its own superheated natural hot spring, which the spa uses to full advantage. Treatments here usually begin with the "bathing ritual": An exfoliating shower (thermal mineral shower gel combined with skin-pummeling water pressure), a soak in two mineral pools, followed by an herbal steam, dry sauna, cool shower, and a rest in a reclining lounge chair. And that's all before your first spa treatment! I did this ritual a couple of years ago and was so relaxed by the time I got out of the shower that I fell asleep in the lounge chair. Almost

missed my Harvest Kur, which would have been a tragedy, because it's among the most unusual spa services I've ever had. First, there's the exfoliation using a grapeseed scrub; then the immersion in a grapeseed oil-infused bubble bath, then a grapeseed mud bodywrap, and a massage using— you guessed it—grapeseed oil. (Note to Mormons and teetotalers: this is as close to drinking wine as you can get without actually tipping a glass).

If tipping a glass or two still sounds appealing after a day of serious relaxation and cash outlay, take Oakville Grade over the Mayacamas Mountains to **Opus One**, the last word in high-end winetasting. A joint venture between wine royals Robert Mondavi and Baroness Philippine de Rothschild, Opus One produces one premium red-wine meritage every year, with a price tag that ranges from $120 to about $350 depending on age, quality, and rarity. Is it worth it? You be the judge—it's $25-a-pop just to sample this nectar of the gods, but for some, that might be all they need to feel they've had a taste of the good life.

Retail Therapy

There's nothing like a little shopping spree to stimulate the economy. If your friends come from a place where haute couture is interpreted as something you need to blow on before putting in your mouth, send them to **Colleen Quen**, **Lily Samii**, or **Jin Wang**.

Quen is the belle of the high-society ball, designing stunning sculptural gowns with mermaid trains and tulip hems, flower-petal collars and Morticia Adams silhouettes, in colors and fabrics that are both brilliantly eye-catching and smolderingly subtle. Each of her cocktail dresses and evening gowns is custom designed, beginning with 36 measurements that ensure the creation will be fitted exactly to your body contours. Quen then sketches her ideas to life before committing them to fabric. The whole process takes about two months.

For a slightly less dramatic look that works for mother of the bride as well as debutante, book an appointment at Lily Samii. Samii's couture dresses are colorful confections: strapless crimson gowns trimmed with bouquets of roses; fanciful beaded and bejeweled creations; off-the-shoulder asymmetrical gowns in lemon-yellow silk or ice-blue satin. Her collection includes a small off-the-rack selection as well as custom couture, with prices ranging from the high hundreds to several thousand.

Though she's no relation to Vera, Jin Wang's custom wedding and evening dresses have similar cachet, making her one of the busiest dressmakers in town. Wang's designs are characterized by clean, elegant lines: strapless fitted bodices with sweeping low backs and just enough swirl to give them glamour.

Men can satisfy their couture yen with a trip down to **Loro Piana**, the Italian family whose cashmere products are legendary on both sides of the ocean. Their recently opened Union Square boutique sells outerwear, wraps, and scarves, and they have a private salon that makes custom men's suits (if you have to ask about the price, you can't afford it).

If you want to buy the chickens, but not the farm, scour the ready-to-wear collections at **Escada** (dresses start at $1000 and run up to $12,000 for a one-of-a-kind gown); **Yves Saint Laurent** ($500 to $5000—a Mombasa handbag will run you about $800); **Max Nugus** (couture daywear suits $1200 to $2500, evening gowns $1800 to $5000—and you'll need an appointment); and **Christian Dior** (anywhere from $600 for a cardigan, to a couple thousand for a dress).

Opus One
7900 St. Helena Highway, Oakville
707-944-9442

Colleen Quen Couture
142 Russ St., Suite 5
415-551-0013

Lily Samii
260 Stockton St., 4th floor
415-445-9505

Jin Wang
111 Maiden Lane
415-397-9111

Loro Piana
212 Stockton St.
415-593-3303

Escada
259 Post St.
415-391-3500

Yves St. Laurent
166 Maiden Lane
415-837-1211

Max Nugus
537 Sutter St.
415-956-6469

Christian Dior
216 Stockton St.
415-544-0394

Accessories

As Imelda Marcos might have said, the decadence is in the details:

April in Paris—French-born designer Beatrice Amblard, who once crafted goods for Hermès, now makes stylish custom handbags from calfskin, java lizard, ostrich, alligator, and other exotic skins in her shop in the Richmond District. The one-of-a-kind purses—classic shapes with fitted over-flaps and 18-karat jeweler clasps—are coveted by an ever-growing legion of high-society devotees.

Paul's Hat Works—At this small, unassuming hattery in the nether regions of the Outer Richmond, master craftsman Michael Harris creates some of the world's finest Panama Montecristi straw hats from "fino" bodies woven in Ecuador. The shop, which has been here since 1912, still uses 19th-century tools to finish and shape each Panama by hand; the result is a $500 hat that feels like silk and will last several lifetimes.

Aftelier—Mandy Aftel, former literary therapist and muse, creates custom perfumes from rare essential oils and distilled natural essences that have attracted the noses of celebs ranging from Kate Hudson and Donovan Leitch, to composer Leonard Cohen. A scent with your name on it will run you about $600.

Judith Ripka—Ripka made fashion headlines in 1997 when she designed the 18-karat pin worn by Hillary Clinton during Bill's inauguration. Known for weighty gold, platinum, and silver neck-laces accented with gemstones, toggle-clasp bracelets, and architectural diamond-and-gold rings, Ripka's commemorative pins for causes such as breast cancer and AIDS are popular with Oprah and of course, San Francisco's always-vigilant PC set.

Tiffany & Co.—Nothing tells people what circles you run in better than a telltale little blue box tied up with white ribbon from Tiffany. An Elsa Peretti pendant will run you about $350, Paloma Picasso earrings $1,500, and a silver baby spoon around $100.

Cartier—Even if you're waiting for your trust fund to kick in before buying that Rolling ring, there's no harm in trying it on. And there's always lay-away . . .

NIGHT

Sure, you could go to see a movie down at the multiplex. Or you could rent Francis Ford Coppola's private screening room for a viewing of *The Godfather* they'll never forget. The small basement movie theater is located in the historic Sentinel Building, the green flatiron tower where Coppola headquarters his **American Zoetrope** production studios and *Zoetrope: All-Story*, his fiction magazine—reason enough to spend a few hundred bucks on 11 of your best friends. Add to the cachet that the Deco screening room is also the site where the Kingston Trio and the Grateful Dead recorded seminal albums and where Martin Sheen recorded voice-overs for *Apocalypse Now,* and now how much would you pay? Did I mention the $200-an-hour fee includes a projectionist (movie rental and popcorn extra)?

Eating the Nest Egg

In San Francisco, dining out—as opposed to grabbing a bite—has always been a fairly spendy proposition, but if you can look at it as an event rather than just a meal, you won't have as much trouble swallowing the bill at the end of the night.

The French Laundry—If you're reading this after your arrival in San Francisco, you're too late. Chef Thomas Keller's fame stretches across continents, and his waiting list reaches nearly as far: reservations are accepted two months in advance. Of course, maybe the gods will smile upon you and you'll luck into a last-minute cancellation. If you should be so blessed, don't spoil it with monetary concerns. Just get yourself up to Yountville and ask for a menu without prices, because this is truly dinner as theater—an elaborate evening in nine acts that will linger in your memory from the first perfect oyster topped with osetra caviar to the last flourish on the Déclinaison au Chocolat.

April in Paris
55 Clement St.
415-750-9910

Paul's Hat Works
6128 Geary Blvd.
415-221-5332

Aftelier
1442A Walnut St.
#369, Berkeley
510-841-2111

Judith Ripka
110 Geary St.
415-399-1995

Tiffany & Co.
350 Post St.
415-781-7000

Cartier
231 Post St.
415-397-3180

American Zoetrope Studios
Sentinel Building,
916 Kearny St.
415-788-7500

The French Laundry
6640 Washington St., Yountville
707-944-2380

Chez Panisse—On the other side of the bay, charming, homey Chez Panisse continues to dazzle diners well into its fourth decade. Founder Alice Waters, the mother of California cuisine, remains a tireless host to the country's longest running dinner party, as well as a relentless champion of locally grown, environmentally harvested produce, fish, and game. Aside from the prices, nothing about this restaurant has changed much in 30-odd years: there are two seatings and one meal served each evening for the fixed price of $75 (on weekends)—a tad dear, perhaps, but one bite of an heirloom tomato and you'll wonder if you've ever really tasted a tomato before.

Harris' Steakhouse—Nothing says success like a giant slab of red meat, and when the waiter at Harris' arrives at your table with that thick, bone-in New York steak or a plate-dwarfing hunk of prime rib, you'll know you've finally made it. If their 21-day dry-aged beef isn't quite over-the-top enough for you, try the Kobe ribeye, a thick cut of boneless, hand-massaged Japanese beef for $65.

Masa's—Perhaps the most highly touted special-occasion restaurant in San Francisco, the fooderati think nothing of dropping a few hundred dollars for chef Ron Siegel's exquisite contemporary French cuisine. Both the menu and the décor are lighter and less traditional than they were under chef Julian Serrano, but the Masa's experience is as

monumental as it ever was (maybe more so—Siegel is the only American to have ever won Japan's famed Iron Chef competition).

Gary Danko—With five Mobil five-star designations and a James Beard award to his name, Danko can charge just about anything he wants. He doesn't. While prices here are steep ($78 for a five-course prix fixe dinner), they're not ridiculous, though the waiting list for reservations at this 75-seat restaurant can sometimes come close. It'll be worth the wait and every penny after a bite of juniper-crusted venison with caramelized endive and cranberry compote, or the signature roast lobster with black trumpet mushrooms and tarragon. Save room for the cheese course, an elaborate affair involving several carts of artisanal, handmade cheeses from points near and far.

Rubicon—A chance encounter with celebrity owners Robin Williams, Robert de Niro, or Francis Ford Coppola draws many folks with big expense accounts here. Others come because of the reputation of Master Sommelier Larry Stone. While Rubicon is definitely one of the spendiest restaurants in town (several entrees top $30), you'll hardly see a single disgruntled face leaving the place at the end of the night.

WHERE TO STAY

For titanium cardholders, the **Four Seasons** is really the only hotel in San Francisco—an ultra-exclusive sanctuary where hotel guests mingle with owners of the luxury skyrise condos whose residences are on the top floors. Hotel features include 1500-square-foot rooms with floor-to-ceiling windows and marble bathrooms with soaking tubs, a premium health club and spa, private limo service, a beauty salon, a highly rated restaurant, and of course Four Seasons' legendary customer service, for which you'll pay through the nose (and thank them for it later).

If you'd prefer something more private and personal, several hotels offer top-floor suites with all the views and the trimmings. The Mendocino Penthouse Suite at the **Prescott Hotel** is one of my favorites—a sumptuously appointed rooftop apartment with two fireplaces, a dining room with a baby grand piano, and a deck with a hot tub from which you can peer down at the twinkling lights of the city below. If you don't feel like going out (and why would you?), order room service from Postrio downstairs.

Chez Panisse
1517 Shattuck Ave.,
Berkeley
510-548-5525

**Harris'
Steakhouse**
2100 Van Ness Ave.
415-673-1888

Masa's
648 Bush St.
415-989-7154

Gary Danko
800 North Point St.
415-749-2060

Rubicon
558 Sacramento St.
415-434-4100

Four Seasons
757 Market St.
415-633-3000

**The Prescott
Hotel**
545 Post St.
415-563-0303

tour 18   Cheapskates

Even in my starving student days, I always liked to think of myself as reasonable, not cheap. My husband, Pete, the sturdy Scotsman, prefers the term "thrifty." But whatever the euphemism, there's a time  in almost everyone's life when your pocketbook is less padded than your resume, and the magic words are "no cover" and "all-you-can-eat." Cheapskates, as you might guess, don't usually make great houseguests. Chances are they spent their last dime to get to San Francisco, and now they're fully expecting to take advantage of your video store card, your medicine cabinet, and all those other little conveniences they're too poor to purchase, until you drive them (on your precious $2.50-a-gallon gas) to the airport.

There's a positive flipside to the cash-poor guest (and his benevolent twin, the saving-up-for-Europe host), however. It involves taking what I like to call the "Cheapskate Challenge": a leisurely, non-desperate stroll through the city, just for the fun of it, seeing how little you can spend. Anyone—even your rich friends (perhaps especially your rich friends)—can find this game entertaining. So leave your money on the dresser and let the cheap inherit the mirth.

MORNING

A good cheapskates breakfast has a two-to-one ratio of large portions to small change. Usually that means a bacon-slinging, dishwater-coffee-pouring, barstool-at-the-counter kinda diner.

Polk Street Station is a classic of the genre. There's more counter space than table seating. The early-bird special—two eggs, bacon or sausage, and toast—is under $4. They have specials with great-old-diner names like the "Caboose" and the "Pullman" (the owner loves trains—even has a model locomotive set in the window), and the regulars look like they haven't budged from a barstool in 30 years. While the neighborhood around Polk and Pine is a little down on its luck, the atmosphere inside—blue collar shirt-off-my-back hominess—more than makes up for it.

Across town, **Art's Café** (see Grandparents) is a tiny place that in another day might have been referred to as a "greasy spoon." What do you want for $5? Belly up to the counter (there's no table seating) and scarf down heaping plates of eggs, hash browns, and bacon. Your cheapskate friends might even have money left over to feed the parking meter (then again, they're probably saving those quarters for laundry).

If you're willing to expand your idea of breakfast beyond eggs and bacon, **Wing Lee Bakery** on Clement

**Polk Street
Station**
1356 Polk St.
415-776-8899

Art's Café
747 Irving St.
415-665-7440

**Wing Lee
Bakery**
503 Clement St.
415-387-1789

offers an incredible array of really fresh, really cheap dim sum straight from the steamer, oven, and frypan. You can put together a gut-busting platter of har gow (shrimp dumplings), cha sui bow (steamed pork buns), pot stickers, and all manner of vegetarian and meat dumpling combinations for less than $5 (most pieces are 60 cents each or three for $1.20). It's not really a sit-down joint, but there are a few tables for eating inside. Or you can opt for take-out and eat it in the minipark around the corner on 10th Avenue.

Down on the waterfront, where mediocre restaurants have been known to charge $10 for an egg, you can get more bang(ers) for your buck, plus views that rival those at all the fancy schmancy places, at **Red's Java House**, the **Java House**, and the **Eagle Café**. Red's is the real thing (see Neo-Bohemians), a rickety old dive for dockworkers on a break. This is a great place to go after an all-night bender. Most of the regulars here order burgers for breakfast (sometimes

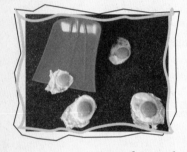

accompanied by a Budweiser), so you won't feel out of place. The prices will warm the cockles of your cheapskate's heart—a full meal for around $4. They might as well be giving it away.

If you want all that gritty, blue-collar atmosphere, but with a few other menu choices, head down the Embarcadero to the Java House on Pier 40. Another old waterfront stalwart (since 1912), the crowd—a mixture of tugboat operators, pier hands, South Beach sailboat owners, pre-game partyers, and yuppies from nearby condo complexes—come here for the three-egg omelets and pancake stacks, which you order at the counter and pick up when they yell. Prices are only about 50 cents more than at Red's, and the view of the South Beach harbor and the bay is, of course, free.

Eagle Café is one of those rare convergences of cheap, authentic and touristy, a turn-of-the-20th-century bar and café with a wooden counter and well-worn stools that was once a favorite hangout of longshoremen and literati. The developers of Pier 39 saved it from the wrecking ball by picking it up lock, stock, and barrel and depositing it on the second level of the complex. Here, you can still get a Bloody

Mary and bacon 'n' eggs breakfast without having to break a $20. After you're done soaking up the Alcatraz views through the large bay windows, you can learn a little something about local waterfront history—gratis—courtesy of the photos and memorabilia posted on the walls.

Where the Air(waves) Are Free

If time flies like an arrow, Internet time flies like one of those bullets in the movie *The Matrix*. When I wrote the last edition of this book, I could only find a handful of places— cafés, hotels, copy shops—that even had public Internet access. Today, they're everywhere, and you don't even need to anchor yourself to an electrical outlet. For cheapskates, the key of course is not finding the cafés with wireless access, but finding ones that don't charge you by the minute (or optionally, where you can freeload off someone else's connection), as well as where you can sit all morning nursing a single cup of coffee or tea and eat/look at/listen to something interesting while you're doing it. Here are some spots where you can nosh and surf and never drop more than the change you grabbed from your friend's ashtray.

Mario's Bohemian Cigar Store—A locale right at the corner of Washington Square Park in North Beach makes this a four-and-a-half-star freebie (there's an official, paid wifi connection, but you can glom onto a free one); the focaccia sandwiches and pints of Anchor Steam bump it up to five.

Caffè Roma—At this iconic North Beach coffeehouse, you can sit and sip exquisitely house-roasted coffee and surf all morning to your heart's content.

Brainwash Café & Laundromat—A dream come true for the penny-pinching multitasker: a hipster café with live (mostly free) music, good beer and snacks, free wifi, and a laundromat.

Maxfield's House of Caffeine—In a town where you can practically get arrested for smoking a cigarette in public, I applaud any place that advertises its vice so boldly. Add on to Maxfield's cachet a locale right next to Mission Dolores (the oldest building in SF, with an often-overlooked, free museum), and their fascinating collection of photographs

Red's Java House
Pier 30, South
Embarcardero at
Brannan St.
415-777-5626

Java House
Pier 40
415-495-7260

Eagle Café
Pier 39
415-433-3689

Mario's Bohemian Cigar Store
566 Columbus Ave.
415-362-0536

Caffè Roma
526 Columbus Ave.
415-296-7942

Brainwash Café & Laundromat
1122 Folsom St.
415-255-4866

Maxfield's House of Caffeine
398 Dolores St.
415-255-6859

chronicling the bullfights that used take place down the street, and you've got at least a half-day's entertainment.

The Canvas Café/Gallery—When this lively café and local art space opened, replacing a gas station, it gave me renewed hope that San Francisco might just have the gumption to resist the systematic Starbucking that's taken place just about everywhere else. The café's key spot across from Golden Gate Park (there's a selection of outdoor tables for leaf-peepers), great lounging sofas, and interesting artistic eye candy makes it a skinflint sightseer's paradise.

NOON

Sightseeing the traditional way can be expensive, but with a little ingenuity you can avoid the excess charges and still have the million-dollar photo ops, a little history and culture, and a gourmet lunch, too.

Hop in the old '78 Civic and head to **Treasure Island**, where the cheap fun begins with crossing the better half of the Bay Bridge and not paying the toll. Sadly, the museum that housed relics from the 1939 Golden Gate International Expo is closed indefinitely, but you can still see the large mural that shows how the island looked in her glory days. Nearby is the hangar that once housed the *China Clipper,* the amphibious plane that flew the wealthy and powerful over

the Pacific between 1939 and 1946. And you can still walk through the interior of what was the passenger terminal, where there is a small commemorative display about the airplane.

Cheapskates with kids may want to make a detour to the **Fire Department's regional training center**, where you can check out the big ladder trucks and maybe catch a fire drill or two. From here walk down to the island's artificial shores and you'll meet the San Francisco skyline eye to eye—an *omigod* view that you won't believe you didn't have to put a quarter into a viewfinder to see. Plans are in the works to develop a shoreline park on the island, expanding the walkable turf, but the views from the sandy shoal are still outstanding, so grab the disposable camera and shoot away. Then spend a little time scouring the island for big movie stars; several of the hangars on this old naval base have been converted to sound studios for Hollywood films, so you never know who you might run into in the commissary (have a pen ready for an autograph; it may be worth something some day). If you're lucky, they might let you stand around and watch a scene being shot. Think of it as a poor man's Universal Studios tour.

Speaking of the commissary, your friend's chintzy heart will fill with joy if you make a reservation for lunch at the **Advanced Culinary Academy**, a school on the island for chefs, run by the Treasure Island Job Corps. For $10, you get a three-course gourmet lunch, beverages included, that rivals anything the big-city restaurants have to offer. Who knows? In a few years, you may get to brag about discovering the next Emeril or Alice Waters. The center is open for lunch only, Tuesday through Thursday (noon sharp), and is served in a genuine former navy galley.

Quarterback, Get the Quarter Back

Clearly, no cheapskate is going to fork over $50 to a scalper for 49ers tickets, and even $30 for a college game is probably too rich for his or her blood. That's why there's **Tightwad Hill** in Berkeley. The knoll just below the big cannon, on the hill above Memorial Stadium's north end zone, is the spot where starving students, penny pinchers, and claustrophobics watch Cal Bears football on Saturdays. Sure, they're not 50-yard-line seats. But you won't be cursing yourself for paying all that money to sit behind the guy wearing one of those beer-caddie hardhats, either. (Warning: the cannon they shoot off after each hometeam touchdown vibrates the seats 100 yards away, so unless you already have tinnitus from standing too close to the speakers at the last Rolling Stones concert, you might want to bring ear plugs.)

For baseballs fans who don't want to fork over $15 to see Barry Bonds knock one over the bleacher seats at SBC Park (but wouldn't mind catching the coveted ball and selling it at auction), there's the **McCovey Cove** walkway, where the cash-poor and the fidgety alike can stand for free

The Canvas Café/Gallery
1200 9th Ave.
415-504-0060

Treasure Island
take the only exit off the Bay Bridge once you've passed the first span.

Fire Dept. Training Center
Building 157, Treasure Island

Advanced Culinary Academy
Building 368, Treasure Island
415-277-2301 or 415-277-2400

Tightwad Hill
above Memorial Stadium, Piedmont Ave. near Hearst, Berkeley

McCovey Cove
SBC Park,
3rd St. at King St.

and spectate for at least three innings of any Giants game. The large viewing windows along the walkway just below the bleachers aren't exactly skyboxes, but you get the added bonus of watching the diehards dive into the bay when a ball makes a splash landing, as well as a water's-edge view of the ferries and sailboats going to and fro.

Golden Gate Park

Just hanging out in the park throwing a Frisbee is a great day out if you ask me, and it doesn't cost a thing. But if you want to see how the paying public lives (without dipping into your own wallet), you'll have to plan ahead. The **de Young Museum** (scheduled to re-open in its new building in 2005) is planning on continuing its free admission days—usually the first or second Wednesday of every month. The de Young's sister museum, the **Legion of Honor Museum** at 34th and Clement, offers free admission every Tuesday. The **Japanese Tea Garden** is free between 5:30 and 6:30 p.m. from May through September, and the **Arboretum** is always free, including the guided tours offered daily at 1:30 p.m.

Most Sundays from April through October, you can also sit on the benches in the Music Concourse and enjoy a

concert of classical standards and rousing patriotic numbers by the **Golden Gate Park Band**, the oldest municipal band in the country, established in 1882. If you haven't seen these guys before, try to imagine your high school concert band, complete with military-style uniforms and a killer arrangement of "Night on Bald Mountain"—only with actual, professional musicians. For most of the group, it's a labor of love. They're paid a pittance, and each year their operating budget gets cut back. So enjoy this city institution while you can. If the band gets your toes tapping, stick around. At 3 p.m. on many Sundays, **Barrio Tango** offers free Argentine tango lessons and dancing until the sun goes down. (Even if you can't get up the nerve to take a crack at it, all those dramatic dips and hip swivels make for good spectacle.)

If you miss the summer park freebies—flower shows, Comedy Day, rollerblade competitions, soccer and tennis matches—there's always **Shakespeare in the Park** in September, the best, free high-culture extravaganza park event of the year. The San Francisco Shakespeare Festival performs the Bard's works (usually comedies) in a glen behind the Conservatory of Flowers weekends throughout the month. Bring a picnic and a lot of sunscreen, spring for a little Trader Joe's $3 vino, and watch as plays like *As You Like It* and *Love's Labour's Lost* are taken out of their traditional contexts and brought to the great outdoors as Indian fables and Roaring Twenties romps.

No-Cover Concerts

The granddaddy of the free concert series is the summer festival at **Stern Grove**. Performers it would normally cost you half a paycheck to see do it for free most Sundays from June through August in this lovely grassy amphitheater surrounded by redwood and eucalyptus trees. Performances range from hip-hop to Hawaiian music, the Preservation Hall Jazz Band to the San Francisco Symphony and Ballet.

Downtown, the **San Francisco Jazz Festival** gets into the act with its annual series of free summer lunchtime and twilight concerts in Union Square, the Crocker Galleria, and Levi's Plaza. Expect the unexpected. Performers might be anything from traditional combos and swing bands to ethnic-industrial-acid jazz groups. Chairs are provided for serious music lovers; casual jazzheads grab a hot dog and stand or sit on the benches or grass.

In spring and summer, radio station **KFOG** hosts an irregular series of free rock and pop concerts in Justin Herman Plaza at the Embarcadero Center. Sometimes they're promoting new bands; sometimes it's a listener appreciation thing (like Kaboom, their annual Sky Concert with fireworks in May). Occasionally you can also hit the big time—such as when U2 played for free because they were making a documentary. However you slice it, there are no ticket lines, no service charge, and no $6 beers (lighters optional).

Though it's usually in an abbreviated format, you can catch some of the hottest acts in rock/alt/modern music

de Young Museum
Golden Gate Park,
Tea Garden Drive
415-863-3330

Legion of Honor Museum
Lincoln Park,
34th Ave. and
Clement St.
415-863-3330

Japanese Tea Garden
Golden Gate Park,
Tea Garden Dr.
415-752-1171

Arboretum
Golden Gate Park,
near 9th Ave.
entrance

Golden Gate Park Band
415-831-2790

Barrio Tango
415-261-0569,
www.barriotango.
com

San Francisco Shakespeare Festival
Golden Gate Park,
Meadow at Arguello
and JFK Blvd.
415-422-2222

Stern Grove
Sloat Blvd. and
19th Ave.
415-753-7048

San Francisco Jazz Festival
415-398-5655

KFOG, 104.5 FM
415-808-5364

promoting their latest albums, live and free, at **Amoeba Music** in the Haight. The largest independent record store in the country, Amoeba books performers ranging from the obscure to the likes of Richard Thompson, Neil Finn, Moby, and the cast of *Hedwig and the Angry Inch*.

Afternoon Aperitifs

Wine tasting in recent years has gotten increasingly spendy, with Napa wineries charging on average $3 to $6 for three or four tastings (but you get to keep that lovely wine glass!). Many Sonoma wineries still offer free tasting, though several now limit the number of wines you can taste. The friendly

folks at **Benziger Family Winery** in Glen Ellen offer close to a dozen wines for free tasting, and you get a bonus freebie in the form of a tram tour of the vineyards, plus there's an interesting exhibit showing how wine is made.

Family Wineries of Sonoma Valley is a collective tasting room where you can sample up to six wines crafted by a variety of homespun winemakers, who are frequently the same people that pour the wines. Besides surveying an interesting panoply of local wines, you'll get an education on varietals—growing conditions, appellations, and the like—and when you're done with the drinking, you can work off the buzz at the bocce court outside.

You don't need to be cheap to enjoy a tour of the **Anchor Brewing Co.** (see the Parents tour), but even people willing to shell out a few bucks for beer will be thrilled that the tasting of the stellar homebrew at the end is free and ample. Tours are offered weekdays and require advance reservations.

If your goal is to drink a lot for free and you don't much care if it's in a factory or a fancy cellar, then **Takara Sake Factory** in Berkeley is for you. In their Japanese-style tasting room, you can stand at the bar and taste cup upon cup of Sho Chiku Bai rice wine or plum wine, until upright is no longer your natural position. Of course, they'll expect you to maybe buy a bottle or two after all this hospitality, but heck, you'll be too soused to care. (If you're still coherent, the adjacent museum, also free, has an interesting exhibit about the sake-making process and the history of sake in America).

If you're into good, inexpensive single-malt scotch (a contradiction in terms?) and you don't mind drinking it in a ramshackle bunker on a golf course in a dodgy part of town, head directly to the clubhouse at **Gleneagles Golf Course**, one of the city's cheapest ($15 for 9 holes on the weekend) and least-populated public golf courses. The bartender at the clubhouse usually doubles as the scheduler, so be patient. You'll be rewarded with 18-year-old Macallan for $5.75 (it's three times that much anywhere else in the city), or maybe splurge and opt for a flight of five whiskeys, each 14 years or older—for around $28.

Finally, if the sun is out and you've got tequila on your mind, take your friends to **Puerto Alegre** in the Mission, where the food's cheap, but the margaritas are cheaper ($15 for a large pitcher). Atmosphere? What atmosphere?

NIGHT

Traditionally, the setting of the sun tends to coincide with the disappearing of the cheapskate's wallet. If you do end up footing the bill, don't fret: it won't end up costing you the arm and the leg, too.

Eat, Drink, and Be Thrifty

San Francisco may very well be the one town where there is a free lunch, or at the very least a super-cheap happy hour. And I'm not just talking chicken wings and chips and salsa. The day the Fairmont's **Tonga Room** shuts down I think I'll have to go into seclusion for a month-long period of mourning. For pure tiki-tacky ambience, there is nothing else in the city that comes close. And it's almost impossible to beat (in volume and price) their enormous, all-you-can-eat happy hour, with its luau-style buffet ($5 from 5 to 7 p.m. Monday through Friday). But the food is merely the flame on the rum drink. At the Tonga you can chow down

Amoeba Music
1855 Haight St.
415-831-1200

Benziger Family Winery
Glen Ellen
707-935-3000

Family Wineries of Sonoma Valley
9200 Sonoma Highway, Kenwood,
707-833-5504

Anchor Brewing Co.
1705 Mariposa St.
415-863-8350

Takara Sake Factory
708 Addison St.,
Berkeley
510-540-8250

Gleneagles Golf Course
2100 Sunnydale Ave.
415-587-2425

Puerto Alegre
546 Valencia St.
415-255-8201

Tonga Room
Fairmont Hotel,
California and
Mason streets
415-772-5278

on chow mein, sip something enormous and blue through a gigantic straw, and bask in the glow of tiki torches and Pirates of the Caribbean cargo nets while listening to a band play "Caribbean Queen" on an island in a swimming pool. Then there's the cocktail menu, which features an amazing array of fruity, umbrella-laden, comes-in-a-coconut-with-smoke-billowing-out-the-sides drinks—all boasting names like the "Scorpion" ("one too many may sting"), and the strangely compelling "Bora Bora Horror!" And then, just when you think it can't get any better, the thunder claps, the lightning flashes, and you're in the midst of a poolside monsoon. Can you stand it? It's *Blue Hawaii* meets the Muppets.

A better deal still is all-you-can-eat oyster night at **El Rio**. Hard to imagine that in a town where six oysters can run you upward of $10, this Mission district bar and club (which proudly boasts the motto "Your Dive" above its doorway) gives them away free every week during Friday happy hour from 5 to 7 p.m. Slurp down as many

Chesapeakes or Blue Points on-the-half-shell as you can stomach, chase them with a very reasonably priced beer, and pat your pocketbook contentedly as you think to yourself: "The world is *my* oyster (you get your own shellfish)." If you happen to miss Friday oyster night (though I can't imagine why you would), the El Rio has other bargains that you won't want to pass up. On Mondays, they have $1 well drinks and Bud Light; on Sundays, spring to fall, they offer free salsa dance lessons and barbecue 3 to 5 p.m. amongst the palm trees and torches on a tropical backyard patio.

Despite the ever-increasing invasion of restaurants like Rose Pistola and Moose's, which threaten to turn North Beach into one solid big-budget zone, there are still several places that offer the traditional five-course family-style dinners for somewhere between $12 and $22. At first you might not think this is a bargain. But consider that you get soup, salad, pasta, an entree (sometimes two entrees), and dessert for that price. Then those pocketbooks are starting to feel pretty hefty, huh? Among the remaining family-style restaurants are **Gold Spike**, **La Felce**, and my favorite, **Capp's Corner**, where you eat next to the bar, and are served dinner by a no-nonsense staff who's seen North Beach trends come and go, and come back again, and never changed a single red checker on their tablecloths.

The cost-conscious consumer will almost always include one pizza dinner on the itinerary. But that doesn't have to mean eating out of the box in front of the TV. Take them to the Monday night all-you-can-eat pizza feed at **Goat Hill Pizza** on picturesque Potrero Hill. For $9, you get to inhale from the unlimited salad bar and choose from a dozen different varieties of hot-from-the-oven pizzas as they're carted around from table to table. The views of downtown are just extra cheese on the pie.

If you don't want to gorge yourself, but would like to eat somewhere that's a cut above Burger King, other inexpensive options include:

Gira Polli—Every day before 5:30 p.m., this popular North Beach eatery offers the most mouth-watering, perfectly roasted whole chickens with potatoes and fresh vegetables for just $10.95 ($7 if you want just the chicken).

Pasta Pomodoro—This mini-chain of fresh, healthy, quick-service (as opposed to fast food) pasta restaurants is a good deal no matter what time of day. Favorite dishes such as gnocchi with Gorgonzola and tomatoes or pasta with mussels, calamari, and scallops are generally priced between $6 and $8.

We Be Sushi—Sushi is not cheap man's food, but We Be, with locations all around the city, makes it almost reasonable. Prices per roll are about half what you'd pay elsewhere, though they're not always so impeccably fresh (as one diner put it: "Good, cheap sushi. Unless, of course, you like really good sushi. Then it's bad, cheap sushi.") Assorted combos run (at last check) about $10. Be sure to read the menu for the rejected alternative names to We Be Sushi. (They tried to name the restaurant "McSushi," but a certain fast food chain said "I don't think so.") My favorite: Sushi and the Banshees.

El Rio
3158 Mission St.
415-282-3325

The Gold Spike
527 Columbus Ave.
415-421-4591

La Felce
1570 Stockton St.
415-392-8321

Capp's Corner
1600 Powell St.
415-989-2589

Goat Hill Pizza
300 Connecticut St.
415-641-1440

Gira Polli
659 Union St.
415-434-4472

Pasta Pomodoro
816 Irving St.
415-566-0900;
2304 Market St.
415-558-8123; and
2027 Chestnut St.
415-474-3400

We Be Sushi
914 Judah St.
415-681-4010;
3226 Geary Blvd.
415-221-9960; and
538 Valencia St.
415-565-0749

California Culinary Academy—A great place for people who want to experience the California cuisine scene but don't want to take out a second mortgage to do it. The academy has trained some of the best chefs in town. But before they can graduate to Jardiniére or Postrio, they have to put in their hours creating culinary masterpieces for school credit. Diners at the academy reap the benefits of their theses. Dinners at the Careme Room are pricey, but Monday through Thursday nights at the basement Academy Grill, you can get a buffet of appetizers, grilled and roasted meats, and dessert for $10-$15. And Friday nights, the $12 prime-rib buffet is a bargain even vegetarians will find hard to pass up.

Axum Café—Big bountiful platters of spicy lentils, tangy chicken, spinach and chickpea purees, and other Ethiopian staples served on doughy injera bread at seriously bargain prices are the draw at Axum, which now has a satellite location in Polk Gulch, at the old Mayes Oyster House.

What Price Culture?

The ultimate victory in a cheapskate challenge is when you can live large and spend small, partaking of those things normally reserved for the leisure class, but paying workingman's prices.

Admission to the Legion of Honor or MOMA won't exactly send you to the poor house, but if your friends are

still kvetching, take them to the **San Francisco Museum of Modern Art Artists' Gallery** at Fort Mason, where they can view museum-caliber paintings, sculpture, photographs, and prints by more than 1,300 emerging and established artists admission-free. The gallery also affords a great opportunity for cheapskates who live here to act like big-time collectors: you can rent and take home artworks, try them out on your wall, and if you really like something, the nominal money you put down as a rental fee goes toward purchase.

First Thursdays at chi-chi downtown galleries are another good way to view museum-quality art without paying admission and also enjoy an evening of free wine and hors d'oeuvres. The first Thursday of every month, galleries that belong to the **San Francisco Art Dealers Association** hold open houses from 5:30 to 7:30 p.m. to promote their current shows. Mosey your way up Geary or Post Street, where many of the galleries are located (there are clusters of galleries at 251 Post and 49 Geary), stopping in at the ones that offer good bite-size edibles (mostly cheese these days) and full glasses of chardonnay. Remember to stand in front of one painting at each place, ponder your wine glass contemplatively, and say something about the work's resonant emotional complexity.

I mention it in the Culture Vultures tour, but penny pinchers will probably appreciate this tip even more. The opera and symphony both offer cheap seats, and if you happen to luck out, they might just be really great seats. For the **San Francisco Opera**, try the box office first thing in the morning on the day of the performance for either standing-room only tickets ($8) or returned/donated tickets (charges vary). A select number of student rush tickets (about half price) go on sale two hours before the curtain. If you want to hear some of the stars of the opera, past and present, do famous arias, you'll have to get your cash-poor friends to show up in September for the annual free Opera in the Park event. Pavarotti and Sills have sung here, as have Thomas Hampson and Frederica von Stade.

The **San Francisco Symphony** sells seats behind the stage for $15, but you'll need to queue up two hours prior to show time and have cash on hand (two ticket limit). Or, if you don't mind a couple of stops and starts, you can attend open rehearsals on select mornings for $15. The price includes donut, coffee, and an informative talk by the music director.

For other theater, dance, and Best of Broadway offerings, hit the **Tix Bay Area** kiosk in Union Square on the day of the show, where you can snag half-off tickets.

The city also still has a couple of bargains for film buffs bemoaning the ever-rising cost of movies. The **Balboa Theater** in the Outer Richmond offers great double features—usually second-runs of major movies just after they've left the big venues—for $7.50. Get there early, grab a

California Culinary Academy
625 Polk St.
415-292-8229

Axum Café
698 Haight St.
415-252-7912,
and 1233 Polk St.
415-474-7743

Museum of Modern Art Artists' Gallery
Fort Mason,
Building A, Marina
Blvd. at Buchanan
415-441-4777

San Francisco Art Dealers Association
415-278-9819

San Francisco Opera
War Memorial
Opera House, 301
Van Ness Ave.
415-861-4008
Opera in the Park,
early September at
Sharon Meadow in
Golden Gate Park

San Francisco Symphony
Louis M. Davies
Symphony Hall,
Grove St. and Van
Ness Ave.
415-552-8000

Tix Bay Area
Stockton St.
between Post and
Geary streets
415-433-7827

Balboa Theater
38th Ave. and
Balboa
415-221-8184

slice of pizza from across the street or a carton of super-cheap Vietnamese food from next door (they let you bring it in), and you can have dinner and a movie for under $20.

Up at UCSF on Parnassus Heights, you can see popular second-run flicks before they go to video for the bargain price of only $4 ($2.50 for kids), at **Cole Hall Cinema**. Showings are usually Thursday and Friday nights from September through May, with the occasional bargain-priced Sunday matinee. The theater is basically a lecture hall, with seats at a steep perch and the screen at the bottom. But frankly, if you'd cushy it up with arm rests and drink cup holders, it wouldn't be all that different from the stadium-style seating that's all the rage at the $10 cineplex.

CITY GUIDE TOURS

So they want to learn something about the city, but they're not willing to shell out a lot of dough for one of those all-inclusive tour-with-lunch deals? No problem. City Guides offers an amazing assortment of informative and entertaining walking tours—all absolutely free. Sponsored by the San Francisco Public Library, the neighborhood jaunts are led by a scholarly stable of history, trivia, and folklore buffs, all volunteers, who clearly delight in what they do. There are some 40 tours to choose from, ranging from Pacific Heights mansions and Gold Rush sites, to "Bawdy and Naughty" and haunted tours. You can catch one almost any day of the week. Most start between 10 a.m. and noon and run a couple of hours. For a recorded schedule and description, call 415-557-4266 or go to www.sfcityguides.org.

WHERE TO STAY

Chances are if they're really cheap, they'll be crashing on your sofa or your floor. Next best alternative is the **Fort Mason Youth Hostel**, where for just $17 a night you get a room on a stretch of the city's most coveted piece of oceanfront real estate. This is truly the Ritz of youth hostels: the rooms are clean and relatively spacious; the kitchen is pristine, with clear-door refrigerators that house individual cubby holes; it's centrally located right between the Marina district and Fisherman's Wharf; and you get panoramic ocean views from here 'til next Tuesday. They also offer free movies, free walking tours, an espresso stand, and other amenities. It's so plush it'll have you thinking twice about your $1,800 one-bedroom apartment with the view of the brick wall.

In the downtown area, **The Mosser** is a hidden gem of a hotel deal. Located a half-block from Yerba Buena Center, the 1913 Victorian, with its stamped-tin elevator doors and iron-and-marble stairways, was recently given a modernist makeover by the same designer who did the ultra-hip W, bringing it up to par with many four-star properties. Rooms, albeit small, now boast wireless keyboards and WebTV, custom platform beds with drawers underneath, wall-unit CD players, bathrobes, and chairs with swivel-arm desks. Some rooms share bathrooms (you still get your own sink/vanity), but consider that all this comes for a price tag of between $70 and $150. Bonus for nightcappers: at Annabelle's, the Mosser's great in-house restaurant/bar, you'll find locals imbibing into the wee hours. Double bonus for autograph-seekers: at the adjacent high-tech recording studio next to the hotel, you might spot the likes of Tracy Chapman. Triple bonus for ecologically concerned cheap-skates: the owner, an avowed environmentalist, puts organic apples in all guest rooms and donates a percentage of the hotel's profits to international reforestation projects.

A beautiful, historic, Italianate Victorian hotel near Fisherman's Wharf for less than $70 a night? Impossible you say? Then you haven't checked out the **San Remo Hotel**, one of the best—if not *the* best—lodging bargain in the city. The hotel was built in 1906 by banker A. P. Giannini to help house earthquake refugees and has been restored to its turn-of-the-20th-century glory. Inside, stained-glass skylights, brass fixtures, and hanging plants give the place a green-house feel. Rooms are small, tasteful, clean, and spare, deco-rated with simple antiques such as pine armoires and iron beds. Neighbors do have to share bathrooms, but they're kept immaculately clean and feature nice touches such as claw-foot tubs and pull-chain toilets. Downstairs in the cocktail lounge and piano bar, you can get hot appetizers in the evening and continental breakfast in the morning.

Cole Hall Cinema
UCSF Medical Sciences Building, 513 Parnassus Ave. at 3rd Ave.
415-476-6932

Fort Mason Youth Hostel
Upper Fort Mason, Building 240, Franklin St. at Bay
415-771-7277

The Mosser
54 Fourth St.
415-986-4400

San Remo Hotel
2237 Mason St.
800-352-7366

tour 19   Politically Correct

You can't swing a dead cat in this town without hitting someone who's got "issues." In San Francisco, we eschew the cause célèbre in favor of the cause du jour. And we vehemently defend our viewpoints for at least a week, until we find another

cause that suits our needs even better. In addition to all the usual popular causes—fair-trade coffee beans, old-growth redwood trees, animal rights—people here rally behind incredibly specific, personal issues, such as the enforcement of pooper-scooper laws, the right to go naked in public, or the folly of introducing nonnative plants to the environment.

In this neck of the woods, being PC (politically correct) is not just a passing fancy, it's a lifestyle choice.

The good thing about being in this protest-happy part of the world is that for everything that's deemed to be PI (politically incorrect), there's probably some faction that's got an argument supporting the opposite viewpoint (and if there isn't, you can usually ad lib something pretty convincing—as long as you back it up with a petition).

MORNING

Here in PCville, even coffee is not without controversy. In fact, the morning beverage adored (and required) by millions is quite the hot-button issue nowadays. In Berkeley, a recent ballot measure tried to make fair-trade coffee (beans that are grown by small farmers employing eco-friendly and non-exploitative practices) a requirement by law.

In the city, the seriously concerned just look for the "fair trade" signs in café windows and eschew Starbucks on principle. And while we're on the subject of Starbucks, let me just take this opportunity to use my book as a soapbox (why? Because I can): Starbucks is the imperialist pig/Stepford Wife of the coffee world. They come in here like CIA mercenaries, scope out an already successful mom-and-pop coffeehouse, offer a nearby landlord three times the rent, and open up next door or across the street. Then they take nice, free-thinking urban youth and brainwash them into mindless droids who can only talk in Starbucks Speak. (Okay, in Starbucks' defense, they do support a number of PC causes, including local schools, literacy programs, and Earth Day activities, and they're making an effort to be socially responsible corporate citizens. But still . . .)

So, where should you go? First choice would have to be **The Beanery** on 9th Avenue, whose beans (including the house blend) come mostly from fair-trade farms and are roasted on the premises. Sip the java but skip the snacks and head up the street to **Arizmendi Bakery** for a brioche knot or corn-cherry scone. Unfortunately, the no-guilt zone

The Beanery
1307 9th Ave.
415-661-1255

Arizmendi Bakery
1331 9th Ave.
415-566-3117

only extends as far as the bakery's politics: nothing at this worker-owned cooperative (named for Basque priest and labor organizer José Maria Arizmendiarrieta) would qualify as Atkins Diet-friendly. However, you may take comfort in the fact that the extra layer of fat forming around your thighs will help insulate you in winter, thus reducing your reliance on natural gas and other non-renewable heating resources.

Later, if all this conscientious consumption gives you the urge to burn a few calories, take a spin around the park on a bike from **Pedal Revolution**, a shop in the Mission District that hires at-risk youth to refurbish second-hand bikes. Their town bikes from KHS (new and used) are great for inner-city riding.

If you're not near 9th Avenue and are still in search of non-offensive coffee, try **Martha & Bros. Coffee Co.**, a small, local operation owned by an extended family of Nicaraguan immigrants. The beans are roasted fresh daily at

a San Francisco roastery, the politics are left-leaning and Third World–sympathizing, and they employ recent immigrants and the elderly. Plus, any place where the World News section of the *Chronicle* is more in demand than the front page or the Datebook has got to be high on the PC scale.

Afterward, if you're at their 24th Street location (there's another branch nearby on Church and Duncan streets), walk down to **Global Exchange**, a "fair trade center" that sells crafts, clothing, jewelry, coffees, teas, music, and furnishings made in developing countries. The shop buys directly from small producers in Third-World nations, paying fair wages and often buying in advance, to help impoverished artisans become economically viable. Far more than just a storefront, Global Exchange, founded in 1988 by San Franciscan Medea Benjamin, is the tangible hub of an international movement that has become one of the world's leading advocates for human rights and environmental/political/social justice. Want to know what Ford is doing about auto emissions? What Mars Chocolate Company is doing to stop child slave labor? What you can do to help free Tibet? It's all here, and some really beautiful Cambodian silk handbags, too.

Down on the waterfront, **Crossroads Café** is located at the serendipitous juncture where social responsibility meets flat-out fabulous. Crossroads may in fact be the best café this side of Potrero Hill (which is saying a lot, considering its proximity to the almighty Farley's). Run by residents of Delancey Street, Mimi Silbert's nonprofit facility, which has helped thousands of addicts start drug-free lives, the café is a combination eatery, training center, bookstore, and secret garden. Get a double dose of do-gooder mojo by enjoying your au lait while perusing *Doing Democracy* by Bill Moyer, and while you're at it, buy a poster—proceeds go to support the foundation. (FYI: if you're looking for a real sit-down meal, **Delancey Street Restaurant**, a full-scale ethnic-American bistro, is next door.)

While it's not in a location that's on any tourist agenda, conscientious consumers might want to make a detour to **Café Phoenix** on the backside of Potrero Hill. Great burgers, tasty pasta, and rock-bottom prices are the least of the reasons to grab a bite here—the café is staffed entirely (except for the chef) by people with mental illnesses, who are either homeless or in danger of becoming homeless. This industrial-zone diner may be the perfect pit stop on your way to **Glide Memorial Church**, in the equally anti-tourist Tenderloin district. If your friends are convinced that religious zeal is the exclusive domain of right-wing conservatives, they need a dose of Glide. The "church without walls," presided over for the last 40 years by the good and powerful Reverend Cecil Williams, will raise your social conscience almost as much as it elevates your spirits. As you sway, sweat, and lift your hands to the joyous harmonies of the gospel chorus, look around: every walk of life is represented here. Prostitutes stand next to homeless Vietnam vets stand next to Marina yuppies stand next to Maya Angelou. If there was a PC hall of fame, this place would be in it.

Pedal Revolution
3085 21st St.
415-641-1264

Martha & Bros. Coffee Co.
3868 24th St.
415-641-4433;
1551 Church St.
415-648-1166; and
2800 California St.
415-931-2281

Global Exchange
4018 24th St.
415-648-8068

Crossroads Café
699 Delancey St.
415-836-5624

Delancey Street Restaurant
600 Embarcadero
(at Brannan)
415-512-5179

Café Phoenix
1234 Indiana St.
415-282-9675

Glide Memorial Church
330 Ellis St.
415-771-6300

NOON

What's so PC about **Mission Dolores**, you may well ask?

I mean, isn't it really just an egregious example of colonialism at its in-your-face worst? Yes and no. The PC credo also states that unless we learn from our past mistakes we are destined to repeat them. And nowhere in San Francisco is this theory more relevant than at the Mission Dolores cemetery, where some 5,000 Costanoan Indians lie buried—victims of white man's diseases and cultural intolerance. Formally named Misión San Francisco de Asis, this Catholic outpost (the third of twenty-one California missions) predates the Declaration of Independence by five days. The actual church, completed in 1791, is the oldest building in San Francisco (so a visit here also earns PC bonus points

under the "respecting your elders" clause) and still boasts its original four-foot-thick adobe walls and redwood-log support beams. From an architectural standpoint, the adobe mission is truly magnificent. Inside the chapel, a dozen or so rows of humble pews lead up to a handpainted, decorative wooden altar replete with religious figures that was crafted in Mexico in 1796. Original Ohlone Indian designs adorn the ceiling, and in the floor, markers indicate the burial sites of several early San Francisco pioneers, including William Leidesdorff, the nineteenth-century African-American businessman who built the first city hall (which goes to show you that San Francisco heard the call of racial tolerance long before it caught on elsewhere). The basilica next door, built in 1918, though not nearly as charming as the mission, contains some lovely stained-glass windows. The real treat here is the cemetery and garden in back, where PC types (and film buffs—this, of course, being one of the major locations in Alfred Hitchcock's *Vertigo*) will no doubt wish to pay homage. The picturesque, serene garden, a fragrant mix of roses, redwood trees, salvia, and native plants,

Mission Dolores
3321 16th St.
415-621-8203

Coit Tower
1 Telegraph Hill
415-362-0808

Commonwealth Club
595 Market St.
415-597-6700

features mostly the gravestones of post–Gold Rush Irish immigrants and Mexican settlers. A small memorial to the Costanoans stands at the back, where most of them are presumed to rest.

Coit Tower

Okay, here's your chance to do some actual, traditional sightseeing without falling off the PC bandwagon. Ostensibly you're taking your friends to Coit Tower to see the PWAP (Public Works of Art Project) murals, not the showstopping views, but since you're up here anyway, what's the harm? The murals, which wrap around the tower's lobby walls, were created by 26 local artists in 1934 under Roosevelt's New Deal reform program. On the surface, they seem to be nothing more than a depiction of Bay Area life at the height of the Depression, with panels illustrating the Financial District, libraries, California industry, agriculture, and so forth. But look a little closer and you'll see why at the time they were considered so subversive that civic leaders voted to close the lobby to the public. On the magazine rack, amid issues of *Esquire,* there's a copy of the socialist newspaper, the *Daily Worker.*

In the library, a man reaches for Marx's *Das Kapital.* Other newspapers sport headlines referring to the destruction of controversial artwork, the 1934 dockworkers strike, and labor issues. After thorough examination, go ahead and take the elevator to the observation deck. The tower was the gift of Lillie Hitchcock Coit, a turn-of-the-century women's libber who preferred chasing fire trucks and swilling bourbon to marriage and maternity.

Commonwealth Club of California

Left-wing or right-wing, everyone gets equal time at the Commonwealth Club luncheons, where the people who are making the headlines and the big decisions speak to an influential crowd of political and professional mucky-mucks. From Madeline Albright to Colin Powell, it's like watching "Nightline" without Ted Koppel.

Seasonally PC

Who says being PC can't be fun? In the summer, the city hosts tons of benefit performances, fund raiser events, and good-cause concerts—a great time to expose your friends to the time-honored San Francisco tradition of guilt-free entertainment. High on the PC charts, the **San Francisco Mime Troupe** has been performing its non-silent brand of left-wing musical-political satire in Bay Area parks for more than 40 years. (In fact, it was a benefit for the Mime Troupe, which had been jailed on obscenity charges after a performance back in 1967, that launched Bill Graham's career as a concert promoter.) The troupe has stayed true to its credo,

slaying capitalist America's sacred cows and lampooning the foibles of modern society, from Watergate and corporate downsizing to genetic engineering, urban gentrification, and war-mongering. Performances take place in parks nearly every weekend throughout the summer and are always free (donations gladly accepted).

Every October, rocker Neil Young gets a cavalcade of emerging and legendary musical talent to do an all-acoustic gig at his **Bridge School Benefit** at Shoreline Amphitheatre. (The Peninsula school, where his son is a student, works with severely handicapped, nonspeaking children.) Though it's certainly not a universal cause like the whales or the rainforests, you can still go and feel good about yourself. The overriding reason to attend is the chance to see the biggest names in the business—Elton John, Pearl Jam, Elvis Costello, Simon and Garfunkel, Tom Petty, Van Halen, Bruce Springsteen—play spontaneous unplugged duets with Neil and each other.

I know it's a long shot, but if your PC friends just happen to be here on April Fool's Day, take them to the annual **Saint Stupid's Day Parade** and join the antiestablishment as they skip down Montgomery Street thumbing their collective noses at corporate America and doing what San Franciscans do best—acting like happy lunatics. Bring an extra pair of socks for the ritual "sock exchange" on the steps of the Pacific Stock Exchange.

Shopping and Snacking

If you'd like to put your paycheck where your principles are, try the **Helpers Homes Bazaar** in Ghirardelli Square, which sells cute crafts, ornaments, and stuffed animals made by disabled adults as part of an organization that houses and works with them. Their miniature furry holiday mice, swathed in gowns made by famous designers such as Ralph Lauren and Diane Von Furstenberg, are a perennial hit and make great gifts.

In the Mission, **Creativity Explored** offers an amazing array of artwork and gift items—paintings, drawings, note-cards, books, T-shirts—all created by adults with develop-mental disabilities. The gallery is worth a visit just to view the rotating exhibits that are created by men and women of diverse ages, ethnic and economic backgrounds, and degrees of disability. Happily, everything in the gallery is also for sale.

Afterward, while you're in the spirit, head down to **St. Anthony's Dining Room** and get a slice of humble pie serving meals to the hungry and homeless. The venerable soup kitchen always needs volunteers. Or treat yourself to a pint of **Ben & Jerry's** ice cream while moseying around Haight Street or North Beach. With 1 percent of the profits going to worthy causes such as Amnesty International and Greenpeace, it's perfectly PC to indulge.

PC in Pacific Heights

It's hard to be PC in Pacific Heights. Amid all the ultra-expensive designer boutiques, the restaurants where a $10 oyster on a plate constitutes a meal, and the shops that sell diamond doggie tiaras, it's hard to know where to turn to patronize places that aren't on the banned list. But they're there. Fillmore Street, for instance, boasts a large number of charitable thrift and secondhand stores where you can often find the cast-off contents from the city's most exclusive closets. **Victorian House** and **Repeat Performance**, a thrift

San Francisco Mime Troupe
855 Treat St.
415-285-1717

Bridge School Benefit
Shoreline Amphitheatre, Mountain View
510-762-BASS

St. Stupid's Day Parade
April 1, on Montgomery St.

Helpers Homes Bazaar
Ghirardelli Square, 900 Northpoint St.
415-441-2650

Creativity Explored
3245 16th St.
415-863-2108

St. Anthony's Dining Room
45 Jones St.
415-241-2600

Ben and Jerry's
Haight and Ashbury
415-626-4143, and
543 Columbus St.
415-249-4684

Victorian House
2033 Fillmore St.
415-567-3149

Repeat Performance
2436 Fillmore St.
415-563-3123

store for the San Francisco Symphony, are the places to look for pre-owned evening gowns (hey—it's a step up from buying them new, and it benefits a good cause).

At the top of Pierce Street is **Alta Plaza Park**, a place where dogs of all walks, trots, and stations in life freely intermingle and poop is scooped indiscriminately. It also affords outstanding views of downtown. Plop yourself down on a warm, grassy spot and watch pedigreed poodles frolic with mangy mutts as their owners look on from a safe distance. If you get bored with that, take a surreptitious tour around romance novelist Danielle Steel's ridiculously enormous estate (the former Spreckels Mansion), located a few blocks east on Washington and Octavia. The sprawling block-long extravaganza, with its glass-enclosed swimming pool and servants quarters, violates just about every principle in the PC handbook—a sobering reminder of the wastefulness and excesses in our society.

People's Republic of Berkeley

Aside from being the PC capital of the Western world, Berkeley is simply a great place to hang out. To be environ-

mentally as well as politically in line (and to avoid sitting in the all-too-common Bay Bridge traffic), take BART to downtown Berkeley and walk up through campus.

Begin with a tour of the major sites of '60s political protest:

Sproul Plaza—This was the birthplace of the Free Speech Movement and site of many a Civil Rights and Vietnam War protest. Park yourself on the steps and imagine student-activist Mario Savio giving his famous "the machine will not work" speech. Then march up toward Sather Gate and pick up political literature at the various recruiting and information dissemination tables. If you're lucky, you'll find some kind of protest that you can either join with or exercise your right to vehemently disagree with.

Even better, pick your own pet peeve, make a couple of signs, and start a movement.

People's Park—From park to political rally site to parking lot to bum campground to volleyball court and back to park again, People's Park proves the adage that what goes around eventually comes around.

Chez Panisse—You can get away with dinner at Chez Panisse, because after all, it is the birthplace of California cuisine and one of the first restaurants to insist on using locally grown, organic produce, which led the way for sustainable organic farming practices in the Bay Area and around the country.

Brennan's—Located in the industrial district down near the waterfront, Brennan's has been serving no-nonsense meals to hard-working men and women since 1878. None of this highfalutin kweezeen that's all over nearby 4th Street, Brennan's is strictly meat-and-potatoes fare for blue-collar folk, old timers, and starving students. Best bets are the brisket, turkey with mashed potatoes, or huge French dip sandwiches. Oh, and make sure to order one of their famous Irish coffees at the bar and mingle awhile with the regulars. They'll have you climbing off that bourgeois pedestal in no time.

Black Panther Legacy Tour—You'll have to cross the border into Oakland, but this may in fact be the most politically aware, if not correct, tour in the Bay Area. Run by ex-Black Panther party chief David Hilliard, the tour recounts the history of the movement and takes you past significant sites—the house where the Panthers organization was founded, the court where founder Huey Newton was tried for killing a policeman in 1967—and brings to light a side of the Free Speech and Civil Rights movements that is rarely examined.

NIGHT

A socially conscious night on the town doesn't have to mean you're collecting for UNICEF while all the other kids are trick-or-treating. San Franciscans, after all, wrote the book on indulgence. (The oh-so-PC beatniks and the hippies

Alta Plaza Park
between Jackson, Clay, Steiner and Scott streets

Sproul Plaza
On the southern edge of campus, where Telegraph Ave. dead-ends at Bancroft Way, Berkeley

People's Park
east of Telegraph Ave. between Dwight and Haste, Berkeley

Chez Panisse
1517 Shattuck Ave., Berkeley
510-548-5525

Brennan's
4th St. and University Ave., Berkeley
510-841-0960

Black Panther Legacy Tour
Tours begin at West Oakland Public Library, 18th and Adeline St., Oakland
510-986-0660

practically killed themselves having fun in the name of bucking convention.)

Enrico's is the perfect example. In the late '50s and early '60s, when former owner Enrico Banducci ran this outdoor café/nightclub, his sidewalk seating and hipster attitude provided a forum (and fodder) for many a beatnik rant. And his willingness to take a chance on unknown entertainers helped launch the careers of performers like Barbra Streisand, Woody Allen, and Bill Cosby. After the strip clubs took over Broadway, Enrico's hit the skids, but like a phoenix rising from the asses (er, ashes), the restaurant came back big-time in the '90s. These days, it's like the main float in the Broadway parade, co-existing happily with strippers, jazz lovers, tourists, and neo-beatniks in the spirit of cooperation and harmony. There's good jazz most nights of the week, and the food is right up there with the best houses of California cuisine.

Those who prefer their bada-bing with a dash more bump and grind will be pleased to note that those cooperative strippers down the street are not on the boycott list, either. The dancing girls at the **Lusty Lady** happen to own

the place as well. The joint with the naked neon hip-shaking gal out front is in fact the first employee-owned and -run strip club in the country. Put that in your G-string and snap it.

Watching a movie about downtrodden people is one thing, but watching a movie about downtrodden people at a venue that supports downtrodden, struggling filmmakers is definitely entertainment for the edified. The nonprofit **Film Arts Foundation** offers training, education, equipment rental, resources, and a forum for independent filmmakers from around the world. Opportunities to see everything from Oscar-winning documentaries to no-budget Super-8 films are numerous: True Stories, their documentary film series is held monthly at the Yerba Buena Center for the Arts screening room; Independent Exposure offers monthly screenings of short films, videos and digital works from around the world, along with beer, wine, and music at 111

Minna Gallery; and their granddaddy event, the Festival of
Independent Cinema, is held every fall at the Roxie and
Castro theaters.

It gets a little stranger at **San Francisco Cinematheque**,
which showcases and champions the work of experimental
film and video artists. The offerings range from installation
art to historical retrospectives and independent features.
(Brechtian analysis of the production and use of napalm,
anyone?) Films are usually screened at microcinemas such as
the SF Art Institute and the Delancey Street theater.

A Note on PC Dining . . .

It's probably easier to pick a PC dining establishment by
ruling out places where you can't eat than by identifying the
places where you can. In other words, forget any restaurant
that serves veal, Chilean sea bass, gill-netted tuna, or endangered game animals; forget fast food joints like Burger King
that tear down rainforests for cattle-grazing land; and skip
seafood such as jumbo shrimp, sailfish, and turtles that are
overfished, raised on water-polluting aquaculture farms, or
endangered. Also nix French restaurants (nuclear testing,
ducks force-fed to make foie gras); Israeli or Palestinian
eateries (depending on your political alignment); places that
use white paper napkins (bleaching process pollutes streams
and paper destroys trees) or styrofoam cups (piling up in
landfills); and any place without handicapped access. And
that's before you've considered all the hidden evils: restaurants that give substandard wages or don't offer health benefits; places that don't hire illegal immigrants or do hire
illegal immigrants, etc. etc. etc. Pretty soon you'll be
reduced to finding a vegan restaurant that's run by battered
women and elderly environmentalists, where all the food is
cooked via solar-heated panels and served on plates made
by struggling Third-World artisans. A person could starve.

The alternative is to do as the PC natives do and say the
hell with it. Use your best judgment, avoid the French food
(did I mention they also eat horse meat?) and never forget
that your body is your temple or other house of nondenomi-
national worship.

Enrico's
504 Broadway
415-982-6223

Lusty Lady
1033 Kearny St.
415-391-3126

**Film Arts
Foundation**
145 9th St. #101
415-552-8760

**San Francisco
Cinematheque**
145 9th St.,
Suite 240
415-552-1990

A Walk on the Waterfront

The south Embarcadero waterfront has a lot to offer the liberally inclined. Starting out in the early evening at the far south end by the 4th Street Bridge, take a stroll down through old China Basin where a small, blue-collar houseboat community has managed to hold its ground against the ever-more-insistent encroachment of big city developments.

The inlet here is the last remaining strand of Mission Creek, which was once part of the much larger Mission Bay, long since filled in to make way for warehouses and dry docks. In the peaceful little channel next to the ongoing Mission Bay construction zone, you can still see seabirds nesting and occasional sea lions bobbing near the docks; the small green strand along the shoreline is the restoration project of the houseboaters, who used their own funds to spruce it up.

Afterward, walk along the waterfront, past the old Sailing Ship Restaurant and Red's Java House (another relic of the old waterfront, where longshoremen still congregate in the wee morning hours over cheap grub and even cheaper coffee), to the portion of the Embarcadero called **Herb Caen Way**. The city's most famous newspaper columnist, beloved by laborers and loft-dwellers alike, championed the underdog and celebrated the assortment of happy misfits who make their home in San Francisco.

Then continue walking south to **SBC Park**, where you can take in a Giants game (you'll have to make a contribution to the Giants Community Fund or buy a ticket for "Until There's A Cure" Day to give this a PC stamp of approval) and then a late dinner at **Acme Chophouse**. Only in San Francisco would a steak, chop, and seafood restaurant come with a social conscience: chef Traci Des Jardins and Operations Director Larry Bain are vocal advocates of humane treatment

PC TOURIST HIT LIST

Cause: Old-growth redwood forests. *Destination:* Muir Woods in Marin or Avenue of the Giants in Humboldt County.

Cause: Whales or other endangered marine mammals. *Destination:* Point Reyes or Monterey, where you can watch the gray whale migration; Año Nuevo State Park near Pescadero, where you can tour the sea elephant breeding grounds; the Marine Mammal Center in Sausalito, where they rehabilitate injured dolphins and sea lions.

Cause: Global warming. *Destination:* Pier 39 or Great America, where you can ride the non-fossil-fuel-burning bumper cars; Critical Mass, the monthly anarchistic bike ride through the streets of San Francisco (last Friday of the month at Justin Herman Plaza).

(recent dinners have included benefits for the Animal
Welfare Institute and Transfair, a fair-trade organization),
and their restaurant is a model for the viability of products
that come from sustainable fishing and farming practices.
Translated to the lip-smacking menu, you can rest assured
the beef is grass-fed, the salmon is wild, Chilean sea bass is
verboten, and even the pigs roam free.

Herb Caen Way
South Embarcadero,
from Brannan to
Mission St.

SBC Park
King St. at 3rd St.
415-972-1800, tick-
ets: 510-762-2277

**Acme
Chophouse**
at SBC Park, 24
Willie Mays Plaza
415-644-0240

tour 20 Extroverts

It seems to be a perpetual lament among the party set that San Francisco just isn't as much fun as it used to be. True, the wild days of dotcom excess are over, and unlike the City That Never Sleeps, San Francisco tends to brush its teeth, hop into its

flannel jammies, and curl up with a good book by midnight.

But that doesn't mean we don't know how to have a good time. Though some of us are becoming less and less inclined to stay up for the third band (and more and more excited by the prospect of watching "The Daily Show" in bed), at least when we do stay up we're usually out there with arms flailing and sweat flying. I've been to other parts of the country where a rousing show of appreciation amounts to standing six feet away from the stage, meticulously avoiding eye contact, and maintaining a face that's chiseled into an expression of moderate bemusement.

Historically, Californians are famous for wearing their fun on their sleeves (and their shoes, and occasionally their wet T-shirts). And while perhaps we've toned it down a tad, faced with the inevitable burden of two-day hangovers and the Monday morning dreads, there are still plenty of places where an extroverted gal or guy on holiday can dance on a table and not raise an eyebrow.

MORNING

After that first cup of good, strong coffee, you'll want to take your chatty, outgoing type to a friendly diner or a place with a good core of regulars and a waitstaff with plenty of attitude. **It's Tops Diner** is one straight out of the books (since 1952), complete with gum-popping waitresses in pink uniforms and cat-eye glasses who look as if they should have night jobs as back-up singers for Lisa Loeb. Counter seating is essential for maximum conversation with the It's Tops clientele, a motley crew that ranges from twenty-something musicians coming off all-night benders to Castro and lower Haight habitués and Union Local 319 workers. Ordering tip: the eggs are damn good, but the blueberry and banana pancakes are the real ticket. For an Edward (or Dennis) Hopper-esque experience, come here during the wee hours— they're open til 3 a.m. most nights—and have a malt made in an authentic stainless-steel 1950s Carnation milkshake machine.

A few blocks away at **Home Restaurant**, the make-your-own Bloody Mary bar may finally offer a worthy replacement to the brunch scene at the late, great Patio. The always-packed restaurant, as known for its sketchy service and dishy morning-after conversations as for its comfort food, delivers a glass with ice and vodka to your table, and the rest is up to you. Concoct a meal of a drink from the

It's Tops Diner
1810 Market St.
415-431-6395

Home Restaurant
2100 Market St.
415-503-0333

massive condiment bar (everything from pickled green beans to anchovy-stuffed olives) or go classic with tomato juice and a solitary celery stalk. Even with reservations, there's usually a wait here, but the evesdropping is so fabulous that no one will mind. Tip: the restaurant holds open a first-come first-served "shared" table in the back for drop-ins, which is ideal for extroverts—you can circumvent the line while providing your friend with a bevy of random, anonymous conversation partners.

Down the street at **La Tasca**, the normally sedate tapas restaurant turns into a hangout for the stimuli-challenged during drag bingo brunch on Sundays. Performer Steven LeMay, coiffed to the ceiling and spitting sarcasm, entertains diners with gender-bending bingo played for yucks and door prizes. It's the perfect solution for the host who isn't feeling inclined to chat with Mr. Nonstop after a long night of bar-hopping.

For all-around gregariousness though, 24th Street in Noe Valley might just win the prize. With three coffee-houses, two bagel shops, and several bakeries crammed into

a four-block stretch, extroverts can turn breakfast into a progressive meal. Best benches and stoops to squat on are outside **Martha & Bros. Coffee Co.**, which is conveniently located next to **Holey Bagel**. The regular coffee klatsch here will rope you into a discussion about jogging, French culture, or what's in the headlines faster than you can say double decaf nonfat latte. The party continues down at **Tully's**, which is spitting distance from Holey's classy cousin, **Noe Bagel**, as well as the homespun **Noe Valley Bakery and Bread Company**.

On Saturday mornings, if you're not sleeping off last night's martinis, show up for the live taping of National Public Radio's *West Coast Live* radio show. Each week, host Sedge Thomson (his name alone is worth the $10 price of admission) interviews a fascinating array of musicians, authors, wits, and wags from locales all around the city and the Bay Area (best bets for good seating are at the Legion of Honor Museum, Fort Mason's Bayfront Theater, and the Freight & Salvage in Berkeley). Audience members are often recruited to create sound effects, tell (almost) true tales of the circumstances that brought them to the show, and participate in regular segments such as "True Fiction Magazine," a hilarious, created-on-the-spot sketch performed by the show's resident improv players.

NOON

Contrary to what some people believe, an extrovert is not what you get when you cross an exhibitionist with a pervert, although you may encounter a little of both at many of the city's favorite freewheeling venues.

Nude Beaches:
Daytime . . .and the Dipping Is Skinny

Nude beaches are great places to take your uninhibited friends. They're also terrific spots to take repressed friends to whom you want to give a big California slap on the ass.

North Baker Beach, the most popular naked spot in the city, has a few drawbacks. It rarely gets warm enough in the city to make lounging around outside in the nude a relaxing pastime (and even the most committed extrovert is helpless against the biological inevitability of shrinkage and high beams). The other possible detraction, at least for some, is that Baker sometimes attracts a largely male (gay) population, particularly at the north end—spillover from Land's End Beach next door. This being said, for the debriefed, Baker Beach still holds an irresistible allure. There's something wildly exhilarating about being able to walk around without clothes on in the middle of the city sipping a Calistoga, taking in spectacular views of the Golden Gate—and not get arrested.

If you're looking for a more blue-collar nude beach experience in the city, try **Fort Funston**. Mellow nakedness takes place primarily on weekdays, and the beach doesn't

attract as many poseurs as Baker. This is a good place to take
extroverts who still have some deep-seated privacy issues.

Down the peninsula, where it's warmer, there are a
number of places to let it all hang out, but a perennial
favorite is the north end of **San Gregorio State Beach** (off
Highway 1, ten miles south of Half Moon Bay). There are
three big advantages to this beach: location, location, and
location. The experience begins with the drive down
Highway 1—the kind of glorious, sea-spraying, cliff-
hanging, sunlight-dancing, so-this-is-what-they-mean-by-

the-Golden-State journey that makes you want
to rent *Foul Play* and sing "Artichoke Fields
Forever" at the top of your lungs. The state
beach sits just off of the Highway 84 turnoff,
where lies the **San Gregorio General Store**, or
as I like to call it, the Center of the Universe. All
trips to the beach here should be prefaced by a
stop at the store. The two sand-washed buildings
(one of which is a post office) are all that
remains of the town of San Gregorio, once a
bustling stop on a turn-of-the-century coastal
stagecoach route. Whatever you've got a
hankering for, it's here—hip waders, Gunther
Gräss novels, righteous Bloody Marys, live bluegrass music, and a wildly diverse-yet-harmonic convergence
of bikers (self-propelled and gas-powered), hippies, yuppies,
beachies, moms, philosophers, and cowboys. I recommend
that you only leave the General Store after having enjoyed a
couple of Bloody Marys, a chat with a few old-timers, and
some guitar pickin'. By the time you get to the beach, your
last vestiges of inhibition will be cast—like so many boxer
shorts—to the winds.

Life of the Party

No other town I know honors extroversion with its own
holidays. In San Francisco we don't have just one, but
several. First and foremost is the **Bay to Breakers Race**,
which is also, of course, a foot race, but really—who cares?
This annual spring ritual every May is about seeing people
running (or walking or getting pushed in shopping carts)

dressed up like giant cocktail weenies or blind Venetians or better yet—not dressed at all (ouch). The most amazing thing about Bay to Breakers is that even if you've never jogged down the street for a carton of milk, you'll find that you have the stamina to get to the finish line. The sheer momentum of this massive conga line, plus the hordes of cheerleaders leaning out of windows and doorways along the way and the bands at every intersection, carries you along the 7.5-mile route. While your friends chat with a group of jogging salmon (who keep turning around and trying to spawn upstream), stop at the top of the Hayes Street hill, look back, and let your extrovert heart swell to three times its normal size.

Bay to Breakers is always followed in short order by Carnaval. While it's not Rio, at **Carnaval San Francisco** the odds of not getting mugged are a whole lot better. This is probably the most multicultural, toe-tapping, hip-shaking festival and parade all year. Samba dancers strut their stuff wearing costumes that put Las Vegas showgirls to shame; enormous stilt-walking puppets undulate down the street; and as Latin rhythms, mariachi trumpets, and Native American chants fill the air, even introverts can't help but sway to the rhythm. After the parade, steer the party over to **La Rondalla** on Guerrero where the cheap margaritas flow like wine. This divey, impossibly narrow Mexican restaurant seems to celebrate Christmas all year round: twinkling colored lights festoon the bars and windows, piñatas and colorful banners hang from the ceilings, and mariachis stand in the corridors playing traditional favorites in your ear. The food is "eh" at best, but the festive atmosphere more than makes up for it.

Much like the Bay to Breakers, **Halloween** is a day when everyone is given carte blanche to dress for excess, act outrageous, and dance in the streets. But unlike the Bay to Breakers, on Halloween you don't have to exercise to participate (unless you count disco dancing or 12-ounce curls). Costumes range from clever to campy to downright amazing. A few of my favorites: the group of guys dressed as bridesmaids chanting "always the bridesmaid, never the bride"; a satyr with hoofed rear legs that moved in sync with his human legs; and the Fruits of the Loom. Since the Castro was

San Gregorio State Beach
40 miles south of San Francisco, on Highway 1
650-879-2170

San Gregorio General Store
Stage Road and Highway 84, San Gregorio
650-726-0565

Bay to Breakers Race
Howard and Spear streets to Ocean Beach
415-359-2800, www.baytobreakers.com

Carnaval San Francisco
held in May along Mission St. near 24th St.
415-920-0125, www.carnavalsf.com

La Rondalla
901 Valencia St.
415-647-7474

Halloween Celebration
Castro and Market streets,
www.halloweensf.com

the birthplace of this annual Born to be Weird party, dressing in drag is always de rigueur. In 1996, the crowds got so big that they moved the official celebration to Civic Center. But the best costumes and characters still roam the sidewalks near Upper Market Street. A word to gawkers: real extroverts wear costumes.

NIGHT

San Francisco's a great town for observing people doing things that you would secretly like to do, if only you had the guts. The beauty of this is that for every person who still clings to a modicum of modesty, there's a whole bunch of crazy, no-holds-barred Mr. Microphones through whom you can be a vicarious extrovert.

Take friends-who-would-be-rock-stars to the **Diamond Heights Yet Wah Restaurant** (upstairs, between Safeway and Rite-Aid), where on Tuesday nights karaoke is king. A Chinese restaurant overlooking the Safeway parking lot might seem like an unlikely place to take out-of-towners,

but where else, I ask you, can you sing "My Way" in front of a room full of enthusiastic and inebriated strangers while munching on really decent Kung Pao chicken? For my money it just doesn't get better than this (apparently I'm not alone in my view; celebrity snapshots attest to cameo appearances by ex-mayor Frank Jordan and other local bigwigs).

If this setting is a bit too suburban, you can also follow the bouncing ball(s) to **The Mint Karaoke Lounge**, where men who would be women who would be torch singers, girls who would be Britney by way of Madonna, and all vocal ranges in between converge to form a more perfect "Reunited"— and it feels so good. This is the ultimate cheeseball karaoke lounge, open for open mic-ers 365 days a year, complete with video enhancement, a full arsenal of bad '70s songs, old queens, young bachelorettes, and a surprising number of very talented singers. Frankly, if you've never seen someone perform "Son of a Preacher Man" or "Endless Love" without the slightest hint of irony, you haven't lived. Go. Sing. Embarrass Yourself.

The **Silver Cloud** down in the Marina offers a similar venue for for this unique form of exhibitionism, but without the camp factor. Here, you're more likely to find brave souls who should have remained shrinking violets and businessmen who've had one too many. Sometimes that's half the reason for going.

If your friends truly enjoy singing in a crowd, and they happen to be in town in December, join the world's largest chorus at Davies Symphony Hall for the **Sing-It-Yourself Messiah**. This is the equivalent of baseball fantasy camp for closet Pavarottis, with the San Francisco Symphony and Chorus providing back-up for an audience of hundreds of wannabes and almost-weres. Lots of people do indeed know the entire score and can even sing it without cracking too many notes. No need to be intimidated by this. It's all just build-up for the Hallelujah Chorus, a massive choral free-for-all that instantly levels the playing field. May the best diaphragm win.

Letting It All Hang Out

Several mainstream San Francisco nightspots specialize in extroversion, notably **Julie's Supper Club**, a mostly yuppie power bar and restaurant, serving great martinis and a satisfyingly chic menu that ranges from lamb tenderloin to grilled salmon. But lurking beneath that White Rain veneer beats the heart of a serious extrovert. This is one of the few places in town where you can dance on the bar and not worry about some yahoo stuffing a dollar in your shoe and expecting more personalized service. The mood is usually boisterous and convivial early in the evening on Fridays and Saturdays, with the rooms equally divided between dinner and cocktails. But by about 10 p.m., after the bachelorette parties have slammed several rounds of tequila poppers and Purple Hooters (and probably opted to skip dinner entirely), things begin to swing. Before you know it, someone's on the bar, and there are stiletto heels weaving in between your daiquiris.

Diamond Heights Yet Wah Restaurant
5238 Diamond Heights Blvd.
415-282-0788

The Mint Karaoke Lounge
1942 Market St.
415-626-4726

Silver Cloud
1994 Lombard St.
415-922-1977

Sing-It-Yourself Messiah
Davies Symphony Hall in December, Grove St. and Van Ness Ave.
415-564-8086

Julie's Supper Club
1123 Folsom St.
415-861-0707

For those who want a bit more XXX for their extrovert bucks, **Bondage a Go Go at the Glas Kat Supper Club** (Wednesday nights) may be just the ticket. The lines start after 10 p.m. at this fairly tame (by Folsom Street standards) leather S&M party. No looky-loos are allowed—in other words, don't come in street clothes. Inside, there are the requisite go go dancers, lots of gals dressed in black latex, an into-the-wee-hours Goth dance scene, fetish contests, and a "fully interactive" bondage play area where you can watch a little whip-and-chain action. Certainly not for the shy or easily scarred; perfect for over-the-top exhibitionists.

Nourishment

Believe it or not, even the life of the party has to eat. Do yourself a favor and take him to a loud, boisterous Thanksgiving-at-the-Waltons kind of place where his antics won't faze anyone. On one end of the cuisine spectrum is **LuLu**, a cavernous interactive party of a restaurant. Sit at one

of the tables around the perimeter for a panoramic view of the whole room in stereo sound. Then let your waiter put together a meal of shared plates—maybe the roasted mussels, wood-fired rosemary chicken, and a couple of the truly sublime pasta dishes. Let your ears do the walking on your long strut to the bathroom and you may get the skinny on who's doing what to whom at City Hall, or any number of intriguing topics.

It's practically impossible to avoid interaction at **Cha Cha Cha**, the perennially popular Cuban/Puerto Rican/Caribbean restaurant in the Haight-Ashbury. Share a pitcher of sangria with whoever's nearby as you wait—sometimes interminably—for a table. If you get chummy enough (and you invariably do), maybe your new best friends will invite you to join them at that huge booth. Order up a mess of tapas to share, and don't forget the jerk chicken or the fried plantains.

Zen and the art of frolicking into the wee hours would seem to be contradictory terms, but leave it to Chip Conley and the creative folks at Joie de Vivre to create a crossroads for hedonism and the peaceable kingdom, where friendly fashionable folk seek transcendence in a Guavapolitan and harmony in a shared plate of five-spice roast duck. The wild popularity of **Bambuddha Lounge**, in a location that's been reincarnated more times than the Dalai Lama, attests to the fact that one does not always come back as a lower life form. The best part: it's in the Phoenix Hotel complex (see below), so extroverts who don't know when to call it quits can divert the conga line directly back to their room.

If you have a hankering for the dance and a yen for the paella, you owe yourself and your uninhibited friends a dinner at **La Bodega**. While there are definitely better places in town to get Spanish food, at those restaurants you don't get to have a tap-off with a real live flamenco dancer while the rest of the diners shake tambourines, maracas, and body parts. From what I can tell, it's a lot easier than belly dancing (though the outfits aren't as enticing).

But if in fact the Dance of the Seven Veils is more what you had in mind, you can bare your midriff and do your best Mata Hari impression at **El Mansour**, a Moroccan restaurant located in the Outer Richmond district. As you sit around low-lying tables on large floor cushions, the scent of cardamon, cinnamon, and cumin waft through the air. Suddenly a belly dancer appears, a vision in jingle bells and tiny finger cymbals, rippling her torso in ways most men dream about. Though they probably won't need a prompt, this is the part where you push your extrovert friends forward, encouraging them with zagareet cries. Then, still heady from glasses of Moroccan wine, they'll proceed to undulate with the natives whilst others look on enviously (or with great relief).

WHERE TO STAY

I suppose an ideal hotel for an extrovert would be something like Jamaica's Hedonism II resort—a place that's more like a commune, where everyone jumps in the hot tub naked and shares a giant Mai Tai. There really isn't a San Francisco equivalent, but there are some good compromises. The rooms on the top floors of the very classy **Mandarin**

Bondage a Go Go at the Glas Kat Supper Club
520 4th St.
415-495-6620

Lulu
816 Folsom St.
415-495-5775

Cha Cha Cha
1805 Haight St.
415-386-5758

Bambuddha Lounge
in the Phoenix Hotel, 601 Eddy St.
415-885-5088

La Bodega
1337 Grant Ave.
415-433-04

El Mansour
3119 Clement St.
415-751-2312

Mandarin Oriental Hotel
222 Sansome St.
415-276-9888

Oriental Hotel, for instance, offer glass-wall bathtubs that look out over the entire city. Soak up the views as you sip a glass of champagne, and for an added vicarious thrill, stand up and see if you can get the attention of that beleaguered business exec burning the midnight oil in the office tower across the way.

If it's a pool party you're after (or an after-hours pool party), there's no place but the **Phoenix Hotel**. This tragically hip Tenderloin no-tell motel is where visiting rock bands and avant-garde filmmakers like to stay. The ranch-style rooms, furnished in '50s rattan funk, encircle one of the city's few outdoor hotel swimming pools, where you can plant yourself by a palm tree with a fruity cocktail and imagine you're in Palm Springs or Negril (never mind the goosebumps). Potential Speedo-to-Speedo encounters with the likes of Flea from the Red Hot Chili Peppers or filmmaker Wim Wenders are just the ticket for most brazen conversationalists. If you're having trouble breaking the ice, perhaps expound on your interpretation of the famous swirl mural that lines the bottom of the pool.

Phoenix Hotel
601 Eddy St.
415-776-1380

Grandparents

Everybody's grandparents are different. Some spend hours in the kitchen making perfect gnocchi; others have perfected the art of the microwave. Some impart pearls of wisdom; others impart fruitcakes and hideous, multicolored sweaters with geometric patterns. Some are sprightly and engaged and keenly aware of developments of the past decade; others think that gas-station jockeys should still wear bow ties and wash windows, and that rock 'n' roll is the devil's handiwork.

My grandmother was a walker. Rain or shine, she loved to take the grandchildren out for a stroll in the woods or down the street, often leaving us in the dust. She was Old World, a woman who insisted her French students call her "Madame Dufer," never "Julia," and who firmly believed children should be seen and not heard (my most vivid memories of her always involve the phrase "schrei nicht so"—"don't scream so"). And though she generally appreciated good food, in her later years, she was most content sitting in a corner booth at Lyon's 24-hour diner with a ham sandwich and a cup of soup.

All this personal reminiscing is by way of saying that grandparents can be difficult people to plan activities for. Sometimes a full day means taking them to a hairdresser and the duck pond, or simply letting them stay at home to cook you strudel/tamales/jook. However, there are two or three universal truths about grandparents. They tend to tire easily, so going places where they can sit down is essential. Their day is often centered around meals, so plan those ahead of time and work your activity schedule around them. And they live to hear about your achievements, big and small, so don't whine when you have to trot out that story about the time you appeared on "Oprah." They're your grandparents. They've earned the right to embarrass you. Get over it.

MORNING

This is a tough time slot for grandparents, because what they consider morning, you probably consider prime sleeping time. No one knows why, but for some reason when you hit the golden years, your meal schedule begins moving incrementally backward until you're eating breakfast at 5 a.m., lunch at midmorning, and dinner at four in the afternoon—hence the origin of the Early-Bird Special. Considering that most cafés aren't open at 5 a.m., and that by the time they are, Grandpa will be ready for lunch, you might want to stock up on Zwieback and waffle mix and use the morning hours as your prime sightseeing time. If you do have a chance to go out for breakfast, think Old School:

Bob's Broiler, a fixture on Russian Hill for more than 30 years, has grandma and grandpa specials. Grandma, for inexplicable reasons, gets the biscuits and gravy; grandpa the piece of french toast, the flapjack and the eggs. Far be it for me to question—the day I was there, a genuine, card-carrying grandpa was ordering just that. Decor includes gray vinyl booths and a long counter with swivel seats. Most amusing item: the prominent sign that says "gift certificates available."

Herb's Fine Foods on 24th Street kills two birds with one stone. You'll enjoy hobnobbing with the Noe Valley "in" crowd and various local celebrities who make a pilgrimage here each weekend (no doubt attracted by the red-leather booths, formica countertops, and crummy coffee). Your grandpa will appreciate the fact that this is a genuine eggs-and-bacon diner from the 1940s. Grab the sports page and talk Yankees over a plate of bangers and flapjacks.

Neighborliness and a sense of family are old-fashioned virtues that seem to have gone out with our grandparents'

era. You know what I mean—the local baker who always gave the kids a treat; the butcher who always shared some words of wisdom. Even though **Katz Bagels** has only been here since 1993, Burt Katz and his son, Mike, are two from the old mold. Lining the walls of their shops are hundreds of wonderful photos of all their friends and neighbors, from babies to bohemians (a hobby of Burt's; he's published several books of local portrait photography). Grandparents from New York will appreciate their traditional boiled bagels, which aren't too chewy ("We wouldn't be able to look at ourselves in the mirror if we made them any other way," says Burt). Bring your bubby, have a sit, a bagel, some lox, and a little over-the-fence chatter.

Art's Café, at Irving and 9th, is a classic counter-and-stool joint for eggs any style and hash browns. Huge portions at rock-bottom prices.

Manor Coffee House is another haven for the blue-haired set (both young and old). This place hasn't changed decor since it was picked up circa 1955 by a tornado in some tiny Midwest town and plunked down on this deliciously frumpy stretch in the inner Sunset. Crowning touch: they still have diet plates consisting of hamburger patties, cottage cheese, and sliced tomatoes.

The Great Benches Tour of San Francisco

To my mind, good benches are worth their weight in wood. From the right perch, you can sit and contemplate city life without having to actually go somewhere. Not to mention the plethora of additional activities you might consider while perching—eating, letting others join you, taking in the views, feeding the ducks, reading the paper, taking a nap. Which is why, for grandparents who want to see it all but maybe don't have the stamina to get there, benches are perfect observation posts on the world. Here is my list of the top ten benches in San Francisco:

1. **Lyon Street at Broadway**—Situated at the end of the toniest block in all of San Francisco, the landing near the top of the Lyon Street steps affords spine-tingling views of the Palace of Fine Arts, the waterfront, and the bay. This bench gets bonus points for friendly joggers (occasionally of the celebrity variety) who wave as they sweat by, and for surrounding flower pots and manicured gardens, which make you feel as if you're in a Merchant Ivory film.

2. **Marina Green kite-flying field**—For sheer volume, there's nothing like the Marina Green. It's a place where sitting on a bench is actually a participatory sport. Aside from the obvious attractions (the views of the Golden Gate Bridge, Alcatraz, and the harbor), there are kite flyers, volleyball players, rollerbladers, and the hoi polloi coming and going from the St. Francis Yacht Club.

3. **Strybing Arboretum in front of the duck pond**—On a sunny Sunday afternoon, the duck pond is a small island of tranquility in a sea of activity. Around you, toddlers chase squirrels, Frisbees fly, couples fight and make up, and trees carry the whispers of a hundred years of dangling conversa-

Bob's Broiler
1601 Polk St.
415-474-6161

Herb's Fine Foods
3991 24th St.
415-826-8937

Katz Bagels
3147 16th St.
415-552-9122

Art's Café
747 Irving St.
415-665-7440

Manor Coffee House
321 West Portal Ave.
415-661-2468

Marina Green
Marina Blvd. at Buchanan St.

Strybing Arboretum
Golden Gate Park, 9th Ave. entrance
415-564-3239

tions. While you toss breadcrumbs to the all-knowing swans, mallards, and turtles (or better yet, get a bag of those wonderful sesame cookies from the Japanese Tea Garden), settle in for a long chat about the old days and all the bad things your father did as a child. The pond is a short walk north from the main entrance.

4. **Palace of Fine Arts eastern benches**—These are the best benches in the city for vicarious wedding crashers. On

weekends in the spring and summer, limos frequently pull up and disgorge happy visions in white lace and bow ties for picture taking. One Saturday afternoon, in a total Annie Leibowitz moment, I saw five bridal parties posed by the banks of the lagoon at the same time. Of course, the other overwhelming reason to bide time here is Bernard Maybeck's magnificent, melancholy pavilion, which begs quiet contemplation. If it's not too cold, try to stick around for sunset, when the palace is lit in all its Panama-Pacific Exposition glory.

5. **Thirteenth Hole at Lincoln Park Golf Course**—The view from the parking lot of the Palace of the Legion of Honor museum is pretty good, but it's even better just below the railing, where a strategically placed bench lets you be part of the golf gallery at the thirteenth hole tee as well as privy to one of the most amazing panoramic vistas of downtown San Francisco anywhere. When you get hungry, mosey up the path to the museum café for a tarragon chicken salad or some homemade potato-leek soup.

6. **Dolores Park at the top of Church and 20th streets**—For some reason (maybe because of its proximity to Mission High School or its fading reputation as a drug dealing area), people sometimes forget about this great sunbathing/dog walking park with its even greater views of the downtown skyline. The benches at the southwest corner are unbeatable for a bird's-eye view of the rolling grassy expanse where the neighborhood's doggie elite meet for playtime, scantily clad Castro habitués laze in the sun, and the city spreads out below like the backdrop of a movie set.

7. **Montgomery and Filbert streets below Grace Marchant Gardens**—This bench, perched midway up the Filbert Street steps, requires a bit of hiking, so it's not for invalid grandparents. But if they're feeling fit and you take it slow, you'll both be rewarded with a sweetheart of a bench, tucked into the overgrowth and looking out over the Embarcadero waterfront to Treasure Island. You can eliminate some of the hike by driving to the top of Montgomery Street, which transects the stairway at about the halfway point. There's actually a great bench here, too, where you can sit among the roses and lilies and gaze out onto the '30s art deco and streamline moderne apartment houses perched on the hillside. If you get peckish, you're only a stone's throw from **Julius' Castle**, a restaurant so fabulously cliché, so yesteryear, it has become, like the cable cars, a sort of camp-cool icon. Settle into a table next to a visiting anniversary couple from Iowa, look out over the misty bay, and reminisce.

8. **Aquatic Park**—The benches just past the steps of Aquatic Park, below the Maritime Museum, were made for grandpas. From here, you can sit and be inspired by the over-60 crowd from the Dolphin Club swimming by you in the bay or stroll over and take in a game of bocce ball with the elderly Italian gents, or hear how Gramps got his medal of valor as you gaze at the *USS Pampanito,* the World War II submarine docked at Pier 45 next door. The view from here isn't half bad, either.

9. **Tiburon waterfront**—If your grandparents are up to it, take the ferry. Otherwise, the drive is also perfectly lovely. After you hit the village and stop for a pastry at the Swedish bakery, stroll a few yards past the ferry landing on the waterfront promenade to one of the benches that looks out over the harbor. Sit, relax, and enjoy the spectacle: Tiburon's well-heeled jogging by with their Jack Russell terriers; tanned, long-legged gals walking off brunch at Sam's; and in the distance, the familiar outlines of San Francisco's skyline etched against the horizon.

10. **Market Street F Line**—A bench seat inside one of these lovingly restored vintage streetcars is a grandparent's E ticket, a bona fide piece of rolling nostalgia in patent leather

Palace of Fine Arts
Bay and Lyons streets
415-567-6642

Lincoln Park Golf Course
34th Ave. and Clement St.

Julius' Castle Restaurant
1541 Montgomery
415-392-2222

Aquatic Park
Beach St. between Larkin and Van Ness

F Line
Muni info:
www.sfmuni.com

and picture windows. The colorful fleet that toddles up and down Market Street originally hailed from places like Hamburg, Blackpool, Milan, Philly, and Paris; each still bears the markings and unique design details of its native city. It's like a rolling history lesson in early-20th century transportation. Grandparents will no doubt enjoy riding the rails they remember from their youths, plus they'll get a tour of downtown from Castro to Fisherman's Wharf all for the old-fashioned Muni senior fare of 35 cents.

NOON

The Bay Area isn't exactly England, with its myriad garden clubs and flower shows, but we have a few places that will delight the retired green thumb. **Filoli**, down in the sylvan enclave of Woodside, is a perfect day outing. A pretty 40-minute drive down Highway 280 to Cañada Road, the Filoli estate (a name cobbled together from the words Fight, Love, Life) was once the residence of water magnate and gold millionaire William Bourn II. The Georgian-style manor house, designed by Willis Polk in 1916, is well worth a visit, but the formal gardens—divided by hedges and patterned borders into a series of unique, separate "rooms"—are the real draw. You can stroll at leisure for hours over the 16 acres of roses, tulips, English cottage flowers, Irish yew

trees, and immaculately sculpted shrubbery. Afterward, have a cuppa and a muffin or biscotti in the tea shop (on Fridays and Saturdays they also have box lunches with half-sandwiches, fruit salads, lemonade, etc.). And make sure to nose around the carriage house gift shop. Spring, of course, is the best season to come, when the gardens are a riot of color, but if you happen to get a grandparents visit around the holidays, Filoli does a wonderful Christmas celebration the week after Thanksgiving (reservations are a must for high teas, luncheons, and concerts). Regular docent-led tours are conducted February through October.

Filoli
Cañada Road,
Woodside
650-364-2880

Allied Arts Guild
75 Arbor Road,
Menlo Park
650-322-2405

We used to visit with my grandmother nearly every weekend when I was growing up, and it became a tradition to go out and have lunch—me, my grandmother, my mom, my aunt, and my cousins—somewhere proper and ladylike. The **Allied Arts Guild** seems as if it were invented precisely for this sort of occasion. Tucked off a quiet residential street in Menlo Park, a stone's throw from El Camino Real and the Stanford Shopping Center, the guild is a time capsule of gentility and quiet, old-fashioned graciousness. A Spanish colonial villa with sand-washed buildings daisy-chained together around a serene Mediterranean courtyard, fountain, and gardens, the complex houses a series of artists' studios and homespun crafts shops as well as a wonderful restaurant run (on a volunteer basis) by sweet little old ladies from the Woodside-Atherton Auxiliary for the Lucile Packard Children's Hospital. The restaurant serves one set meal every day for $10.95, including soup, salad, an entree, rolls, and dessert. The portions are just perfect—not too big, not too small—and all the menus are based on home recipes from auxiliary members, who also do all the cooking and serving (proceeds benefit the hospital). As you sit in the warm, terra cotta-tiled dining room with its cozy fireplace, munching on turkey pot pie, chicken Monterey, rhubarb apple crumble, or lemon crisp, the volunteers walk around in green smocks, pouring lemonade and tea and offering motherly advice. The whole thing takes you back to the days of PTA bake sales. To complete the effect, you can purchase guild recipes for 75 cents; they're all neatly filed, grandmother-style, on 3x5 index cards on a rack by the entrance. Afterward, take a turn around the garden, browse for garden ornaments or glass animals in the quaint shops, and be sure to take note of the frescoes, done by a student of Diego Rivera in the 1930s, inside the studios on the east side.

Tea Time

No grandparents' visit would be complete without a good old-fashioned heart-to-heart (the kind you never have with your parents, because, well, they'd think all that angst, lack of motivation, and inability to commit was because of something they failed to do as parents). And there's no better setting for it than at tea—strong brew, finger sandwiches, miniature pots, the works. **Lovejoy's Antiques and Tea Room** in Noe Valley is a small, dainty parlor where you can drink Taylors of Harrogate out of real china teacups and eat teeny tiny sandwiches from little terraced silver caddies. The whole place is exquisitely "pinkies out," from the antique velvet settees and lace doilies that look like they're straight out of Grandma's front room to the flowery china teapots. Grandmas go ga-ga over those soft, white, crustless sandwiches made with things like cucumber and cream cheese or bay shrimp and mayonnaise. If she's not watching her cholesterol, also order up a helping of crumpets or scones served with double Devon cream. Gramps will no doubt pooh-pooh the whole idea until he gets wind of the Ploughman's Platter, which involves thick, crusty bread, English cheeses, pickled onions, oak-smoked Finnan haddock, and other weird side dishes that you only hear about when grandparents are around.

Across town, tucked away in a barely discernable storefront in the Outer Richmond (I drove past it twice), **Tal-Y-Tara Tea & Polo Shoppe** offers what is perhaps the ultimate English tea experience. Those who remember the Waters-Upton Tea Room from days of old will be delighted to find the family happily ensconced in this quaint parlor, still

serving their famous "motorloaf" (a secret-recipe bread loaf made with molasses, walnuts, and buttermilk that is hollowed out to hold finger sandwiches for "motoring") and sherry trifle, and a huge array of hard-to-find Anglo teas (among them Kinnells and Jackson of Piccadilly). Steer Nana past the saddles and riding crops and *accoutrement de polo*—the tea room doubles as a "shoppe" for English equestrian gear—to one of the cabbage-rose print settees or a table on the sheltered garden patio, and spend the afternoon flipping through *Horse & Hound*.

A little less cozy (and a little more blueblood), the **Palace Hotel** is worth an excursion with or without the tea.

It's served on Saturdays in the magnificent Garden Court, one of the most beautiful rooms in all of San Francisco. The historic stained-glass dome ceiling casts the nostalgic light of yesteryear over the gilded, marble-columned ballroom, calling to mind an era of white gloves, dance cards, and gentlemen with waxed moustaches. No place else serves as elegant a tea—perfect, dainty finger sandwiches, pristine little teapots, and the kind of deferential service that grand-mothers long ago chalked up to fond childhood memory.

For Eastern bloc (and Far Eastern bloc) grandmas who prefer good strong tea with a cube of sugar and sans doilies, head to the **Samovar Tea Lounge** in the Castro. Named for the Russian metal urn *cum* teapot (they do a weekly Russian tea service of jam-infused black tea, Russian-style, from the samovar), this überhip "tea lounge" caters to a whole new generation of sippers who are as interested in where the tea is harvested (sustainable family tea estates) as what it tastes like. On Monday nights, you can ensure your inheritance if you take your babushka to the Knitter's Tea, a free-for-all of knitting, drinking, and kibbitzing with the least frumpy set of needle-wielders you'll ever meet. The watercress on the tea-smoked chicken-and-muenster sandwich is Sunday nights, when the gang gets together to listen to old-time radio shows, such as "The Whistler" and "Amos and Andy."

A Little (More) Lunch

Chances are, if your grandparents live nearby or have visited San Francisco over the years, they have fond memories of places that no longer exist, such as the City of Paris store, which stood on the site of what is now Neiman Marcus. The **Rotunda** restaurant on the mezzanine level of Neiman's manages to recapture some of that old magic from the days when "going downtown" was an outing you looked forward to for weeks. The restaurant sits beneath the historic stained-glass dome that was the hallmark of City of Paris and encir-cles the inner atrium of the store like a balcony at the opera house, with most tables looking out over bustling Union Square. This a favorite haunt of the Ladies Who Lunch: hats and gloves (and lots of Chanel jewelry) are still the protocol.

Lovejoy's Antiques and Tea Room
1351 Church St.
415-648-5895

Tal-Y-Tara Tea & Polo Shoppe
6439 California St.
415-751-9275

Palace Hotel
Market and New Montgomery St.
415-512-1111

Samovar Tea Lounge
498 Sanchez St.
415-626-4700

The Rotunda at Neiman Marcus
150 Stockton St.
415-362-4777

The lobster club sandwich is the thing to order, but if that's too heavy, perhaps a nice chicken salad, or high tea service after 2 p.m.

Seafood places out in the avenues are not like the new wave of haute seafood restaurants—Aqua, Farallon, or Plouf—where you might take your parents, yuppie friends, or a date. These are, you know, *Avenue* places, bastions of nontrendy neighborhoodiness, havens for the unhip, but

boasting big menus of every variety of fish cooked every which way you can think of. At **Pacific Café**, way out on Geary, you won't find barely seared tuna or seafood foie gras—just fresh fish: broiled, poached, grilled, sautéed, or fried. A throwback to the formica-and-wood-paneled décor of the '70s (it opened in '74), the homey restaurant is the kind of no-fuss, no-muss mom's-style cookin' that pleases young and old alike. Bonus: Grumpy grannies who don't like to wait for a table can be mollified with bottomless glasses of free white wine.

The Mission district seems the most unlikely spot for an old-time soda fountain, but the **St. Francis Fountain**, bless its heart, has been here since 1918, churning out homemade ice cream and dishing up the kind of classic 1940s diner food that makes grown grannies weep. Ideally, grandparents should come here with their blasé children and not-yet-cynical grandchildren. Sit at one of the straight-back wooden booths and order a double-decker liverwurst, cheese, and tomato sandwich, cottage cheese topped with pineapple, or a frankfurter plate. Then, after you've dispensed with the nutritional formalities, let the old-timers do what they do best—spoil their grandchildren. The hard part will be deciding between the banana split special, a double-dip soda, a scoop of strawberry shortcake ice cream, or pie à la mode (or even better, topped with cheese).

NIGHT

A night on the town for many grandparents might be a brief affair. If they're tired, settle down to a cup of tea and

"Charlie Rose" and don't complain (it's not like you would have gotten into Delfina anyway). If they've still got some energy left, keep in mind that loud, crowded places aren't very conducive to those with hearing aids and bad hips.

Though you gave up on organized religion years ago, you should make an exception for Evensong at **Grace Cathedral** Thursday evenings at 5:15 p.m. For one thing, the men's and boys' chorus is truly exceptional and uplifting; for another, the concert is free. Your grandparents will get to enjoy the city's most impressive neo-Gothic structure, which was modeled on Notre Dame, and you won't have to tell them you don't actually go to church anymore. Recovering Catholics, agnostics, and those of various other faiths can be reassured by the fact that this is a "House of Prayer for All People." (If you miss Thursday, there's another Evensong service Sunday at 3:30 p.m.)

Talkies and Two-Step

Take in an early picture show at the **Castro Theatre**, which frequently offers excellent grandparents material—reissued classics, Frank Capra fests, old MGM musicals—plus a preshow performance on the mighty Wurlitzer. If they're visiting in July, keep an eye open for the Silent Film Festival—an annual ode to the time before talkies, when Gloria Swanson and Mary Pickford ruled the silver screen. Most of the films are shown to organ and piano accompaniment, but occasionally a complete live orchestra sits in the pit the way they did in the old days.

A nice drive is always a safe bet with grandparents. While I recommend the town of Sonoma as a place to take parents, there is one spot up there where grandparents rule: **Little Switzerland**. Located about two miles west of town, this Swiss restaurant/bar/beer garden is a retirees paradise, but also an absolute gas for younger folk who have forgotten that old people know how to have fun, too. I came here one weekend with some friends and ended up eating sausage and sauerkraut, drinking Jäegermeister, and dancing the polka with some 75-year-old guy who had better moves than John Travolta. I had to retreat to the beer garden out back for a

Pacific Café
7000 Geary Blvd.
415-387-7091

**St. Francis
Fountain**
2801 24th St.
at York
415-826-4200

Grace Cathedral
1100 California St.
415-749-6300

Castro Theatre
429 Castro St.
415-621-6120

**Little
Switzerland**
Riverside Dr. and
Grove St., Sonoma
707-938-9990

breather, while he just kept on going. Most weekends, Little Switzerland transforms into a small Oktoberfest, with live German polka and oompah-pah bands, and a family-style buffet meal (usually consisting of hearty dishes like pot roast and potato salad, bratwurst and sauerkraut, roast chicken, or spaghetti) served at long tables with red-checkered table-cloths. Elderly types from all around come and sit and eat and then enjoy a spin (or a slow two-step) around the room. Maybe you could even set your grandma up with some nice elderly gentleman.

Dinner Out

Grandparents grew up in a time when vegan wasn't even a word, so cut them some slack. Take them to an old-fash-ioned place with white tablecloths that still speaks surf and turf. Here's a quick run-down of suggestions.

Alfred's—Not too much has changed (except the loca-tion) in sixty-odd years at this traditional, clubby steak-house where pre-dining cocktails are a must. Go for a fat T-bone, New York, or porterhouse steak—dry-aged and

mesquite-grilled—and of course the requi-site baked Idaho potato on the side.

La Felce—One of the anchors of the North Beach family-style restaurants of yore, La Felce still serves the full-on six courses—antipasti, salad, soup (probably minestrone or pastina in broth), pasta, a hearty chicken, veal, or beef dish, and spumoni ice cream—and does it with some style and flavor. After dinner, take a slow stroll around Washington Square Park and admire Saints Peter and Paul Church—if not for its magnificent spires, then for the fact that Joe DiMaggio went to school here.

Fior d'Italia—A half-block away from La Felce, Fior d'Italia has the unique distinction of being the oldest docu-mented Italian restaurant in the country, opened in 1886. Though its old-style touches—tuxedoed waiters, double-spoon service, private dining rooms—might be considered hokey by some, those people are not your grandparents.

Think how many points you'll score by reserving the Tony Bennett Room, a tribute to the crooner who used to make this restaurant his home away from home.

Joe's of Westlake—Though it's not related to the venerable Original Joe's in the Tenderloin, Westlake Joe's has been around almost as long, serves many of the same dishes, and is in an area that your grandparents won't be frightened by. Plus, there's plenty of parking, and while the atmosphere is nice, it's not overly dressy. Huge hamburger-steaks are the ticket here, served on sourdough rolls; there's also a variety of steaks, chops, and surf 'n' turf combos.

Eating In

If she wants to cook, let her cook. Besides, when was the last time you sat down at your own kitchen table for a nice home-cooked meal that you didn't have to make yourself? (Safeway barbecued chicken doesn't count.) Or maybe Grandpa is tired of that fancy California cuisine and just wants some familiar comfort food. Some suggestions on where to find supplies:

Lucca Ravioli Company—Key items include wonderful homemade ravioli (if Nona's cooking, it'll give her more time to perfect the sauce) and cannoli, great coppa and prosciutto, and dozens of imported Italian goodies.

Lehr's German Specialties—Ever since Speckmann's closed, I've been mourning the loss of a place to get good pumpernickel, knödel, and Bavarian wurst. Little did I know that directly across the street, in a 30-year-old shop that appeared to specialize in glass vases and gifty tchotschkes, was a treasure trove of German and Austrian edible delicacies. An entire aisle is devoted to chocolate, another to soups and sauces (six types of knödel!), and a whole corner to Christmas goodies—pfeffernüssen to stollen.

Haig's Delicacies—This mecca for Middle-Eastern edible imports carries hard-to-find items like halvah, kefir, and Turkish coffee. Haig's also makes some of the best baba ghanoush I've ever had—just the right amount of garlic and fire-roasted aroma. There's also a good smattering of gourmet packaged items from India and Indonesia,

Alfred's
659 Merchant St.
415-781-7058

La Felce
1570 Stockton St.
415-392-8321

Fior d'Italia
601 Union St.
415-986-1886

Joe's of Westlake
11 Glenwood Ave.,
Daly City
650-755-7400

Lucca Ravioli Co.
1100 Valencia St.
415-647-5581

Lehr's German Specialties
1581 Church St.
415-282-6803

Haig's Delicacies
642 Clement St.
415-752-6283

including sambal oulek, a wonderful Indonesian red-pepper paste that beats Chinese chili sauce hands-down.

Cinderella Bakery, Deli, and Restaurant—The bakery attached to this small Russian restaurant is like your

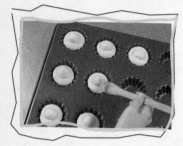

babushka's own kitchen—Russian wheat bread fresh from the oven, piroshki fried or baked, stuffed cabbage rolls, and hamand taschen (cookie popovers filled with prune or poppyseed filling). Be forewarned, the smells are so tempting you may find your-self sitting down to a meal of borscht and syrniki (cottage-cheese fritters). You'll also be happy to learn that the mystery of the name "Cinderella" has finally been solved. One of the Russian regulars informed me that Cinderella is actually a character from Russian fairy tales as well, where she is known as the "Snow Maiden."

East Coast West Delicatessen—The closing of Shenson's left a gaping hole in the Jewish deli firmament, so you really have to root around to get a decent kosher meal this side of Berkeley. Israel & Cohen on Geary is more of a market; there's a little store and café on Irving and 20th that caters to orthodox set; but probably your best bet for a sit-down, New York-style nosh is East Coast West on Russian Hill, where you can feast on big pastrami sandwiches, white fish, brisket, and matzo ball soup until it's time to call your mother, who's sitting all alone, in the dark, wondering why you love your bubby more than the woman who labored for 20 hours giving birth to you.

Yamada Seika Confectionery—This tiny Japantown store specializes in manju, traditional sweet-bean pastries wrapped in tubular-shaped sweet-sticky rice dough—a rare find in the Bay Area. It's a great little shop to get your sweet fix, even if your grandmother is from Oslo, not Osaka.

Schubert's Bakery—This adorable little slice of French/German confection in the middle of Little Chinatown makes perfect fluffy, spongy cakes, iced petit fours, coffee cakes, and cream-filled pastries—in short, everything your grandmother was told she shouldn't eat, but did anyway, regularly, and lived to be 102. Fill up a box with miniatures and don't miss the Princess cake with icing made of marzipan.

WHERE TO STAY

Let me begin with the following disclaimer: no self-respecting grandchild shuffles his or her grandparents off to a hotel if he or she can at all help it. Grandparents get the bed; you get the sofa or the floor. That's the protocol. Of course your grandparents may very well prefer a hotel to a house full of screaming toddlers or a bathroom shared by four other people. In that event, I suggest putting them up at an old-fashioned hotel that still knows how to hold doors and coddle eggs.

A luxury hotel out of another era, **Campton Place** offers the kind of meticulous attention to detail and deft little touches that you thought went out with the Eisenhower era. The rooms are lovely, but more important, the staff here (there are approximately 178 employees for 117 rooms) will make sure your grandparents are comfortable and can get what they want, exactly when they want it, exactly the way they want it. The house car or limo will be waiting for them when they get to the front door; the on-site laundry and drycleaner will have their suits cleaned and pressed (with loose buttons fixed) in as little as two hours; their special dietary needs will be accommodated without even blinking (the full five-star restaurant menu is available for room service); the hotel is literally steps from Union Square so they won't have to schlep all over town to shop; and they'll even allow cats and small dogs to bunk with the grandparents in their room. It's like having your own private San Francisco pied-à-terre.

If grandpa was in the service, or even if he wasn't, the hotel find of the decade—and definitely one for the "who knew?" list—is the **Marines Memorial Club** on Sutter Street, two blocks from Union Square. Built in 1926 as the first women's club west of the Mississippi, it is now a full-service hotel and memorial to the Marine Corp, a "tribute to those that have gone before; and a service to those that carry on," where folks can bunk up in stately colonial-themed rooms complete with marble baths, cherrywood armoires, coffee makers, cable TV, downtown views, and full complimentary breakfast and happy hour cocktails for as little as $100 and change ($150 for non-members). Add on

Cinderella Bakery, Deli, and Restaurant
436 Balboa St.
415-751-9690

East Coast West Delicatessen
1725 Polk St.
415-563-3542

Yamada Seika Confectionery
1955 Sutter St.
415-922-3848

Schubert's Bakery
521 Clement St.
415-752-1580

Campton Place
340 Stockton St.
415-781-5555

Marines Memorial Club
609 Sutter St.
415-673-6672

to the amenities a skyroom restaurant and bar with a piano player that's so below the radar you'd be lucky to find more than a dozen folks up here on a busy night; a Club One fitness center with swimming pool (free to members and guests); a business center with free Internet; a lobby that displays revolving exhibits on Marine Corps history; a museum and library with panoramic views, overstuffed chairs, and a huge array of periodicals current and historic where granddad can raise a glass to his fallen comrades; and an average guest age of around 65—and you've pretty much hit grandparent Nirvana.

The over-the-top theme rooms at **Noe's Nest**, Noe Valley's oldest B&B, aren't to everyone's taste, but if you want your grandparents to stay in the 'hood, and they feel at home in a room that looks like the house they just left (rose-colored fabric wallpaper, floral bedspreads, lacy doilies, French fans, skirts around the nightstand), the French Provincial Room here is the ticket. The inn has some other advantages for the elderly: a full kitchen where Owner Sheila Ash serves a "Brooklyn breakfast" (a good-size nosh), a private entrance, a lovely little sheltered front deck and garden, and no stairs to contend with for those with limited mobility.

Sometimes the best perk you can offer a visiting grandparent is a good night's sleep. At the **Pan Pacific Hotel**, sweet dreams are ensured with spacious, graciously appointed rooms that feature (among other amenities) TVs in the bathroom and a button for the on-call personal butler. But the perk de resistànce is the hotel's custom-made pillows, crafted on-site to your specifications (thick, thin, hard, soft, with feathers, or hypoallergenic). Hard to believe such a thing still exists in this day and age.

Noe's Nest
3973 23rd St.
415-821-0751

**Pan Pacific
Hotel**
500 Post St.
415-771-8600

tour 22 Weary Young Families

They bring you their tired, their weary, their toddlers yearning to be fed. And it's up to you to show them a good time. No pressure. It's only their first real vacation since they had the kids, and they've only been looking forward to it like felons look forward to parole. So now you have to come up with an itinerary that will be fun for grown-ups and also accommodate cranky babies, feeding schedules, nap time, and short attention spans.

Being a parent of a toddler myself these days, and having towed said toddler to several urban centers, I have a few words of advice to pass along to prospective hosts:

- Don't get too ambitious. If you plan a day's itinerary and only end up accomplishing one of the five items, you're doing better than most. As anyone who has little children knows, putting them on your timeline is a frustrating and self-defeating proposition.

- Confine your energetic outings to the morning and early afternoon. Save the late afternoon for more mellow stuff. Do not plan to visit museums in the afternoon unless there's some kind of sit-down activity for the kids, or you risk a dressing-down from a docent who looks just like your third-grade teacher.

- If you're going to visit grown-up places (and you are, because let's face it—this vacation is for Mommy and Daddy), make sure they're places where screaming babies won't be a problem.

- Pack a goody bag filled with "distractions"— toys, crayons and coloring books, Cheerios, stuffed animals, hand puppets, etc. You never know what little children are going to find fascinating, or more importantly, boring.

- Don't expect to expand the children's palates with weird, ethnic cuisines, unless you don't mind getting sushi spit all over the front of your shirt. It is the rare child that appreciates "interesting" foods. Most likely they will want familiar things—peanut butter and jelly, McNuggets, macaroni and cheese, pizza.

- Really want to give depleted parents a vacation to remember? Offer to take the kids to the playground, library, or zoo so your friends can recharge their batteries (and their romance) with a stroll on the beach and a sunset cocktail.

MORNING-NOON

They'll be up at the crack of dawn, so grind the beans the
night before and set the coffeepot timer on "stun." One cup
won't be nearly enough, so after you've propped your eyelids
open, pack up the pram and head down to Noe Valley,
where you can join in the 24th Street Stroller Derby while
you sip a double half-caf latte. These days, you can't say the
words "Honey, don't touch that" without half the population
of Noe Valley turning around to see if you're talking to their
kid. The neighborhood is positively crawling with babies
and new moms and dads, all socializing, sunning, and jock-
eying for stroller position on the benches in front of Holey
Bagel, Tully's, Starbucks, Martha & Bros. Coffee Co.,
Phoenix Books, and the playground at Alvarado School. On
Saturdays, the recently installed **Noe Valley Farmer's Market**
makes for a pleasant compromise: kids can listen to live
music (usually folky guitars) while they snack on fresh-off-
the-tree tangerines and apples; parents can shop for organic
produce, locally farmed honey, dried fruits, nuts, and the
like while they soak up the sunny vibes.

Over in the Inner Sunset, the **Canvas Gallery and Café**,
pivotally located at the 9th Avenue entrance to Golden Gate
Park, offers good coffee, comfy seating (indoors and out),
and an interesting array of whimsical, colorful art that will

intrigue adults and entertain youngsters. (My son played "hide behind
the legs of the six-foot-lady-with-the-
big-pink-lips" for a good half-hour
one morning.)

Afterward, stroll through the park
to the **arboretum** for a spin around
the duck pond—don't miss the turtles
sunning on the northside rocks. If
things are going well—i.e., the kids (and sleep-deprived
parents) haven't run out of gas—walk out the north gate,
past the Japanese Tea Garden and de Young Museum, to JFK
Drive. Just below the bridge near 10th Avenue is the "blue"
playground, a favorite of city parents everywhere. With
climbing structures for both big and little kids surrounded
by spongy landing platforms, a sandbox, swings, a nearby

pedestrian tunnel (that echoes!), and a sunken location sheltered from fog and wind, it's a nice, stress-free spot to sit, have a snack, and enjoy the park.

Other don't-miss park attractions include:

Children's Playground and Carousel—Built in 1887, this was the first children's playground in the United States to be constructed in a public park. The swings and slides have been augmented over the years by a geodesic climbing structure/jungle gym and other modern playground fare, but the most popular attraction here is still the historic Herschell-Spillman Carousel. Built in 1914 and still boasting its original band organ, the restored carousel features hand-carved and hand-painted horses, as well as a pig, a gazelle, an ostrich, a tiger, and an old-fashioned sleigh. The carousel currently operates from June through September.

Stow Lake—This is a great late-afternoon activity. Pack a couple of peanut butter sandwiches and some juice boxes and rent a pedal boat (the rowboats are too much work; the motorboats are not very PC). Let the kids work the rudder—that is, until you crash into Strawberry Island. Boats rent by the hour, and the lake's not that big, so take your time. And don't forget to bring breadcrumbs for the ducks. If you're feeling ambitious, hike up Strawberry Hill for the views of the city and the top of sparkling Huntington Falls.

Pedal-Powered Surreys—The bicycles-built-for-six with baby seats in front look a lot easier than they are, so if you don't feel like huffing and puffing (or getting out and pushing them back up the hill to the rental office at Stow Lake), this may not be for you. They are, however, a fun way to tour the park on a languid Sunday afternoon.

Buffalo Paddock—It still seems weird to me to see real, live buffalo walking around in Golden Gate Park, but there they are at the western end. You probably won't get close enough to pet one, but little ones might find those horned, shaggy heads a little intimidating anyway.

Spreckels Lake—Just west of the paddock is this popular model boat pond, where little boys have been known to go into hyperactive overload while watching the remote-controlled sailboats and yachts cruise the lake.

Noe Valley Farmer's Market
24th St. between Church and Sanchez
415-248-1332

Canvas Gallery and Café
1200 9th Ave.
415-504-0060

Arboretum
9th Ave. and Lincoln

Children's Playground and Carousel
Golden Gate Park at Sharon Meadow near Stanyan St.

Stow Lake
Golden Gate Park on Stow Lake Drive opposite 17th Ave.

Pedal-Powered Surreys
Stow Lake Boathouse
415-668-6699

Buffalo Paddock
Golden Gate Park near 36th Ave.

Spreckels Lake
Golden Gate Park opposite 36th Ave.

Trains, Cable Cars, and Great Big Ships

For little kids, something as simple as riding **BART** (Bay Area Rapid Transit) constitutes entertainment. An acquaintance of mine has spent entire weekends taking his grandson to no particular destination on buses and trains and streetcars. My nephew dawdled away a day climbing on a single fire truck. So when you're thinking about your grown-up destination, factor in a kid-friendly way to get there.

Start off with a streetcar or bus ride to **Union Square**. Take in the sights and the shops until the kids start to get fussy, then make a detour into the **Disney Store**, where big-screen cartoons and trailers for the next Disney animated classic will keep them occupied while you shop for Nemo baseball caps. Another great shop stop for kids is **Sanrio**, home of the popular Japanese character Hello Kitty and her friends Spotty Dotty and Kerokeroppi. While its location on the bottom floor of the San Francisco Centre isn't exactly

high-profile, this flagship store does carry every single licensed product Sanrio makes, down to the last key chain.

Next tour the lobby of the venerable **Westin St. Francis Hotel**, making sure to stand under the large clock in the corner: it's been a meeting place for San Franciscans since the turn of the 20th century. Don't leave the St. Francis without riding the famous outdoor glass elevators to the top of the hotel—an E ticket for the short set and, for adults, a fabulous bird's-eye view of downtown, the Bay Bridge, and Coit Tower.

The other great glass elevator ride is at the **Hyatt Regency** in the Embarcadero Center. The architecture of the hotel is unusual in that the hallways and balconies look inward, with plants and lights cascading down the sides of a seventeen-story lobby atrium. The high-speed elevators face the atrium and the ride up feels like what would happen if they turned a high-rise building inside out.

You might want to make this part of Day Two's itinerary, but if your guests are not too tired, catch the Powell-Mason cable car heading to Fisherman's Wharf and get off at Washington and Mason streets, home of the **Cable Car Barn and Museum**. Kids could probably spend the whole afternoon standing on the observation platform watching the cable wind around the giant wheels. But if they lose interest, there are also a couple of restored, vintage cable cars to check out while parents watch the movie about the history of the cable car and how it works.

From here, climb back on the cable car and take it to the end of the line. Then make your way down to **Hyde Street Pier**, where the kids can climb through a ship galley, raise a sail, or pretend they're Captain Hook as they spin the steering wheel on the square-rigger *Balclutha* or the *C.A. Thayer.* In the spring and fall the park hosts sea music concerts and chantey singing; in September, there's the annual Festival of the Sea, with boat rides and all kinds of hands-on maritime activities for children.

Before nap time (theirs, not yours), indulge in a little chocolate decadence at the **Ghirardelli Chocolate Manufactory and Soda Fountain**. While you wait for your Emperor Norton (a hot fudge banana split) or your Alcatraz Rock (rocky-road ice cream in a shell of hard chocolate), go to the mini-production center at the back of the room and watch melted milk chocolate slosh around in big vats.

And if you're already down here, you can't bypass Pier 39. Best bets for the attention-span-challenged include the carousel, the sea lions, and **Aquarium of the Bay**, a people-mover that transports you "under" the ocean through two clear, acrylic tunnels, where you're surrounded by hundreds of fish. Upstairs there are also touch tanks with bat rays and starfish. Afterward, grab a bite at the **Bubba Gump Shrimp Company**, a loud, touristy restaurant inspired by the movie *Forrest Gump*. Definitely not haute cuisine (or haute atmosphere), the place has other charms: great bay views and all kinds of cool stuff on the walls for kids to look at. In addition to fare such as pizza, corn dogs, and burgers, more advanced palates might dive into coconut or barbecued shrimp or the Bucket of Boat Trash—deep-fried shrimp, lobster, and other undersea goodies.

BART Info
415-989-2278

Union Square
between Stockton, Powell, Geary and Post streets

Disney Store
400 Post St.
415-391-6866

Sanrio
San Francisco Shopping Centre, Powell and Market streets
415-495-3056

Westin St. Francis Hotel
335 Powell St.
415-397-7000

Hyatt Regency
5 Embarcadero Center
415-788-1234

Cable Car Barn and Museum
1201 Mason St.
415-474-1887

Hyde Street Pier
at Aquatic Park, end of Hyde St.

Ghirardelli Chocolate Manufactory and Soda Fountain
900 North Point
415-775-5500

Aquarium of the Bay
Pier 39
415-623-5300

Bubba Gump Shrimp Company
Pier 39
415-781-4867

The next day, for a waterfront experience that's completely the opposite of Pier 39, take your train enthusiasts big and small to the **Golden Gate Railroad Museum** in Hunter's Point. Yes, Hunter's Point. And before you dismiss

this idea as being too, um, "scenic" for little children and delicate Midwestern sensibilities, let me explain. The old Hunter's Point naval shipyard on the Bay is like the land that time forgot, related to the surrounding gritty housing projects in name only. On a spit way down at the end of Evans Avenue, next to the old railroad tracks, you'll see Southern Pacific, State Belt Railroad and other retired (read: discarded) trains that once made California the glamorous queen of rail travel. A group of volunteer locomotive enthusiasts, some of them former employees, decided to restore the cars and make them available to the public. Sporting names such as the Daylights, the California Zephyr, Cascade, Sunset, and Lark, the collection and its keepers have re-created a time when San Francisco was the epicenter of train transportation. Kids get to climb aboard steam engines, see photos of the trains in their glory days, and explore sleeper cars, old-time diner lounges, and even a railway Post Office car. Best part: They can take a ride on one of the engines and sound the train whistle.

For parents, the best time to visit the museum is in May or October during **Open Studios**, when the more than 300 artists who now occupy a number of the old navy buildings open their studios to the public. You can actually ride a train from the railroad yard to Building 101, where the main contingent of artists is housed. During Open Studios, they usually augment their art with live music and good food. A win-win all around.

Museums They Can Handle

So this isn't exactly stimulation for adult minds. Once in a while you gotta give in.

Coyote Point Museum—Located a short drive down the Peninsula in San Mateo, this hands-on nature museum is

a great, bite-size alternative to the Academy of Sciences,
located on a picturesque stretch of the Bay. Outside, a sunny
garden path dotted with benches leads past foxes, river
otters, and a large aviary. Kids can peer inside a honeybee
hive and then grab dress-up wings and antennae or
beekeeper masks and pretend they're making honey.
Zig-zagging ramps that take you from "sea level" to "mountaintop" make for hours of entertainment for energetic 3-
year-olds. Best bet for friends with kids in the aforementioned age bracket: come on Toddler Tuesdays (second and
fourth Tuesdays of the month), when the museum offers a
variety of discovery activities aimed at ages 2 to 5.

Bay Area Discovery Museum—The indoor/outdoor
interactive museum, designed for kids ages one to 10, is
located in east Fort Baker, on the waterfront at the base of
the north end of the Golden Gate Bridge. If the kids are still
in Bjorns or strollers, make this an all-morning outing by
parking in the south end lot, walking across the bridge and
down Alexander Avenue to the complex of historic army
buildings that house the museum. Once there, toddlers can
hang out in the Tot Space exploring bat caves, pint-size
houses, and rooms with squishy floors. Older kids can
check out special programs that range from scientific explo-
rations of the planet to interactive exhibits based on
"Sesame Street," "Arthur," and other popular children's
shows. You'll also find a construction zone, a crawl-through
"underwater" tunnel, and a miniature train depot; recent
renovations have added an expanded arts-and-crafts space,
and Lookout Cove, a bayside area with water play activities,
a shipwreck, and a miniature Golden Gate Bridge.

San Francisco Fire Department Museum—This is the
place to take boys like my aforementioned nephew, who are
entranced by anything to do with trucks and who go
ballistic at the sight of a fire engine. The collection of
historic fire-fighting memorabilia includes one of the first
fire engines in San Francisco, which was shipped around the
Horn in 1849, as well as an 1897 steam fire engine and an
old hook-and-ladder truck. Plus, the museum is attached to
a firehouse with a real working fire pole. Mom and Dad
might enjoy reading about the glory days of San Francisco's

Golden Gate Railroad Museum Hunter's Point Shipyard 415-822-8728

Open Studios 934 Brannan St. 415-861-9838, www.artspan.org

Coyote Point Museum 1651 Coyote Point Drive, San Mateo, 650-342-7755

Bay Area Discovery Museum Fort Baker, first Sausalito exit after crossing the Golden Gate Bridge on Highway 101, Sausalito 415-487-4398

San Francisco Fire Department Museum 655 Presidio Ave. 415-558-3546

fire department, especially the volunteer units that operated during the Gold Rush and the Great Earthquake of 1906.

Asian Art Museum—No, not for the fine art, but for the storytelling on Sundays and first Saturday of the month

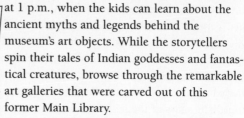

at 1 p.m., when the kids can learn about the ancient myths and legends behind the museum's art objects. While the storytellers spin their tales of Indian goddesses and fantastical creatures, browse through the remarkable art galleries that were carved out of this former Main Library.

Gulf of the Farallones National Marine Sanctuary Visitor Center—While technically not a museum, the center offers a wonderful display that's great for small children, including a touch tank filled with anemones, clams, urchins and the like, a button where you can listen to recordings of seabirds, and sand tables where kids can dig for shells and starfish.

Randall Museum—Kids will love looking at and petting the museum's resident animals—chickens, rabbits, turtles, and owls. Grown-ups can take in the astounding views from the top of Corona Heights. Both will love the working model-railroad town located in the basement.

Wells Fargo History Museum—An authentic 19th-century Pony Express stagecoach that you can climb into, real gold nuggets from the Gold Rush, and stuff belonging to the notorious stagecoach robber Black Bart are the main attractions at this small Financial District museum, located inside the bank of the same name.

Hiller Aviation Museum—More than 40 airplanes, helicopters, and inventive flying craft hang from the ceiling and fill the hangar of this museum, which chronicles aviation history from 1869 into the future.

Shanghai Surprise

With all the funny little toys and colorful candies in open bins at the shops along Grant Avenue in Chinatown, you'll be lucky if you get from one end to the other without a temper tantrum. Fortunately, most things in the sidewalk stands go for pocket change. My favorite "must have" items from childhood include the candies wrapped in paper that melts in your mouth, the Chinese nesting dolls, and the little chirping bird pins.

On many Sundays throughout the year, you can get an abbreviated version of the Chinese New Year parade when Lion Dancers prowl Grant Avenue scaring off evil spirits. Light firecrackers or pop those little gunpowder caps as the colorful, 30-foot lion with the blinking eyelids bobs, weaves, and snakes its way down the street. Afterward, take the gang to the **Far East Café**, where you can sit in mysterious, curtained, wooden compartments and pretend you're in a Charlie Chan movie. The restaurant, which dates back to 1920, offers all the classic, safe Chinese-American dishes that kids like: sweet and sour pork, sizzling rice and won ton soup, chow mein, and chop suey (a hash of bean-sprouts, noodles, pork, and sauce that was supposedly invented in San Francisco).

For dessert, pay a visit to one of Chinatown's fortune cookie factories. At the tiny **Golden Gate Fortune Cookie Company** on Ross Alley you can watch little old ladies sitting at ancient-looking machines pick up flat cookie disks and fold them around a metal peg into their familiar shapes. Then buy a big bag of sesame, almond, or traditional fortune cookies to munch on.

The family-owned **Mee Mee Bakery** on Stockton Street, one of the oldest cookie bakeries in the city, is a bigger operation, producing dozens of different kinds of fresh-daily Chinese cookies, including ginger, walnut, sesame, and maca-roons. The bakery offers the added allure of fortune cookies that contain your own, personal fortune. If you buy the prepackaged kind, just make sure they aren't the ones with the racy messages (save those until after the kids are asleep, when sex-starved parents can really appreciate them).

Parking It

It's big, it's green, it comes equipped with a children's play-ground, a cheap, uncrowded bowling alley, a swimming pool, cool things to climb on, and a lovely little restaurant where you can get a gourmet sack lunch. It's the Presidio,

Asian Art Museum
200 Larkin St.
415-379-8800

Gulf of the Farallones National Marine Sanctuary Visitor Center
West Crissy Field
415-561-6625

Randall Museum
199 Museum Way,
off Roosevelt Way
415-554-9600

Wells Fargo History Museum
420 Montgomery St.,
415-396-2619

Hiller Aviation Museum
601 Skyway Road,
San Carlos, 650-654-0200

Far East Café
631 Grant Ave.
415-982-3245

Golden Gate Fortune Cookie Company
56 Ross Alley
415-781-3956

Mee Mee Bakery
1328 Stockton St.
415-362-3204

which should begin with a walk around the Main Post and Fort Scott (with requisite stops to climb on the cannons and guns) and a dip into the visitor center and bookstore. Afterward, pony up for a few frames at the **Presidio Bowling Center** next to the parade grounds, which, while not the locals-only secret it used to be (like the tennis courts, gym and swimming pool), is still relatively uncrowded and reasonably priced. There's plenty of free parking, and after

you're done throwing two-handed gutter balls, you can walk down the road to **Desiree**, Anne Gingrass's little epicurean hideaway (open for breakfast and lunch only) and drown your sorrows in a perfectly grilled ham-and-cheese or vegetable sandwich and a bag of fresh-baked sugar cookies. Then if you're up for it, splash around at the YMCA swimming pool, which has open swim hours every day, or if you don't feel like getting wet, head to the southern end of the Presidio and **Julius Kahn Playground**. While there are plenty of kiddie parks in town where you can fritter away a pleasant afternoon, not many of them offer an architectural survey of the city's most extravagant and glamorous mansions.

Afterward, exit out the Lombard Street gate and push the stroller across Marina Boulevard, following the waterfront road that skirts the Golden Gate yacht harbor, until you reach the Wave Organ. This is a unique musical instrument composed of some twenty granite pipes that sit at various depths in the breakwater, creating harmonic sounds when the ocean hits them. The best concert is at high tide.

Monsters and Merry-Go-Rounds

I'm not a huge advocate of the Metreon center for small children (a half-hour here winds them up as much as a handful of candy bars and a Power Rangers marathon), but make an exception for **Where the Wild Things Are**, the giant, interactive storybook on the fourth floor, which is based on Maurice Sendak's famous book. Enormous tree slides, a mirror maze, flowers that bloom at the push of a button, whack-a-mole, and monsters that dance when you step on certain areas of the floor are just some of the surprises at this inventive, truly fun amusement center. And when the kids finally crash, there's the Night Kitchen restaurant for french fries, pizza, and a big glass of milk.

Get Outta Town

Though parents may have delusions that this will be fun ("we'll take turns!"), let me tell you from experience, wine tasting with small children is a pain in the butt. Kids are generally not welcomed in wine-tasting rooms, and chasing a little one around a barn while your other half gets sloshy on cabernet just makes for feelings of resentment. A nice compromise is the **Rouge et Noir Cheese Factory**, located nine miles southwest of Petaluma, off the road that continues at the end of D Street. The Thompson family has been making seriously wonderful and wonderfully stinky French and Austrian cheeses (Camembert, Brie, Schloss, breakfast cheese) for five generations. The factory sits on five acres of lawn dotted with picnic tables, surrounding an idyllic duck pond. Get your cheese, your bread, your garlic-stuffed olives, and your nice bottle of wine, plunk yourself down at one of the tables or on the grass, and let the kids run around or feed the ducks while you kick back and live the life.

Going to hear live music with kids (unless it's "The Wiggles" in concert) can be frustrating in the same way that winetasting is. One of you ends up running around while the other guiltily half-listens to the music—that is, if they even let the kids into the show. So one of the happiest discoveries of my parenting life thus far has been the afternoon shows and barbecues at **Rancho Nicasio**, a bucolic little spread in the rolling hills of Marin County, just west of Novato. Part restaurant, part music venue, part town square, the ranch hosts great concerts year round, attracting musicians such as Maria Muldaur, Box Set, Dave Alvin, and New Riders of the Purple Sage. On select summer weekends, they set up the outdoor stage and the grill for afternoon all-ages shows where Moms and Dads can kick back on a lawn chair with a glass of wine and an ear of corn, listening to real live grown-up music, while little kids twirl on the deck, roll in

Presidio Bowling Center
at the corner of Montgomery and Moraga in the Presidio
415-561-2695

Desiree
inside the San Francisco Film Centre, Presidio, 39 Mesa St.
415-561-3456

Julius Kahn Playground
in the Presidio, Pacific Ave. near Spruce St.

Where the Wild Things Are
Metreon, 3rd floor, 101 Fourth St.
415-369-6000

Marin French Cheese Co. (Rogue et Noir Factory)
7500 Red Hill Road, Petaluma
800-292-6001

Rancho Nicasio
1 Old Rancheria Road, Nicasio
415-662-2219

the grass, throw horseshoes, or lick their saucy fingers. It's a bona fide miracle.

Great Kids' Tours

The key to success with children and structured activities is that they should be short on talk and long on rewards:

Basic Brown Bear—Select a teddy bear from among dozens of styles, and then have a ball filling him with soft innards. Tours of the factory are offered nearly every day.

Jelly Belly Factory—This factory in Fairfield is where the Goelitz Candy Company, the inventor of those gourmet bubble gum, pina colada, and (yuck) popcorn jellybeans, makes its sweet, chewy creations. Tours take you through the production rooms, and include at the end (on weekdays) lots of free samples. They also make a full range of gummi candies.

Mrs. Grossman's Sticker Factory—Don't know about you, but I went through half a factory's worth of stickers during potty training alone. Andrea Grossman, the woman who launched the stickers-by-the-yard craze some 20 years ago, is now the largest sticker manufacturer in the United States. Her Petaluma factory offers free daily tours, where kids can watch as millions of stickers get printed, packaged, and shipped. After the tour, you can go to the sticker art room to decorate your own postcard and you get a package of stickers to take home. The visitor center also houses a museum of sorts, where hundreds of "classic" stickers are on display.

San Francisco Zoo—All kids love the zoo; nothing new there. But if your friends are here in July, take them on the Night Tour, when kids get to feed giraffes, watch the nocturnal animals prowl around, and see what animals do after dark. There's also entertainment and a barbecue picnic dinner. During the rest of the year, the zoo's greatest hits include the lemur habitat, the Primate Discovery Center, the Lion House (where you can watch the big cats feast on raw meat), and the children's petting zoo.

DINNER

Not every meal out has to be at Pizza Hut or McDonald's. Here are some less-greasy options (for more ideas, see Nieces/Nephews):

Chenery Park—At last, a grown-up white-tablecloth restaurant that does more than just put up with children. Tuesdays "kids bring the parents" nights have become something of a phenomenon in sleepy Glen Park, when foodies with four-year-olds descend on the southern-inspired restaurant (think chicken-fried steak, gumbo, and meatloaf with blue-cheese-smashed potatoes) for a night of dining, drinking, and the sort of mayhem only a parent—and a patient waitstaff—could endure. Lucky for you, you're surrounded by other parents who will only sigh with relief when your little angel throws his chicken fingerlings across the room, providing a diversion from what's going on at their table.

Café Pescatore—Despite its location near the Wharf, this is a very good Italian restaurant, rivaling many North Beach eateries. The pasta dishes are exceptional, and the seafood is fresh and not oversauced. For kids, there are simple dishes like spaghetti with butter, spaghetti Bolognese (with meat sauce), penne pasta with fresh veggies, and wood-fired pizzas.

Mel's—I've eaten here with friends who had two fidgety little ones crawling all over the place, and the waiter never even batted an eye. The menu of mostly comfort food—meatloaf, turkey and mashed potatoes, triple-decker BLTs—seems to bridge the generation gap. Kids get theirs served inside a cardboard car, and they'll honor requests like a scrambled egg with "no things in it."

Hornblower Dining Yachts—Not for the easily seasick, this is an entertaining way for families to sightsee around the bay and eat a nice meal at the same time. No high chairs, but you can and should bring strollers with locking wheels. If sailing the high seas turns out not to be their thing, at least the kids cruised for half price.

Rainforest Café—Sensory overload for young and old alike, this Disney-style theme restaurant is done up like a

Basic Brown Bear
The Cannery,
2801 Leavenworth St.
415-409-2806

Jelly Belly Factory
2400 North Wattney Way,
Fairfield
707-428-2838

Mrs. Grossman's Sticker Factory
3810 Cypress Drive, Petaluma,
800-429-4549

San Francisco Zoo
off Great Highway at Sloat Blvd.
415-753-7080

Chenery Park
683 Chenery St.
415-337-8537

Café Pescatore
2455 Mason St.
415-561-1111

Mel's
2165 Lombard St.
415-921-3039, and
3355 Geary Blvd.
415-387-2244

Hornblower Dining Yachts
Pier 33
415-788-8866

CHINA BEACH

If it's warm enough (you know, that one day during the year), and you want to visit the ocean, the beach to take little kids to is China Beach, located in the refined confines of Sea Cliff (end of Seacliff Avenue, 415-239-2366). The small, sheltered cove has (relatively) clean bathrooms, a small enough stretch of sand that kids can't run completely out of sight, picnic tables, a pier, and in summer months, a lifeguard. Very civilized. Afterward, walk up Seacliff Avenue past the mauve house flying the flag with the blue wolf on it—that's where Robin Williams lives.

rainforest jungle with vines, waterfalls, and life-size gorillas, elephants, snakes, and birds that move and make noise. The giant tropical fish tank is a big draw; the gorilla that occasionally goes a bit ape may frighten little ones. Biggest surprise—the food is decent.

El Mansour—Moroccan food may be iffy for little ones, but there's always rice and bread. And they'll love sitting on cushions on the floor and eating with their fingers while the belly dancer clangs her finger cymbals and shimmies around the room.

Sapporo-Ya—Big bowls of ramen noodle soup (noodles made right on the premises) are the main attraction at this little restaurant on the second floor of the Japantown center. My kid loves 'em, and afterward, we always go downstairs to the photo booths, where you can get your picture on a dozen miniature Hello Kitty stickers.

WHERE TO STAY

The best accommodations for friends with little children (who go to bed early, and eat dinner and take a bath even earlier) is a fully stocked house—preferably one that's been baby-proofed. Short of that, you might suggest the **Donatello**. Located in the heart of downtown, this hotel is a rare find in the city: a four-star property that is operated by a timeshare vacation company, and as such boasts spacious rooms (400 square feet) that come equipped with microwaves, toasters, bar sinks, comfy sofas, and VCRs. The hotel even has a complimentary video library in the lobby. For grown-ups, there's also a nice Jacuzzi and his-and-her saunas.

Hotels are fine and good, but camping out is way better. For folks who want the benefits of camping (campfires, s'mores, stargazing, beach-combing, leaf-peeping) without the mess, the cold, or even the tent, there's **Costanoa**, Joie de Vivre's upscale campground and lodge just south of Pescadero. Accommodations range from pitch-your-own-tent to adorable canvas tent-cabins, to a full-on lodge with all the trimmings (massage, sauna, hot tub). After you've hit the tidepools and barked at the elephant seals (Año Nuevo State Park is a mile down the road), head back and cook up dinner on the barbecue (premarinated fixin's provided at the general store/café) or sit down for a meal of fresh-caught local salmon or stuffed chicken breast. Now that's what I call camping.

For price, location, and the all-important outdoor swimming pool, it's hard to top the **Hotel Del Sol**, a revamped motor lodge that is done up like a sunny California beach house. The flurry of family-friendly features include suites with kitchenettes, bunk beds, board games, toys, and child-friendly furnishings; a pillow lending library; free parking on the premises; and complimentary kites, beach balls, and sunglasses for exploring the surrounding Marina waterfront.

Rainforest Café
145 Jefferson St.
415-440-5610

El Mansour
3119 Clement St.
415-751-2312

Sapporo-Ya
1581 Webster St.
415-563-7400

The Donatello
501 Post St.
415-441-7100

Costanoa
200 Rossi Road at
Hwy. I, Pescadero
650-879-1100

Hotel Del Sol
3100 Webster St.
415-921-5520

Culture Vultures

There are the culture sparrows—small-town folk for whom San Francisco is indeed the Big City, who come here looking to soak up the kind of big city culture they can't get at the state fair. These sorts of guests can inspire you to finally getting around to seeing that Diane Arbus exhibit at MOMA. On the negative side, as host, it may mean having to go to Beach Blanket Babylon for the umpteenth time.

Then there are the culture vultures—those voracious, guidebook-toting trivia buffs whose appetite for the arts is insatiable. They come here to peck meat off the city's cultural bones until not even a scrap of street theater is left. For them, no museum is too small, no piece of historical minutia too obscure, no dance group too interpretive. The benefits are obvious: you'll finally go to the places you often thought about visiting back when you first moved here. Places that sounded lofty and intellectually intriguing and definitely black turtleneck. On the dark side, you may find yourself in an audience of six, watching some extremely bad theater, with no hope of making an inconspicuous exit. Either way, it's an "experience."

MORNING

Being culturally conscious doesn't just mean staying awake during the third act, it means taking a big spoon and dipping it into San Francisco's bubbling ethnic melting pot. Start Saturday off with a whirlwind education in the deep-rooted tradition of Mexican muralism on a **Precita Eyes Mural Arts Center** tour of the Mission district. The neighborhood is a hotbed of public murals (more than sixty in an eight-block area), most of which tell the history of the Chicano and Latin community. The tour is led by artists who work with the center and know all the stories behind the murals and the people who did them. Pay special attention when you get to Balmy Alley, where practically every garage, doorway, and cement wall is covered with art.

Mural buffs will also want to seek out the city's notable Diego Rivera frescoes. The one with the easiest access is inside the **San Francisco Art Institute** between North Beach and Russian Hill. "The Making of a Fresco Showing the Building of a City, 1931" is well worth the hike up Chestnut Street to the skylit gallery off the courtyard. Filling the entire north wall, the painting depicts portraits of artists and patrons working on the mural-within-the-mural, as well as Rivera himself, sitting on the scaffold, his back to the viewer.

Less accessible, but worth the effort—especially if your friends want a little Frida Kahlo thrown in with their Diego—is the Pan American Unity mural (1940) at **City College** out on Ocean Avenue. Rivera's wife is depicted in the third panel of this sweeping work, which according to Rivera, is about "the marriage of the artistic expression of

Precita Eyes Mural Arts Center
2981 24th St.
415-285-2287

San Francisco Art Institute
800 Chestnut St.
415-771-7020

City College (Diego Rivera mural)
50 Phelan Ave.
415-239-3127

the North and of the South on this continent." This fresco, along with "The Allegory of California" at the **San Francisco City Club** above the Pacific Stock Exchange, may be viewed by appointment and on tours scheduled by the Mexican Museum (415-441-0404).

Next head down to **Fort Mason**, where you can expand your worldview across three continents at the Museum of Craft & Folk Art, the Museo Italo Americano, and the African-American Historical and Cultural Society.

The **Museum of Craft & Folk Art** is dedicated to contemporary craft, American folk art, and traditional cultural art. Exhibits cross media and geographical bound-

aries, with shows ranging from Japanese textiles to quilts, war toys, and Native American glass. The gift shop is a great source of Christmas presents and interesting souvenirs for the folks back home.

Museo Italo Americano doesn't have a huge space or a vast collection, but like the Italian contingent in North Beach, a little devotion goes a long way. Your paisano friends from New York will admire the tenacity of this small society, which has dedicated itself to preserving Italian culture in this western outpost. The shows consist mostly of contemporary Italian and Italian-American painting, etchings, and photography, as well as works that foster appreciation of modern Italian culture and art. They also have regular screenings for and by Italian filmmakers.

The **African-American Historical and Cultural Society** is more of a resource center and research facility for those interested in the history of African-Americans on the West Coast, but the exhibitions (often mounted in the nearby Bayfront Gallery) can be truly exceptional. FYI: a new, expansive **Museum of the African Diaspora**, scheduled to open in late 2005, will occupy three floors of the new St. Regis Museum Tower in the Yerba Buena district. It will celebrate the culture of African-descended people and the African

American experience through interactive exhibits and first-person oral histories collected from people of all ages, backgrounds, and socio-economic levels.

More Alternative Museums

Of course you'll want to make a pilgrimage to the quadruple crown of local museums—the de Young (reopening in 2005), the Legion of Honor, MOMA, and the Asian Art Museum—but once you've done that, try something a little more obscure.

Wells Fargo History Museum—Actual gold nuggets found in the streams up north in the 1850s and a genuine Concord stagecoach are the main attractions here, a fun little slice of western pioneering history in the middle of the Financial District.

Telephone Pioneer Communications Museum—San Francisco's first skyscraper, the magnificent Timothy Pflueger-designed Pacific Telephone building houses a small but fascinating collection of early telephone ephemera: a replica of Alexander Graham Bell's original telephone, San Francisco's first telephone book, antique switchboards, and other early communications devices.

Pacific Heritage Museum—Located on the site of the old U.S. Subtreasury and the city's first mint, you can still see the original coin vaults from strategically placed windows. The museum features Thai decorative and ceremonial objects, costumes, ancient Chinese pottery, calligraphy, and old photographs that trace San Francisco's ties to the Pacific Rim.

Main Library—The library hosts some terrific exhibits about the life and times of San Francisco, ranging from a historic look at Angel Island to fond remembrances of the wacky and wonderful denizens who gave the city its character. Lots of other interesting memorabilia—souvenir programs from the opening of the Golden Gate Bridge, postcards from the Pan-Pacific Expo—can be found inside the glass cases of the San Francisco History Room.

San Francisco City Club
310 Pine St.
415-441 0404

Fort Mason
Buchanan St. and
Marina Blvd.
415-979-3010

Museum of Craft & Folk Art
Fort Mason Center,
Building A
415-775-0991

Museo Italo Americano
Laguna St. and
Marina Blvd.
415-673-2200

African-American Historical and Cultural Society
Building C, Fort
Mason
415-441-0640

Museum of the African Diaspora
St. Regis Museum
Tower, 3rd and
Mission streets
415-358-7200

Wells Fargo History Museum
420 Montgomery
415-396-2619

Telephone Pioneer Communications Museum
140 New
Montgomery St.
415-542-0182

Pacific Heritage Museum
608 Commercial St.
415-399-1124

Main Library
Grove and Larkin
streets
415-557-4400

The Art Mart

There are dozens of galleries in this town, some of which sell serious art to collectors and people who know, others which sell schlock to people who don't know. I don't pretend to be an arbiter of either, but I know what I like. Here is a brief rundown of places probably worth a second look.

Southern Exposure—Local artists mingle with the community that supports them at this large, sunny, nonprofit gallery. Many emerging talents have been discov-

ered here and gone on to fame and fortune. Just consider the roster of names on their "box set" (a collection of editions donated by various artists to support SoEx's programs): Enrique Chagoya, Rebeca Bollinger, Castaneda/Reiman, Barry McGee, and Rigo.

Paul Thiebaud Gallery—Owned by the son of artist Wayne Thiebaud, this is a prime spot to view and purchase paintings by the Bay Area artist, whose works grace the halls of many a museum of modern art. Included in the mix are several of Thiebaud's San Francisco street scenes and his famous cakes and pies.

Art Exchange—If your friends are interested in purchasing art, but their last names aren't Trump or Getty, take them to Art Exchange. This gallery sells original, quality cast-offs from museums and private collections, at very reasonable and occasionally remarkable prices. Media include sculpture, painting, prints, and works on paper. The racks and bins can be like a bargain basement sale at the Met.

Thomas Reynolds Fine Art—Looking for art as souvenir? Ignore your first instinct to go to Fisherman's Wharf and steer them instead to Thomas Reynolds, located in the chic Upper Fillmore district. Reynolds, a former magazine editor, carries a wonderful range of San Francisco cityscapes by emerging, talented local artists, including James Stagg and white-hot Thai artist Veerakeat Tongpaiboon.

SoMa Goes SoHo

The South of Market art boom shows no signs of slowing down. Besides the big draws—the San Francisco Museum of Modern Art (MOMA) and the Yerba Buena Center for the Arts—the district around 3rd and Mission/Howard will soon be home to the splendid Mexican Museum, the Jewish Museum, and the Museum of the African Diaspora. But it's the alleyways and sidestreets that offer some of the most interesting alternatives to the oil-on-canvas diet you're fed downtown.

On a whirlwind tour, your first stop should be the airy upstairs aerie of **Crown Point Press**, a working atelier specializing in etchings and woodblock prints that has collaborated over the years with such artists as Richard Diebenkorn, Nathan Oliveira, and John Cage. Hardwood floors and skylights create a warm, welcoming atmosphere that's almost like being inside someone's incredibly tastefully decorated flat. Tucked into a corner is **Califia Books**, a studio selling exquisite letterpress editions and artist-made books. Afterward, stop in next door for lunch at the wonderful Cal-Asian restaurant, **Hawthorne Lane**. Culture snobs (and foodies) will appreciate the fact that owner David Gingrass was one of the original stars of Wolfgang Puck's Postrio. But unlike Postrio, you won't have to wait two weeks to get in (and even if it is booked up, the tables at the front of the house are always reserved for walk-ins).

Just behind MOMA is **Aurobora Press**, a fine-art printing press dedicated to monoprints and monotypes, as well as a small body of work that's produced on-site. The gallery is housed in a stunning former firehouse built in 1907 with bricks from the rubble of the Great Earthquake.

Around the corner is 111 **Minna Street Gallery** which, like 330 Ritch Street, doubles as a performance and events space. Contemporary paintings, sculpture, and pop art (their exhibit of "anti-Barbies," which included the now quasi-famous Trailer Trash Barbie, was stupendous) are rounded out by a rockin' happy hour, complete with eclectic live music, and the odd art-film screening.

Next, stop in at **Meandra**, the newly founded **San Francisco Design Museum**. This largely undiscovered

Southern Exposure
401 Alabama St.
415-863-2141

Paul Thiebaud Gallery
718 Columbus Ave.
415-434-3055

Art Exchange
645 Chestnut St.
415-956-5750

Thomas Reynolds Fine Art
2291 Pine St.
415-441-4093

Crown Point Press
20 Hawthorne Lane
415-974-6273

Califia Books
20 Hawthorne Lane
415-284-0314

Hawthorne Lane
22 Hawthorne Lane
415-777-9779

Aurobora Press
147 Natoma St.
415-546-7880

111 Minna Street Gallery
111 Minna St.
415-995-4949
(recorded info)
415-974-1719

Meandra/San Francisco Design Museum
Metreon, 2nd floor,
101 4th St., www.
meandra.org

museum showcases eye-popping design in all its forms—a perfect fit given its setting on the second floor of the flashy, hi-tech Metreon center. Exhibits span media from advertising and package design to furniture and industrial products. A glowing footbridge leads to the Action Theater, where they host films and lectures. Future exhibits promise a fascinating array of work from robots, to wearable art and game design.

Farther west, **San Francisco Camerawork**, entering its

third decade, provides exposure (sorry) for emerging and mid-career photographers at the local, national and international level. Its galleries, in a space shared by New Langton Arts, have featured works by artists such as Talking Heads founder David Byrne; its lectures have brought in names like Robert Mapplethorpe and William Wegman.

Obviously, if you're a culture vulture looking for carrion South of Market, the **Museum of Modern Art** is your prime destination. But even for voracious appetites, the whole museum in one day can be a bit much. If you're watching your intake, make room for the permanent collection of paintings, which includes a couple of important Matisses, Robert Indiana's famous "Love," and works by Salvador Dali, Diego Rivera, and Robert Arneson, among others. The multimedia installations are always intriguing (if not occasionally perturbing), and the fifth floor is worth going to just so you can walk across the see-through metal bridge under that amazing cylindrical skylight. The one thing that you absolutely shouldn't miss is the MOMA store, which is second only to the Met's shop. The modern-art jewelry alone will keep you in Christmas presents for years, and the bookshelves offer a great selection of quirky little volumes by local artists, which will occupy your friends for hours.

NOON-NIGHT

Nothing whets the cultured appetite more than a night at the symphony, ballet, or opera. Lucky thing for your visiting arts animals that we have world-class entries in all three categories.

Getting tickets to the **San Francisco Opera** can be a challenge even if your name is Getty, but you can often find extra seats the night of the performance. A small number of student rush tickets ($15) go on sale at the box office at 11 a.m. until 30 minutes before showtime. Season-ticket holders who can't make it for one reason or another also occasionally donate their tickets so that some lucky soul—maybe you—gets primo seats spitting distance from the soprano. If your pals are just overwhelmed by the grandeur of Wagner and don't care where they sit, there's also a limited number of standing-room-only spots available behind the orchestra section for $10, but you'll have to get to the box office by 10 a.m. the day of the performance. After intermission, if there are open seats, the ushers will usually let you sit down.

San Francisco Symphony tickets are a little easier to procure on short notice. Even if the performance is officially sold out, you can queue up for $15 to $20 center terrace tickets two hours prior to curtain time (two tickets per person, cash only, and not during choral performances). In some ways, although the sound may not be as pristine as in the boxes, it's a more thrilling experience for visitors. The seats are located on the stage, directly to the side of and behind the orchestra, so you can practically read the brass section's scores. And the reverse view looking out to the audience allows you to experience the full architectural splendor of Davies Hall.

The **San Francisco Ballet** also offers a limited number of same-day tickets (discounted for students, seniors, and members of the military). Hit the box office after 12 noon on a performance date and you'll often luck into leftover single seats—some of them amazingly good.

For a real behind-the-scenes look at the historic **War Memorial Opera House**, join the guided tour offered hourly on Mondays from 10 a.m. to 2 p.m. You get to go backstage among the props and sets and learn about the history of the

San Francisco Camerawork
1246 Folsom St.
415-863-1001

Museum of Modern Art
151 3rd St.
415-357-4000

San Francisco Opera
301 Van Ness Ave.
415-861-4008

San Francisco Symphony
Louise M. Davies Symphony Hall, Van Ness Ave. between Hayes and Grove streets
415-864-6000

San Francisco Ballet
box office in the War Memorial Opera House, Van Ness and Grove streets
415-865-2000

War Memorial Opera House
300 Van Ness Ave.
415-864-3330

...AND EVEN MORE BOOK-STORES

Borderlands Books (866 Valencia St., 415-824-8203)—Send your *Lord of the Rings*–obsessed friends to this charming store that sells nothing but science fiction, fantasy, and horror books. The staff knows all—even what is carved on the walls in Moria.

SF Mystery Bookstore (4175 24th St., 415-282-7444)—The place to hit before the plane ride home, this neighborhood treasure specializes in mysteries, suspense novels, hard-boiled detective fiction, and true-crime drama.

A Different Light (489 Castro St., 415-431-0891)—One of the few bookstores in the country devoted to gay and lesbian literature.

Marcus Books (1712 Fillmore St., 415-346-4222)—This small shop specializes in African and African-American literature.

Book Bay at Fort Mason (Fort Mason, Building C, Buchanan St. and Marina Blvd., 415-771-1076)—This is where the city's public libraries send their cast-offs. Great prices, especially on big sale weekends.

Modern Times Bookstore (888 Valencia St., 415-282-9246)—Left-leaning, socialist, and feminist works.

Eastwind Bookshop (1435 Stockton St., 415-772-5888)—Everything you've ever wanted to know about Chinese medicine, acupuncture, Buddhism, martial arts, and other mysteries of the east.

building and some of the landmark performances held here (it was, for instance, the site of the first American performance of the Nutcracker Ballet). The tour also includes architectural and acoustic highlights of Davies Symphony Hall and the Herbst Theatre—all for $5.

You can work up a powerful hunger listening to Liszt, and Mentos at intermission won't do much to assuage it. Just around the corner from the symphony hall, on a funky, industrial sidestreet in a nouveau metal-corrugated building, is chic little **Vicolo Pizzeria**. Sit and discuss Handel's harmonics over a cornmeal thin-crust pizza topped with goat cheese and artichoke hearts.

For something a little more substantial and cozy, try **Stelline** or **Bistro Clovis**, both extremely popular with the symphony/opera crowd. The former is a checkered-tablecloth Italian trattoria; the latter an authentic and unpretentious French bistro. Be forewarned: if you dine beforehand, you might end up sacrificing the first act in order to linger over a steaming plate of polenta with pesto and Gorgonzola, or a rich, decadent cassoulet.

While you're down here, why not walk around and show off the rest of the Civic Center? **City Hall**, with its soaring French Renaissance copper dome and stately granite columns (it rises some 16 feet higher than the nation's capitol) is like the sun around which all other civic buildings rotate. Located at the city's very center, it's viewable for miles from the west side of town. Even more impressive than the exterior is City Hall's enormous interior rotunda, at the base of the grand stairway, down which you can picture French kings descending with 30-foot trains in tow.

Across the street, the Veterans' Building and Herbst Theatre, next to the Opera House, was the site of the signing of the United Nations charter in 1945.

If you're dealing with serious performance art aficionados who are obsessed with Isadora Duncan, in search of a lost musical score, or dying to see the San Francisco Ballet perform *Romeo and Juliet* even though it's not in this season's repertoire, head upstairs to the **San Francisco Performing Arts Library and Museum**. The small gallery shows rotating exhibits on performing arts—from puppetry to opera to vaudeville—mostly as they relate to San Francisco. A short video shows clips of various productions, and an extensive library has just about every book on the arts ever written, plus archives on conductors, choreographers, costumes, theatrical and dance companies, and artists. You can even listen to old recordings of rare musical scores.

If your guests still can't find what they're looking for, head to Hayes Street and **Richard Hilkert Booksellers**, where they might rub shoulders with the likes of symphony conductor Michael Tilson Thomas while sifting through the stacks for a book on costumes or interiors of the world's great opera houses. The sophisticated and natty Hilkert has amassed a comprehensive collection of volumes on interior design and the arts, which are wedged into every nook and cranny and piled all the way to the ceiling. If their field of intellectual interest is even narrower and more obscure, take heart—there's a bookstore in San Francisco that's got you covered. Among them:

The Limelight—This one-stop shop for aspiring film-makers and screenwriters has books on film technique, TV production, method acting, and a large selection of unbound (and occasionally yet-unpublished) recent-release and classic screenplays.

Drama Books—This largely overlooked shop expands on the Limelight theme with a broad spectrum of books about stage and screen—everything from biographies on theater legends to manuals on costume and stage design.

Vicolo Pizzeria
201 Ivy St.
415-863-2382

Stelline
330 Gough St.
415-626-4292

Bistro Clovis
1596 Market St.
415-864-0231

City Hall
between Polk and Van Ness, and McAllister and Grove
415-554-4000

San Francisco Performing Arts Library & Museum
4th floor, Veterans' Memorial Building, 401 Van Ness Ave.
415-255-4800

Richard Hilkert Booksellers
333 Hayes St.
415-863-3339

The Limelight
1803 Market St.
415-864-2265

Drama Books
134 9th St.
415-255-0604

Socialist Action Bookstore—Catch up on the latest plot to overthrow the government or oppress workers at this bookshop-cum-lecture room. Among the selection are works by Leon Trotsky and Malcolm X, biographies of Che Guevara, and books on the history of labor strikes.

Vedanta Society Bookstore—Half the reason to go here is the building—best described as Queen Victoria meets the rajah. The small store inside sells books about eastern religion and Indian philosophy.

William Stout Architectural Books—From neoclassic to postmodern, this shop carries just about every volume on architecture you'd ever want to shake a slide rule at, as well as a healthy helping of books on art, graphics, and design.

Fields Book Store—Devoted to "soulful and scholarly books from the world's spiritual traditions," Fields carries an esoteric selection ranging from tomes on crop circles and tarot kits, to the gospel of Mary Magdalene and the I Ching.

Good Vibrations—As the ad says, this is "a clean, well-lighted place" for sex toys and erotica, how-to and self-help manuals, photography, and lots of books about "doing it."

City Lights Bookstore—The birthplace of the Beat goes on. Under the all-watchful eye of poet/publisher Lawrence Ferlinghetti, City Lights continues to promote and provide great poetry and fiction by the bards of the Beat generation and their progeny.

California Historical Society—The best collection in town of books on, about, and written by San Francisco and San Franciscans—from tales of western pioneers to Ambrose Bierce, Mark Twain, Joan Didion, and the architectural history of Russian Hill. A must for local history hounds and tourists.

Bound Together Book Collective—The all-volunteer bookstore has been offering up literature for budding anarchists since 1976. For your convenience, the collection is categorized by themes such as conspiracy, drugs, magick, spirit and the like. They also serve as the mailing address for the Prisoners' Literature Project.

Theatah

The San Francisco theater scene is a curious animal—a mixed bag of brilliant, experimental works on their way to bigger and better things and flea-bitten road company productions on their last tour leg. The mainstream culture vulture might be satisfied with a night out at the **Golden Gate** or **Orpheum** theaters, where the Best of Broadway comes through every year. The Golden Gate has hosted just about every blockbuster musical that's ever graced a New York stage, from revivals of *Hair* and *Grease* (two different plays, mind you) to *Damn Yankees, Cats,* and *State Fair,* but it's been eclipsed in recent times by the Orpheum, which snagged the revival of *Showboat* and the mega-musical *Lion King.*

ACT is of course the standard-bearer for quality repertory dramas in this neck of the woods. The caliber of the performers and the productions are consistently superior, and tickets can be hard to come by (for last-minute, day-of-the-performance seats, try the TIX kiosk on Union Square).

For more alternative offerings (black turtleneck optional), the choices are varied and often hit or miss. The **Magic Theatre** in Fort Mason has championed some exceptional new playwrights over the years and has also served as a launching pad for big names looking to work out kinks before moving on to Broadway. Sam Shepard, artist-in-residence in the '70s, brought many of his early plays to light here. More recently, he and the Magic staged *The Late Henry Moss* with a star-studded cast that included Sean Penn and Nick Nolte. Other notable performances have included former *Saturday Night Live* regular Julia Sweeney's one-woman show and John Leguizamo's odd, funny, and disturbing character study, *Freak.*

The Marsh in the Mission district is a self-described "breeding ground for new performance" and a great place to catch quirky and hilarious works such as Charlie Varon's *Rush Limbaugh in Night School* and new monologues by Josh Kornbluth.

Cinema

San Francisco is no Hollywood north . . . thank god. This is a town where movie stars walk around unimpeded by autograph hounds and have to flash their SAG cards to get preferential seating in restaurants. On the other hand, when it comes to indie, underground, and cult films, cutting-edge

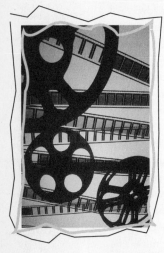

digital video, or all manner of niche festivals, San Francisco has few rivals. In an average year, the city hosts 20 to 30 film fests, from the granddaddy **San Francisco International Film Festival** (April–May) and the **Mill Valley Film Festival** (October), to ethnic celebrations (black, Asian, Latino, Armenian, Arab, German, Italian to name but a few), and ones devoted to offbeat and downright odd genres (foreign horror, silent films, film noir, sex workers).

But even if there's no major film event happening, there are plenty of interesting filmic experiences to be had outside the normal avenues of the multiplex. **111 Minna Street** Gallery has monthly screenings sponsored by the Film Arts Foundation (see Politically Correct). **The Werepad** offers a beatnik lounge, DJ music, and a cheesy menu of B movies for exploitation-flick fans (see Neo-Bohemians). And the **Red Devil Lounge**, an R&B/jazz/funk/rock club, alternates live bands with short films and art every Monday night. It's a mixed bag both from a music and movie perspective, but where else can you combine drinking, dancing, and movie viewing and only pay one cover charge?

Architectural Intrigues

No cultural exploration of the city would be complete without a look at a few of its architectural icons, and in San Francisco, that means first and foremost the Victorians. First stop should be the **Haas-Lilienthal House** on Franklin Street, the only historic Victorian in the city that is also a museum that is open to the public. The magnificent Queen

Anne Victorian was built in 1886 for William Haas, whose descendants went on to own Levi Strauss and the Oakland A's, and who eventually donated the house and its original furnishings to the city. The tour is run by the Foundation for San Francisco's Architectural Heritage, which also conducts Pacific Heights architectural walking tours. From here head to the top of **Liberty Street**, where you can still see huge Queen Anne, Stick/Eastlake, and Italianate Victorians—the kind they had all over town before the 1906 earthquake. Then move on to Postcard Row, that stretch of restored Victorians on **Alamo Square** that's in all the opening credits of the TV shows. The best view of them is from the top of Hayes Street, with the downtown skyline providing a backdrop so perfect it looks fake.

Even though it's been moved a couple of times and is now tucked safely off the street, the house at 329 Divisadero Street is worth a peek because it's purportedly the oldest house in San Francisco (circa 1850). Around the corner at 1111 Oak Street, the **Abner Phelps House** is one of the few examples in the city of early Gothic revival style and is almost as old as the Divisadero house.

WHERE TO STAY

Sumptuous, cozy, and just steps from the opera house, the **Inn at the Opera** was originally built in 1927 as a place to house visiting opera singers and still is a favorite of guest soloists and cultural royalty.

Around the corner and up the stairs, the **Albion House Inn** is a charming, low-key, moderately priced inn on Gough Street. Part of the Hayes Valley scene long before there was a Hayes Valley scene, the inn seems to attract a nice, middle-class, middle-aged crowd. There's a grand piano and fireplace in the main room for anyone who wants to start a sing-along, and the walls are filled with whimsical, lyrical paintings by artist-in-residence, Sachal.

In the heart of the theater district, the **Monticello Inn** is a spit-spot boutique hotel that caters to book lovers, owned by the Kimpton Group. The connection between the décor (early Americana colonial) and the reading selection is

SF International Film Festival
415-561-5000,
www.sfiff.org

Mill Valley Film Festival
415-383-5256,
cafilm.org

111 Minna Street Gallery
111 Minna Street,
415-974-1719

The Werepad
2430 3rd St.
415-824-7334

Red Devil Lounge
1695 Polk St.
415-447-4730

Haas-Lilienthal House
2007 Franklin St.
415-441-3004

Liberty Street
between 29th and
21st streets, Castro,
and Noe

Alamo Square
at Steiner and
Grove streets

Abner Phelps House
on Oak St. between
Divisadero and
Broderick streets

Inn at the Opera
333 Fulton St.
415-863-8400

Albion House Inn
135 Gough St.
415-621-0896

Monticello Inn
127 Ellis St.
866-778-6169

CITY ARTS AND LECTURES

Culture Vultures who live in small towns and can only hear the likes of John Updike, David Sedaris, Tobias Wolff, Spike Lee, or Calvin Trillin on NPR's "Fresh Air" will devour these one-on-one interviews and intimate "conversations" like it was pizza day at the cafeteria. They are usually held at the Herbst Theatre, 401 Van Ness Avenue, 415-392-4400.

Thomas Jefferson, whose Virginia home is the aesthetic and intellectual inspiration for the inn. Weekly readings by local authors are held in a large living room-style library and lounge, where there's also a nightly wine reception. Even better—guests can order books from an "honor bar" in their room that connects to Border's Books & Music up the street and have their favorite novel, magazine, or CD delivered in a half-hour.

The **Hotel Rex** looks like an overgrown literary salon from the 1920s—furnished like you might have envisioned Ina Coolbrith's Russian Hill flat or poet George Sterling's (the man who first called San Francisco "the cool, gray city of love") North Beach haunt. Along with regularly scheduling book readings and signings, the hotel hosts numerous authors, so you never know who you might bump into in the elevator or at the bar.

Dolled up like a Hollywood movie palace circa 1940, the **Hotel Bijou** finally gives visiting film lovers a place to hang their hats. Movie stills adorn the walls, rooms are named for films shot in San Francisco (with little background biographies on the bedstands), there's a bulletin board showing current movie schedules, and a phone booth in the lobby connects to an information line that tells you what films are being shot in the city and how you can sign up to be an extra. Best of all, every night guests are treated to a free double feature (all films set in SF) in the adorable Petite Theatre Bijou, which has real theater seats, red velvet curtains, and a concession stand with Junior Mints and M&Ms.

ABOUT THE AUTHOR

Bonnie Wach has worked as an editor and writer at just
about every San Francisco magazine that has ever existed.
Currently she writes columns about food and local travel for
the *SF Weekly* and the *San Francisco Chronicle* newspapers.
Her work has also appeared in *Via*, the *New York Times
Magazine*, *Travel + Leisure*, *Health*, and various travel guides.
She lives in San Francisco with her husband, son, and
frequently a whole bunch of houseguests.